A Stanley Gibbons
Thematic Catalogue

COLLECT
RAILWAYS ON STAMPS

Howard Burkhalter

Second Edition, 1990

D0925853

Stanley Gibbons Publications Ltd.
London and Ringwood

*By Appointment to Her Majesty The Queen
Stanley Gibbons Ltd., London
Philatelists*

Published by **Stanley Gibbons Publications Ltd**
Editorial, Sales Offices and Distribution Centre:
5 Parkside, Christchurch Road, Ringwood,
Hants BH24 3SH

**First Edition – October 1986
Second Edition – February 1990**

© Stanley Gibbons Publications 1990

ISBN 0-85259-237-X

Item No. 2888 (90)

Printed in Great Britain by Grosvenor Press (Portsmouth) Ltd, Portsmouth, Hampshire

Revised Timetable

When the first edition of *Collect Railways on Stamps* appeared in October 1986 we envisaged a steady sale to the relatively small number of railway thematic collectors with a new edition in five years or so. It is sometimes very pleasant to be proved wrong.

The original printing of the first edition sold out by mid-1988 leaving enough unfilled orders to require an immediate reprint. This was a most encouraging trend for the SG thematic catalogue range. Work on a second edition of *Collect Railways on Stamps* was then put in hand and plans drawn up to extend this series of catalogues to other subjects.

Railways have, of course, always been popular, owing their place in everyone's imagination to a mixture of romance, adventure and their vital contribution to the development of the modern world. It is certainly significant that the first railway commemorative was issued, by Peru, as early as 1871. Since then almost every aspect of railway equipment and operation has been depicted on stamps. With the growth of thematic collecting after 1945 it is, perhaps, not surprising that it should become a major collecting topic.

This second edition has been revised by Howard Burkhalter to include all issues which have appeared in *Gibbons Stamp Monthly* Catalogue Supplements up to the December 1989 magazine. There are now over 5,700 stamps listed, all identified by standard SG catalogue numbers and priced either as singles or in sets. Once again we have had the advice of Andrew Fowler, of Paper Heritage, concerning current market values and many of the foreign listings especially have increased considerably in price. The index section, covering subjects from Allegorical designs to Wagons and including sections for named trains and locomotives, has been updated to cover all the new stamps.

We do hope that railway collectors will find this second edition as useful as its predecessor and we look forward to planning any timetable changes needed in preparation for the next.

David J. Aggersberg

About This Book

This catalogue is a listing of stamps depicting railway themes issued by countries throughout the world. It is based on the Stanley Gibbons *Stamps of the World Simplified Catalogue*, published annually in three volumes. This second edition contains over 5,700 stamps including 650 new listings. It has been updated so that it includes all railway stamps which have appeared in the *Gibbons Stamp Monthly* catalogue supplements up to and including the December 1989 issue.

What is included

All issues, including overprints and surcharges, depicting railway views as listed in the *Stamps of the World Catalogue*. Miniature sheets are included when they contain stamps different from those in the regular stamp sets.

What is excluded

All stamp variations of watermark and perforation which are outside the scope of the *Stamps of the World*. The lists also exclude stamps showing aerial cableways, trackless tram (or trolley) buses, or other self-propelled vehicles that do not operate on rails.

Countries Section

This section lists in alphabetical order, with prices, the various countries and territories that have issued railway stamps. Within each country the stamps are listed in chronological order with year of issue and catalogue number taken from the *Stamps of the World Catalogue*.

Each railway stamp is described so as to identify the subject depicted.

Index Section

This section lists all railway related items which have appeared on stamps by the subject of the design. Under each entry are given, in alphabetical order, the countries and catalogue numbers of the stamps which depict that particular railway related item. Sections are also provided for named locomotives and named trains (eg "The Orient Express"). Each entry includes reference to all designs showing that particular locomotive or named train for whichever country is involved.

made the Gibbons catalogues and monthly supplements available to me, and without whose assistance this catalogue would not have had its present shape or value.

Howard J. Burkhalter
Auburn, November 1989

Railway Names and Terms

The recognised English names and terms have been used. The terms are those generally accepted by the railway industry and recognized by enthusiasts. Some terms may vary from country to country.

Acknowledgements

I would like to thank all who kindly assisted me in the preparation of this edition particularly A. Dyson, A. Fowler, L. Merrill, A. Pollock, T. Smith and, especially my wife, Susan, for her understanding and encouragement.

Special thanks to David Aggersberg, Catalogue Editor of Stanley Gibbons Publications Ltd., who kindly

Books on Railways

A large number of books on railways are available. I have found these particular books, beside stamp catalogues, most useful.

Rixon Bucknall *Trains*, Grosset & Dunlap, New York, 1971.

Earl Clark *Directory of World Electric Lines*, Cincinnati, Ohio, 1971.

Derbibooks *Trains around the World*, Booksales, Inc., Secaucus, NJ, 1975.

O. S. Nock *World Atlas of Railways*, Mayflower Books, Inc., New York, 1978.

H. Sampson *Jane's World Railways*, Jane's Year Books, London, U.K.

The Author

Howard Burkhalter lives in Auburn, New York, United States. Howard (69) is retired from the New York Telephone Co. as Central Office Manager after 40 years service. He is a devoted railway enthusiast both in modelling, collecting railway items and prototype operation. Howard has also been a railway thematic stamp collector for 39 years, enjoys railway research and has written many railway thematic articles in addition to this catalogue.

Stanley Gibbons Ltd.

Head Office, Auction Room, Shop and Rare Stamp Departments
399 Strand, London WC2R OLX.
Offices open Monday – Friday 9.30 a.m. to 5 p.m.
Shop open Monday – Friday 9.30 a.m. to 6 p.m. and Saturday 10 a.m. to 4 p.m.
Telephone 01 (071 from May 1990) -836 8444 and Telex 28883 for all departments.

Stanley Gibbons Publications Ltd: Mail Order and Editorial Departments: 5, Parkside, Christchurch Road, Ringwood, Hants BH24 3SH
Telephone 0425 472363 and Telex 41271

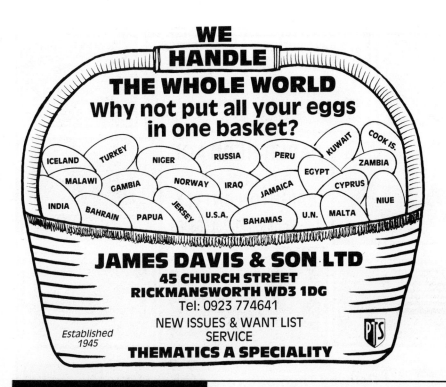

Countries Section

Arrangement

The various countries and territories are listed in the same order as in *Stamps of the World*. Those few which are not in alphabetical order are covered by cross-references. Each entry includes the geographical location and details of the currencies used. The dates quoted against these currencies are those on which they were first used for stamps in this catalogue.

Illustrations

These are three-quarters of actual size. One design from each issue is depicted, but only those overprints and surcharges required for identification are included.

Listings

These are divided into years by dates and into individual issues by illustrations.

For philatelic details the *Stamps of the World*, or the 22 volume standard catalogue, should be consulted.

A † against the catalogue number indicates an issue where unlisted stamps in the set show designs unrelated to railways.

Miniature sheets are indicated by a **MS** prefix.

Appendix

Some countries have issued stamps which are either in excess of postal needs, or which have not been made available to the public in reasonable quantities at face value. Such issues are recorded in Appendix sections at the end of the country listing concerned. Miniature sheets are not included in such entries.

Prices

Those in the lefthand column are for unused stamps and those in the righthand column for used.

Issues where all the designs depict railways are priced as sets only; single stamps and those from "broken" sets are priced individually.

Our prices are for stamps in fine average condition, and in issues where condition varies we may ask more for the superb and less for the sub-standard.

The price of unused stamps are for lightly hinged examples for those issued before 1946, thereafter for examples unmounted mint.

Prices for used stamps refer to postally used examples, though for certain issues it is for cancelled-to-order.

The minimum price quoted is 5p which represents a handling charge rather than a basis for valuing common stamps.

The prices quoted are generally for the cheapest variety of stamps but it is worth noting that differences of watermark, perforation, or other details, outside the scope of this catalogue, may often increase the value of the stamp.

All prices are subject to change without prior notice and we give no guarantee to supply all stamps priced. Prices quoted for albums, publications, etc. advertised in this catalogue are also subject to change without prior notice.

Guarantee

All stamps supplied by us are guaranteed originals in the following terms:

If not as described, and returned by the purchaser in the original transaction, we undertake to refund the price paid to us. If any stamp is certified as genuine by the Expert Committee of the Royal Philatelic Society, London, or by B.P.A. Expertising Ltd., the purchaser shall not be entitled to make any claim against us for any error, omission or mistake in such certificate.

Consumers' statutory rights are not affected by the above guarantee.

ADEN

Arabian Peninsula
16 annas = 1 rupee

1949

32† 2½a on 20c Silhouette of steam locomotive   40   75

ADEN PROTECTORATE STATES

Arabian Peninsula
1949 16 annas = 1 rupee
1967 1000 fils = 1 dinar

Kathiri State of Seiyun

1949
As No. 32 of Aden

16† 2½a on 20c Silhouette of steam locomotive   25   40

Qu'aiti State in Hadhramaut

1949
As No. 32 of Aden

16† 2½a on 20c Silhouette of steam locomotive   20   30

Appendix

The following stamps have either been issued in excess of postal needs, or have not been made available to the public in reasonable quantities at face value. Miniature sheets, imperforate stamps, etc. are excluded from this section.

1967

"Stampex", London. "Empire State Express" (on United States No. 301, inverted centre) 10f.

AJMAN

Arabian Peninsula
100 dirhams = 1 riyal

Appendix

The following stamps have either been issued in excess of postal needs, or have not been made available to the public in reasonable quantities at face value. Miniature sheets, imperforate stamps, etc. are excluded from this section.

1970

"Expo '70" World's Fair, Osaka, Japan (Monorails). 1d.

1971

Olympic Games, Munich (German trams). 8d, 10d.

ALBANIA

South-east Europe
100 qint = 1 lek

1947

468	1q Construction of Durres–Elbasan Railway		
469	4q Construction of Durres–Elbasan Railway		
470	10q Construction of Durres–Elbasan Railway		
471	15q Construction of Durres–Elbasan Railway		
472	20q Construction of Durres–Elbasan Railway		
473	28q Construction of Durres–Elbasan Railway		
474	40q Construction of Durres–Elbasan Railway		
475	68q Construction of Durres–Elbasan Railway		
		Set of 8	70·00 25·00

1948

498	0 lek 50 Construction of Durres–Tirana Railway		
499	1 lek Construction of Durres–Tirana Railway		
500	1 lek 50 Construction of Durres–Tirana Railway		
501	2 lek 50 Construction of Durres–Tirana Railway		

502	5 lek Construction of Durres–Tirana Railway		
503	8 lek Construction of Durres–Tirana Railway		
504	12 lek Construction of Durres–Tirana Railway		
505	20 lek Construction of Durres–Tirana Railway		
		Set of 8	65·00 25·00

1950

532	5 lek Steam locomotive		
533	8 lek Steam locomotive		
534	12 lek Steam locomovtive		
		Set of 3	10·00 13·00

1951

569†	5 lek Railway tracks	2·00	2·50

1969

1294†	25q Shkurte Vata (railway worker) and railway tracks	1·25	35

1971

1475†	15q Freight wagons	50	15

1972

1532† 25q Diesel locomotive 75 10

1974

1720† 1 lek 20 Railway construction .... 1·00 45

1976

1846† 25q Railway tracks 50 30

1853† 80q Railway workers and track 60 30

1978

1986† 1 lek 60 Train and lorry .... 2·50 70

1981

2112 80q Railway tracks
2113 1 lek Railway tracks

Set of 2 1·40 80

1984

2220† 2 lek 20 Railway tracks and train on
viaduct .... 1·75 1·25

1986

2310† 1 lek 20 James Watt (inventor of steam
locomotive) 90 55
MS2312† 1 lek 90 James Watt .... 1·50 1·10

2319 1 lek 20 Diesel train and track 60 20

COLLECT MAMMALS ON STAMPS

A Stanley Gibbons thematic catalogue on this popular
subject. Copies available at £7.50 (p. + p. £2) from:
Stanley Gibbons Publications Ltd, 5 Parkside,
Christchurch Road, Ringwood, Hants BH24 3SH.

ALGERIA

North Africa
1930 100 centimes = 1 franc
1964 100 centimes = 1 dinar

1930

93†	5c + 5c Oran Railway Terminus	3·50	3·75
94†	10c + 10c Railway viaduct, Constantine	3·50	3·75

1951

As No. 1107 of France overprinted **ALGERIE**
307 12f + 3f Travelling Post Office sorting van 3·00 4·00

1957

372 40f Electric train crossing viaduct .... 1·00 20

1970

550† 30c Diesel train on bridge 30 15

1977

711 20c Tunnel and railway tracks in El
    Kantara Gorges
712 60c Tunnel and railway tracks in El
    Kantara Gorges
713 1d Tunnel and railway tracks in El Kantara
    Gorges
                    Set of 3 1·50 50

1987

975† 3d30 Diesel locomotive and passenger
    train .... 1·00 80

1989

1012 2d New railway track 40 35

ALLENSTEIN

Central Europe
100 pfennig = 1 mark

1920

Nos. 114/15 *of Germany overprinted* **PLEBISCITE OLSZTYN ALLENSTEIN**
11†	1m25 Tram, General Post Office, Berlin ..	50	45
12†	1m50 Tram, General Post Office, Berlin ..	50	45

Nos. 114/15 *of Germany overprinted in oval* **COMMISSION D'ADMINISTRATION ET DE PLEBISCITE OLSZTYN–ALLENSTEIN**
25†	1m25 Tram, General Post Office, Berlin ..	45	45
26†	1m50 Tram, General Post Office, Berlin ..	45	45

ANGOLA

South-west Africa
1955 100 centavos = 1 escudo
1977 100 lweis = 1 kwanza

1955

511 5c Map of Angola showing railway lines
512 20c Map of Angola showing railway lines

513 50c Map of Angola showing railway lines
514 1e Map of Angola showing railway lines
515 2e30 Map of Angola showing railway lines
516 4e Map of Angola showing railway lines
517 10e Map of Angola showing railway lines
518 20e Map of Angola showing railway lines
                              Set of 8   4·50   75

1965

633† 1e50 Fire extinguishers on tracks at
          petroleum refinery   60   5
640† 7e Captain Trofilo Duarte Railway Bridge   1·60   40
642† 12e50 Captain Silva Carvalho Railway
          Bridge ....   2·25   80

1970

697† 4e50 Beyer-Garratt steam locomotive .. 1·25 1·25

1974
No. 511 overprinted **1974 FILATELIA JUVENIL**
729   5c Map of Angola showing railway lines   35   50

1976
No. 517 overprinted **DIA DO SELO 15 Junho 1976 REP.**
          POPULAR DE
734   10e Map of Angola showing railway lines   1·25   75

1977
No. 518 overprinted **REPUBLICA POPULAR DE**
742† 20e Map of Angola showing railway lines   1·40   40

1980
No. 697 overprinted **REPUBLICA POPULAR DE**
751† 4e50 Beyer-Garratt steam locomotive .. 1·00 1·00

COLLECT SHIPS ON STAMPS
The largest Stanley Gibbons thematic catalogue to date
– available at £10.95 (p. + p. £2) from:
Stanley Gibbons Publications Ltd, 5 Parkside,
Christchurch Road, Ringwood, Hants BH24 3SH.

ANGUILLA
West Indies
100 cents = 1 dollar

1984

613† $1 Sydney Harbour Bridge (on Australia
          No. 144)   70   55

ANTIGUA
West Indies
1949 12 pence = 1 shilling
20 shillings = 1 pound
1951 100 cents = 1 dollar

1949

114† 2½d Silhouette of steam locomotive 40   40

1974

388† 2c Train guard   5   5
392† $1 American express train ....   1·50   1·25

411† $1 Railway map of Natal and Transvaal,
          1899   80   90

1975
No. 392 surcharged
424† $5 on $1 American express train .... 5·00 8·00

1979

606† $2 British Advanced Passenger Train
(APT) and commuter railcar .... 1·00   75

International Year
Of The Child   **1979**

615† $2 Toy train .... 1·00   90

1980

645† $4 Donald Duck riding toy train .... 2·50   2·25

No. 606 overprinted **LONDON 1980**
650   $2 British Advanced Passenger Train
(APT) and commuter railcar .... 1·25   1·25

1981

681   25c Diesel locomotive No. 15
682   50c Narrow-gauge steam locomotive

683   90c Diesel locomotives Nos. 1 and 10
684   $3 Steam locomotive hauling sugar cane
                                Set of 4   2·75   2·75
MS685 $2.50 Antigua sugar factory, railway
yard and sheds .... 1·75   1·75

1982

765† $1 "Roosevelt Special" Train 80   55

1983

785†   60c Diesel train 80   45

1984

893† $1 Gandhi leaving London by train, 1931   1·50   1·25

1986

1014   25c "Hiawatha Express"
1015   50c "Grand Canyon Express"
1016 $1 "Powhattan Arrow Express"
1017 $3 "Empire State Express"
                                 Set of 4   3·25   3·00
MS1018 $5 "Daylight Express" .... 3·50   3·75

1061† 25c Mickey Mouse dressed as Santa
Claus on toy train 25 25

1987

1101† 15c Siemen's Electric Locomotive, 1879 15 10

1988

MS1209† Two sheets (a) $5 Mickey Mouse
and monorail, EPCOT Centre, Florida (other
sheet shows EPCOT Centre)
Set of 2 sheets 4·50 4·75

ARGENTINE REPUBLIC

South America
1921 100 centavos = 1 peso
1985 100 centavos = 1 austral

1921

492 3c Small steam locomotive
493 5c Small steam locomotive

494 10c Small steam locomotive
495 12c Small steam locomotive
Set of 4 5·75 1·25

1921
As No. 493, but smaller and inscribed "BUENOS AIRES AGOSTO
DE" 1921
496 5c Small steam locomotive .... 1·00 15

1921
As No. 496, but inscribed "REPUBLICA ARGENTINA"
511 5c Small steam locomotive .... 1·00 25

1947

790 5c Argentine–Brazil International Bridge 10 10

1948

MS808a Two sheets 55c First train, 1857
(sheets contain seven other designs)
Set of 2 sheets 13·00 13·00

1949

809 10c Winged railway wheel on rail 15 5

1951

828† 5c Steam locomotive 15 5

1957

907 40c *La Portena* (early locomotive)
908 60c Diesel locomotive (air)
Set of 2   50   20

1958

924† 40c Railway locomotive and Arms of
Argentina and Bolivia   25   5

1980

1673 300p Zarate–Brazo Largo Bridge   50   20

1983

1855† 4p Locomotive *La Portena*   90   50
1856† 5p Tram . . . .   1·25   50

1984

1890† 20p Antonio Oneto and Puerto Deseado
Railway Station   45   25

1986

2023 20c Old Railway Station, Trelew City   30   15

1988

2091† 5a Tram tracks, Caminito   50   10
2099† 50a Tram tracks, Caminito   10   5

2110 50c "Cereals" (mural), Nueve de Julio
Station, Buenos Aires Underground
Railway (detail showing men stacking
sacks)
2111 50c Detail showing sacks
2112 50c Detail showing men loading lorry
2113 50c Detail showing horse and cart
Set of 4   15   15

2114 1a + 50c Steam locomotive *Yatay* and
tender, 1888
2115 1a + 50c Electric passenger coach,
1914
2116 1a + 50c Type "B-15" locomotive and
tender, 1942
2117 1a + 50c Type "GT-22" electric
locomotive, 1988
Set of 4   55   55

2139 5a Underground train, Buenos Aires 50 45

OFFICIAL STAMPS

1922

No. 499 overprinted in block capitals for use in various Ministerial Offices

OD27B†	5c overprinted **M.G.**	4·50	1·50
OD27D†	5c overprinted **M.I.**	6·00	4·50
OD27E†	5c overprinted **M.J.I.**	3·50	1·50
OD27aF†	5c overprinted **M.M.**	3·50	1·50

ARMENIA

North-west Asia
100 kopeks = 1 rouble

1922

193† 5(k) on 2000r Erivan Railway Station .... 12·00
194† 10(k) on 2000r Erivan Railway Station .... 12·00

ASCENSION

South Atlantic
12 pence = 1 shilling
20 shillings = 1 pound

1949

As No. 114 of Antigua

52† 3d Silhouette of steam locomotive .... 1·40 1·00

AUSTRALIA

Oceania
1932 12 pence = 1 shilling
20 shillings = 1 pound
1966 100 cents = 1 dollar

1932

144 2d Sydney Harbour Bridge
142 3d Sydney Harbour Bridge
143 5s Sydney Harbour Bridge
          Set of 3 £350 £170

1947

220† 3½d Ladle wagons in steel mill, Newcastle 15 40

1954

278 3½d Locomotives of 1854 and 1954 ...... 15 5

1956

292† 1s Trams on Collins St., Melbourne 40 30

1958

305 4d Silver mine wagon, Broken Hill 15 5

1970

453 5c Symbolic track and diesel locomotive 15 10

COLLECT BIRDS ON STAMPS

New second edition available at £8.50 (p. + p. £2) from:
Stanley Gibbons Publications Ltd, 5 Parkside,
Christchurch Road, Ringwood, Hants BH24 3SH.

1979

705† 35c Ferry M.V. *Lady Denman* under
Sydney Harbour Bridge 50 75

715 20c "Double Fairlie" type locomotive,
Western Australia
716 35c Locomotive *Puffing Billy*, Victoria
717 50c Locomotive, Pichi Richi Line, South
Australia
718 55c Locomotive, Zig Zag Railway, New
South Wales
Set of 4 2·25 2·50

1982

864 27c Sydney Harbour Bridge (on stamp
No. 143) 30 25

1988

1148† $1 Sydney Harbour Bridge . . . . 95 1·00

OFFICIAL STAMPS

1932
Nos. 144 and 142 overprinted **OS**
O134† 2d Sydney Harbour Bridge . . . . 8·00 2·75
O135† 3d Sydney Harbour Bridge . . . . 20·00 7·50

ALBUM LISTS
Write for our latest list of albums and accessories. This
will be sent on request.

AUSTRIA
Central Europe
100 groschen = 1 schilling

1923

559† 240k Tram in Main Square, Linz . . . . 3·50 4·50

1935

774† 2s Train on Tauern Railway Viaduct . . . . . . 5·00 5·50

1936

799† 24g(+24g) Karl Ritter von Ghega and
train on bridge . . . . 2·50 3·25

1937

812 12g Steam locomotive *Austria*
813 25g Modern steam locomotive
814 35g Electric locomotive
Set of 3 1·75 1·50

1945

924† 4g Mine wagons at Erzberg open-cast
mine 5 5

947† 60g Krauselklause Railway Viaduct
     Semmering (violet) 5   8
948† 60g Krauselklause Railway Viaduct
     Semmering (purple) .... 1·50 1·40

1947
As Nos. 947/8, but colour changed
1080† 60g Krauselklause Railway Viaduct
      Semmering (red) .... 5·00 1·25

1948

1088† 10g + 5g Rebuilding Laabenbach
      Viaduct, Neulenbach 20   20
1089† 20g + 10g Work wagons at Vermunt
      Lake Dam 20   20
1090† 30g + 10g Train at Danube Port,
      Vienna 30   30
1091† 40g + 20g Steam train at Erzberg
      open-cast mine 12   12
1092† 45g + 20g Steam locomotive and
      Southern Railway Station, Vienna .. 5 5
1094† 75g + 35g Tracks at Vienna Gas
      Works 8   8
1095† 80g + 40g Tank wagons at oil refinery 8   8

1952

1234 1s Karl Ritter von Ghega (railway
     engineer) .... 4·75 90

1955

1270† 1s Western Railway Station, Vienna .... 6·50 15

1957

1312† 2s50 Danube Bridge, Linz 35   5

1961

1364 3s Multi-unit electric train 70   40

1962

1392 3s Electric locomotive and first steam
     locomotive *Austria* 85   45

1963

1408 3s + 70g Vienna "101" Post Office and
     railway shed 65   80

1967

1505 3s50 Locomotive of 1867 45   25

1971

1624†   2s Railway tracks at nitrogen factory,
Linz   30   25

1626   2s Electric train on Semmering Line   40   15

1974

1719†   2s 19th-century postman and mail
transport   35   15

1977

1793   1s50 Steam locomotive *Austria*, 1837
1794   2s50 Type "214" steam locomotive, 1928
1795   3s Type "1044" electric locomotive, 1974
                      Set of 3   1·25   75

1978

1800   3s Underground train, Vienna   65   20

1979

1857   2s50 Series "52" goods locomotive   35   15

1980

1882   4s Falkenstein Railway Bridge   30   20

1982

1937   6s Linz–Freistadt–Budweis horse-drawn
railway   50   30

1983

1980   3s Modling–Hinterbruhl Electric Railway
tram No. 5, 1883   40   20

1984

2027   3s50 Electric train on Schanatobel
Bridge
2028   4s50 Electric train on Falkenstein Bridge
                      Set of 2   95   65

1985

2053   4s50 Electric train, Boheimkirchen 40 20

1986

2099   4s Nineteenth-century steam tram and modern electric articulated tram, Salzburg 40 25

1987

MS2129   6s 150th Anniversary of Austrian Railways emblem 55 55

1988

2157   4s Steam locomotive *Aigen*, Muhlkreis Railway, 1887
2158   5s Modern electric tram and Josefsplatz stop, Vienna
                     Set of 2 80 45

STANLEY GIBBONS STAMP COLLECTING SERIES

Introductory booklets on *How to Start, How to Identify Stamps* and *Collecting by Theme*. A series of well illustrated guides at a low price.
Write for details.

2182   6s + 3s Loading railway mail van at Pardubitz Station, 1914 .... 80 80

1989

2202   5s Steam locomotive, Achensee Rack-railway 45 25

BAHAMAS

West Indies
1949 12 pence = 1 shilling
20 shillings = 1 pound
1966 100 cents = 1 dollar

1949

As No. 114 of Antigua

196†   2½d Silhouette of steam locomotive 35 60

1970

348†   11c Train and Globe 70 25

BAHRAIN

Arabian Peninsula
12 pies = 1 anna
16 annas = 1 rupee

1938

No. 255 of India overprinted **BAHRAIN**

28†   4a Mail train .... 80·00 40·00

BANGLADESH

Indian sub-continent
100 paisa = 1 taka

1980

157† 10t Steam locomotive 80 85

1983

218† 5t Steam train 65 50

223† 20p Inside railway travelling post office 5 5
227† 1t Kamalapur Railway Station, Dhaka 5 8

1987

289† 7t Express diesel train 30 35

OFFICIAL STAMPS

1983
Nos. 223 and 227 overprinted **Service**
O34† 20p Inside railway travelling post office 10 10
O38† 1t Kamalapur Railway Station, Dhaka 10 10

BARBADOS

West Indies
1949 12 pence = 1 shilling
20 shillings = 1 pound
1950 100 cents = 1 dollar

1949
As No. 114 of Antigua
267† 1½d Silhouette of steam locomotive 25 25

1979

639† 10c Unloading H.A.R.P. gun on railway
wagon 10 5
640† 12c H.A.R.P. gun on railway wagon
under tow 20 12

1981

665† 12c Bathsheba Railway Station 10 10
667† 45c Animal-drawn tram 30 25
669† $1 Railway Station, Fairchild Street 60 85

BARBUDA

West Indies
100 cents = 1 dollar

1974
Nos. 388 and 392 of Antigua overprinted
152† 2c Train guard (optd **BARBUDA 13
JULY 1922**) 15 15
153† 2c Train guard (optd **BARBUDA 15
SEPT. 1874 G.P.U.**) 15 15
160† $1 American express train (optd
BARBUDA 13 JULY 1922) .... 2·50 4·00
161† $1 American express train (optd
BARBUDA 15 SEPT. 1874 G.P.U.) .. 2·50 4·00

No. 411 of Antigua overprinted **BARBUDA**
201† $1 Railway map of Natal and Transvaal,
1899 .... 1·50 1·25

1977

369† 95c "Voskhod" rocket on railway flat car 65 55

1979
No. 606 of Antigua overprinted **BARBUDA**
455† $2 British Advanced Passenger Train
(APT) and commuter railcar .... 1·00 80

No. 615 of Antigua overprinted **BARBUDA**
467† $2 Toy train .... 1·25 75

1980
No. 455 overprinted **LONDON 1980**
497† $2 British Advanced Passenger Train
(APT) and commuter railcar .... 2·00 1·10

1981
Nos. 681/5 of Antigua overprinted **BARBUDA**
541 25c Diesel locomotive No. 15
542 50c Narrow-gauge steam locomotive
543 90c Diesel locomotives Nos. 1 and 10
544 $3 Steam locomotive hauling sugar cane
Set of 4 3·25 2·10
MS545 $2.50 Antigua sugar factory, railway
yard and sheds .... 1·50 1·75

1983
No. 785 of Antigua overprinted **BARBUDA MAIL**
660† 60c Diesel train 45 35

1985
No. 893 of Antigua overprinted **BARBUDA MAIL**
772† $1 Gandhi leaving London by train, 1931 1·25 90

1986
Nos. 1014/18 of Antigua overprinted **BARBUDA MAIL**
881 25c "Hiawatha Express"
882 50c "Grand Canyon Express"
883 $1 "Powhattan Arrow Express"
884 $3 "Empire State Express"
Set of 4 3·50 3·50
MS885 $5 "Daylight Express" .... 4·25 4·50

1987
No. 1101 of Antigua overprinted **BARBUDA MAIL**
951† 15c Siemen's Electric Locomotive, 1879 15 15

BASUTOLAND
Southern Africa
12 pence = 1 shilling
20 shillings = 1 pound

1949
As No. 114 of Antigua
38† 1½d Silhouette of steam locomotive 25 25

COLLECT SHIPS ON STAMPS
The largest Stanley Gibbons thematic catalogue to date
– available at £10.95 (p. + p. £2) from:
Stanley Gibbons Publications Ltd, 5 Parkside,
Christchurch Road, Ringwood, Hants BH24 3SH.

BAVARIA
Southern Germany
100 pfennig = 1 mark

RAILWAY OFFICIAL STAMPS

1908

Stamps as design above overprinted **E**
R133 3pf Arms
R134 5pf Arms
R135 10pf Arms
R136 20pf Arms
R137 50pf Arms
Set of 5 5·00 9·00

BECHUANALAND
Southern Africa
12 pence = 1 shilling
20 shillings = 1 pound

1949
As No. 114 of Antigua
138† 1½d Silhouette of steam locomotive 25 25

BELGIAN CONGO
Central Africa
100 centimes = 1 franc

1894

Inscribed "ETAT INDEPENDANT DU CONGO"
21† 50c Railway bridge over the M'pozo
(green frame) .... 2·50 90
33† 50c Railway bridge over the M'pozo
(ochre frame) .... 5·25 60

1909
No. 33 overprinted **CONGO BELGE**
41† 50c Railway bridge over the M'pozo ...... 4·50 2·50

As No. 21, but colour changed and inscribed "CONGO BELGE"
59† 50c Railway bridge over the M'pozo
(bistre frame) .... 4·00 3·25

As No. 21 but inscribed "CONGO BELGE BELGISCH CONGO"
65† 50c Railway bridge over the M'pozo (olive
frame) .... 3·25 1·50

1915
As No. 65, but colour changed
75† 50c Railway bridge over the M'pozo (lake
      frame) .... 6·50 1·25

1918
No. 75 surcharged with red cross and premium
83† 50c + 50c Railway bridge over the
      M'pozo .... 50 1·25

1921
No. 65 surcharged
93† 15c on 50c Railway bridge over the
      M'pozo 25 50

1922
No. 75 surcharged
101† 5c on 50c Railway bridge over the
       M'pozo 60 50

1948

292 2f50 Railway train and map of
      Matadi–Leopoldville Railway .... 1·75 20

BELGIUM

Western Europe
100 centimes = 1 franc

1946

1197† 1f35 + 1f15 Train and Ostend Arms 35 25

1949

1275† 50f Forms of postal transport .... 24·00 9·00

1955

1563† 1f20 + 30c E. Walschaerts (locomotive
       engineer) .... 10·00 3·50

1956

1584 2f Electric train and railway bridge 90 10

1957

1609† 4f + 2f Goods train .... 5·00 5·00

1611 2f Tracks, Zeebrugge Harbour 70 10

1958

1651† 20f Mail train .... 3·00 3·00

WHEN YOU BUY AN ALBUM LOOK FOR THE NAME "STANLEY GIBBONS"
It means Quality combined with Value for Money.

1963

1855 6f Winged railway wheel in "Transport" 45 25

1969

2108 3f Mail train 25 8

1972

2274 7f "UIC" (International Railways Union)
      on coupled wagons 35 20

1976

2445 6f50 Modern electric train 35 5

2446 6f50 Underground train, Brussels 40 5

1978

2520† 10f Railway signal as arrows on map of
       Europe 60 15

1979

2556 8f Railway Parcels stamp, 1879 .... 35 5

1983

2745 7f50 Horse tram
2746 10f Electric tram
2747 50f Tram with trolley
                              Set of 3 2·25 1·00

2754 11f Graphic representation of Midi
      Railway Station, Brussels 55 30

2757† 20f "Night Trains" (P. Delvaux) .... 1·25 30

1984

2779† 11f Electric commuter train 50 25

1985

2826 9f Class "18" steam train, 1896
2827 12f Locomotive *Elephant*, 1835
2828 23f Class "23" tank engine, 1904
2829 24f Class "1" Pacific locomotive, 1935
              Set of 4   3·25   1·00
MS2830 50f Class "27" electric locomotive,
1979 ....   2·25   2·00

2834† 23f Aerial view of Zeebrugge Harbour
       showing railway tracks   85   25

NEWSPAPER STAMPS

1928

Railway Parcels stamps of 1923 overprinted **JOURNAUX
DAGBLADEN 1928**
N443 10c Winged railway wheel
N444 20c Winged railway wheel
N445 40c Winged railway wheel
N446 60c Winged railway wheel
N447 70c Winged railway wheel
N448 80c Winged railway wheel
N449 90c Winged railway wheel
N450 1f Winged railway wheel
N451 2f Winged railway wheel
N452 3f Winged railway wheel
N453 4f Winged railway wheel
N454 5f Winged railway wheel
N455 6f Winged railway wheel
N456 7f Winged railway wheel
N457 8f Winged railway wheel
N458 9f Winged railway wheel
N459 10f Winged railway wheel
N460 20f Winged railway wheel
              Set of 18   38·00   12·00

1929

Railway Parcels stamps of 1923 overprinted **JOURNAUX
DAGBLADEN**
N505 10c Winged railway wheel
N506 20c Winged railway wheel
N507 40c Winged railway wheel
N508 60c Winged railway wheel
N509 70c Winged railway wheel
N510 80c Winged railway wheel
N511 90c Winged railway wheel
N512 1f Winged railway wheel
N513 1f10 Winged railway wheel
N514 1f50 Winged railway wheel
N515 2f Winged railway wheel
N516 2f10 Winged railway wheel
N517 3f Winged railway wheel
N518 4f Winged railway wheel
N519 5f Winged railway wheel
N520 6f Winged railway wheel
N521 7f Winged railway wheel
N522 8f Winged railway wheel
N523 9f Winged railway wheel
N524 10f Winged railway wheel
N525 20f Winged railway wheel
              Set of 21   60·00   22·00

RAILWAY PARCELS STAMPS

1879

P63 10c Winged railway wheel
P64 20c Winged railway wheel
P65 25c Winged railway wheel
P66 50c Winged railway wheel
P67 80c Winged railway wheel
P68 1f Winged railway wheel
              Set of 6   £1600   50·00

1882

P69 10c Steam locomotive ....   10·00   80
P73 15c Steam locomotive ....   7·00   7·00
P75 20c Steam locomotive ....   35·00   2·50
P77 25c Steam locomotive ....   35·00   2·75
P78 50c Steam locomotive ....   32·00   20
P81 80c Steam locomotive (yellow) ....   35·00   35
P84 80c Steam locomotive (brown) ....   35·00   45
P86 1f Steam locomotive (grey) ....   £170   1·25
P87 1f Steam locomotive (purple) ....   £170   1·25
P88 2f Steam locomotive ....   £130   35·00

1895

P96	10c Steam locomotive (black & brown)
P97	15c Steam locomotive (black & slate)
P98	20c Steam locomotive (black & blue)
P99	25c Steam locomotive (black & green)
P100	30c Steam locomotive (black & orange)
P101	40c Steam locomotive (black & green)
P102	50c Steam locomotive (black & red)
P103	60c Steam locomotive (black & lilac)
P104	70c Steam locomotive (black & blue)
P105	80c Steam locomotive (black & yellow)
P106	90c Steam locomotive (black & red)
P107	1f Steam locomotive
P108	2f Steam locomotive

Set of 13 £325 13·00

1902

10c to 90c as 1895 *issue, but colours changed*

P109a	10c Steam locomotive (slate & brown)
P110	15c Steam locomotive (purple & slate)
P111	20c Steam locomotive (brown & blue)
P112	25c Steam locomotive (red & green)
P113	30c Steam locomotive (green & orange)
P114	35c Steam locomotive (green & brown)
P115	40c Steam locomotive (mauve & green)
P116	50c Steam locomotive (mauve & pink)
P117	55c Steam locomotive (blue & purple)
P118	60c Steam locomotive (red & lilac)
P119	70c Steam locomotvie (red & blue)
P120	80c Steam locomotive (purple & yellow)
P121	90c Steam locomotive (green & red
P122	1f Winged railway wheel
P123	1f10 Winged railway wheel
P124	2f Winged railway wheel
P125	3f Winged railway wheel
P126	4f Winged railway wheel
P127	5f Winged railway wheel
P128	10f Winged railway wheel

Set of 20 8·75 4·00

1915

Stamps of 1912 overprinted **CHEMINS DE FER SPOORWEGEN**
and winged railway wheel

P160	5c Heraldic lion
P161	10c King Albert
P162	20c King Albert
P163	25c King Albert
P164	35c King Albert
P165	40c King Albert

P166	50c King Albert
P167	1f King Albert
P168	2f King Albert
P169	5f King Albert

Set of 10 £2500

1916

P201	10c Winged railway wheel
P202	15c Winged railway wheel
P203	20c Winged railway wheel
P204	25c Winged railway wheel
P205	30c Winged railway wheel
P206	35c Winged railway wheel
P207	40c Winged railway wheel
P208	50c Winged railway wheel
P209	55c Winged railway wheel
P210	60c Winged railway wheel
P211	70c Winged railway wheel
P212	80c Winged railway wheel
P213	90c Winged railway wheel
P214	1f Steam locomotive
P215	1f10 Steam locomotive ("FRANKEN")
P216	1f10 Steam locomotive ("FRANK")
P217	2f Steam locomotive
P218	3f Steam locomotive
P219	4f Steam locomotive
P220	5f Steam locomotive
P221	10f Steam locomotive

Set of 21 £150 30·00

1920

P259	10c Winged railway wheel (blue)	1·25	35
P280	10c Winged railway wheel (red)	35	25
P260	15c Winged railway wheel (olive)	1·50	65
P281	15c Winged railway wheel (green)	25	25
P261	20c Winged railway wheel (red)	1·50	35
P282a	20c Winged railway wheel (green)	60	25
P262	25c Winged railway wheel (brown)	1·75	50
P283	25c Winged railway wheel (blue)	60	25
P263	30c Winged railway wheel (mauve)	14·00	14·00
P284	30c Winged railway wheel (brown)	60	25
P285	35c Winged railway wheel	75	50
P265	40c Winged railway wheel	75	25
P286	50c Winged railway wheel (bistre)	4·25	40
P287	50c Winged railway wheel (red)	75	25
P266	55c Winged railway wheel (brown)	3·25	2·00
P288	55c Winged railway wheel (yellow)	2·25	2·25
P267	60c Winged railway wheel (purple)	6·50	45
P289	60c Winged railway wheel (red)	75	25
P290	70c Winged railway wheel	2·75	35
P269	80c Winged railway wheel (brown)	25·00	50
P291	80c Winged railway wheel (violet)	2·40	25

P270	90c Winged railway wheel (blue)	6·50	45
P292	90c Winged railway wheel (yellow)	18·00	18·00
P293	90c Winged railway wheel (red)	5·00	40
P271	1f Steam train (grey)	55·00	80
P272	1f10 Steam train (blue)	11·00	85
P273	1f20 Steam train (green)	4·50	30
P274	1f40 Steam train (brown)	4·50	30
P275	2f Steam train	55·00	60
P276	3f Steam train (mauve)	60·00	50
P277	4f Steam train	60·00	70
P278	5f Steam train (brown)	60·00	60
P279	10f Steam train (orange)	60·00	45

1920

P294	1f Steam train (brown)	5·00	25
P296	1f10 Steam train (red)	1·75	25
P297	1f20 Steam train (orange)	2·00	25
P298	1f40 Steam train (yellow)	8·50	1·00
P299	1f60 Steam train	17·00	50
P300	2f Steam train	18·00	35
P301	3f Steam train (red)	18·00	35
P302	4f Steam train	18·00	35
P303	5f Steam train (violet)	15·00	35
P304	10f Steam train (yellow)	90·00	4·00
P305	10f Steam train (brown)	15·00	35
P306	15f Steam train	15·00	35
P307	20f Steam train	£200	1·25

Nos. P294/307 differ from Nos. P271/9 in that the engine carries three headlamps instead of one, the make-up of the train is different and the last coach is clear of the curved frame.

1922

P341	2f Winged railway wheel
P342	3f Winged railway wheel
P343	4f Winged railway wheel
P344	5f Winged railway wheel
P345	10f Winged railway wheel
P346	15f Winged railway wheel
P347	20f Winged railway wheel
	Set of 7 £100 85

COLLECT MAMMALS ON STAMPS

1923

Values from 1f are in a similar horizontal design

P375	5c Winged railway wheel
P376	10c Winged railway wheel (red)
P377	15c Winged railway wheel
P378	20c Winged railway wheel (green)
P379	30c Winged railway wheel (purple)
P380	40c Winged railway wheel (olive)
P381	50c Winged railway wheel (red)
P382	60c Winged railway wheel (orange)
P383	70c Winged railway wheel (brown)
P384	80c Winged railway wheel (violet)
P385	90c Winged railway wheel (slate)
P386	1f Winged railway wheel (blue)
P388	1f10 Winged railway wheel
P389	1f50 Winged railway wheel
P390	1f70 Winged railway wheel
P391	1f80 Winged railway wheel
P392	2f Winged railway wheel (olive)
P393	2f10 Winged railway wheel
P394	2f40 Winged railway wheel
P395	2f70 Winged railway wheel
P396	3f Winged railway wheel (red)
P397	3f30 Winged railway wheel
P398	4f Winged railway wheel (red)
P399	5f Winged railway wheel (violet)
P400	6f Winged railway wheel (brown)
P401	7f Winged railway wheel (orange)
P402	8f Winged railway wheel (brown)
P403	9f Winged railway wheel (purple)
P404	10f Winged railway wheel (green)
P405	20f Winged railway wheel (pink)
P406	30f Winged railway wheel (green)
P407	40f Winged railway wheel (slate)
P408	50f Winged railway wheel (bistre)
	Set of 33 £110 4·25

1924
*No. P394 surcharged **2f30***

P409	2f30 on 2f40 Winged railway wheel	2·75	30

1934

P655	3f Steam locomotive *Goliath*
P656	4f Steam locomotive *Goliath*
P657	5f Steam locomotive *Goliath*
	Set of 3 9·00 3·25

1935

P689	10c Diesel locomotive			
P690	20c Diesel locomotive			
P691	30c Diesel locomotive			
P692	40c Diesel locomotive			
P693	50c Diesel locomotive			
P694	60c Diesel locomotive			
P695	70c Diesel locomotive			
P696	80c Diesel locomotive			
P697	90c Diesel locomotive			
P698	1f Locomotive *Le Belge*			
P699	2f Locomotive *Le Belge*			
P700	3f Locomotive *Le Belge*			
P701	4f Locomotive *Le Belge*			
P702	5f Locomotive *Le Belge*			
P703	6f Locomotive *Le Belge*			
P704	7f Locomotive *Le Belge*			
P705	8f Locomotive *Le Belge*			
P706	9f Locomotive *Le Belge*			
P707	10f Locomotive *Le Belge*			
P708	20f Locomotive *Le Belge*			
P709	30f Locomotive *Le Belge*			
P710	40f Locomotive *Le Belge*			
P711	50f Locomotive *Le Belge*			
P712	100f Locomotive *Le Belge*			
		Set of 24	£450	38·00

1938

P806	5f on 3f50 Winged railway wheel and posthorn			
P807	5f on 4f50 Winged railway wheel and posthorn			
P808	6f on 5f50 Winged railway wheel and posthorn			
		Set of 3	7·50	50

1939

P856	20c Seal of the International Railway Congress	
P857	50c Seal of the International Railway Congress	
P858	2f Seal of the International Railway Congress	

P859	9f Seal of the International Railway Congress			
P860	10f Seal of the International Railway Congress			
		Set of 5	15·00	16·00

Design as Nos. P806/8, *but surcharged* **M. 3Fr**

P867	3f on 5f50 Winged railway wheel and posthorn	35	10

1940

As Nos. P399 *and* P404, *but colours changed*

P876	5f Winged railway wheel (brown)			
P877	10f Winged railway wheel (black)			
		Set of 2	4·75	4·25

Nos. P376, P378/86, P392, P396, P398/408 *overprinted with* **B** *in oval*

P878	10c Winged railway wheel			
P879	20c Winged railway wheel			
P880	30c Winged railway wheel			
P881	40c Winged railway wheel			
P882	50c Winged railway wheel			
P883	60c Winged railway wheel			
P884	70c Winged railway wheel			
P885	80c Winged railway wheel			
P886	90c Winged railway wheel			
P887	1f Winged railway wheel			
P888	2f Winged railway wheel			
P889	3f Winged railway wheel			
P890	4f Winged railway wheel			
P891	5f Winged railway wheel			
P892	6f Winged railway wheel			
P893	7f Winged railway wheel			
P894	8f Winged railway wheel			
P895	9f Winged railway wheel			
P896	10f Winged railway wheel			
P897	20f Winged railway wheel			
P898	30f Winged railway wheel			
P899	40f Winged railway wheel			
P900	50f Winged railway wheel			
		Set of 23	12·00	8·50

1941

As Nos. P376, P378/86, P392, P396, P398/408 *but colours changed. Values from* 1f *are horizontal*

P911	10c Winged railway wheel (olive)	
P912	20c Winged railway wheel (violet)	
P913	30c Winged railway wheel (red)	
P914	40c Winged railway wheel (blue)	
P915	50c Winged railway wheel (green)	
P916	60c Winged railway wheel (grey)	
P917	70c Winged railway wheel (green)	
P918	80c Winged railway wheel (orange)	
P919	90c Winged railway wheel (lilac)	
P920	1f Winged railway wheel (green)	
P921	2f Winged railway wheel (brown)	
P922	3f Winged railway wheel (grey)	
P923	4f Winged railway wheel (olive)	
P924	5f Winged railway wheel (lilac)	
P925	5f Winged railway wheel (black)	
P926	6f Winged railway wheel (red)	
P927	7f Winged railway wheel (violet)	
P928	8f Winged railway wheel (green)	
P929	9f Winged railway wheel (blue)	
P930	10f Winged railway wheel (mauve)	
P931	20f Winged railway wheel (blue)	
P932	30f Winged railway wheel (yellow)	
P933	40f Winged railway wheel (red)	
P934	50f Winged railway wheel (red)	
	Set of 24 25·00 1·50	

1942

P1090 10c Engine driver
P1091 20c Engine driver
P1092 30c Engine driver
P1093 40c Engine driver
P1094 50c Engine driver
P1095 60c Engine driver
P1096 70c Engine driver
P1097 80c Engine driver
P1098 90c Engine driver
P1099 1f Platelayer
P1100 2f Platelayer
P1101 3f Platelayer
P1102 4f Platelayer
P1103 5f Platelayer
P1104 6f Platelayer
P1105 7f Platelayer
P1106 8f Platelayer
P1107 9f Platelayer
P996 9f20 Platelayer
P1108 10f Railway porter (red)
P1109 10f Railway porter (sepia)
P997 12f30 Engine driver
P998 14f30 Railway porter
P1110 20f Railway porter
P1111 30f Railway porter
P1112 40f Railway porter
P1113 50f Railway porter
P999 100f Electric train

Set of 28   48·00   27·00

1945

P1116 3f Mercury
P1117 5f Mercury
P1118 6f Mercury

Set of 3   35   20

1946
As 1938 *issue*
P1162 8f on 5f50 Winged railway wheel and
         posthorn
P1163 10f on 5f50 Winged railway wheel and
         posthorn
P1164 12f on 5f50 Winged railway wheel and
         posthorn

Set of 3   2·25   30

ALBUM LISTS
Write for our latest list of albums and accessories. This
will be sent on request.

1947

P1203   100f Level crossing .... 10·00   20

P1204   8f Archer
P1205   10f Archer
P1206   12f Archer

Set of 3   4·00   50

1948
Nos. P1204/6 *surcharged*
P1229   9f on 8f Archer
P1230   11f on 10f Archer
P1231   13f50 on 12f Archer

Set of 3   4·25   50

P1250   9f "Parcel Post"
P1251   11f "Parcel Post"
P1252   13f50 "Parcel Post"

Set of 3   16·50   20

1949

P1277   50c Locomotive *Le Belge*, 1835
P1278   1f Locomotive, 1862
P1279   2f Locomotive, 1875
P1280   3f Locomotive, 1884
P1281   4f Locomotive, 1901
P1282   5f Locomotive, 1902
P1283   6f Locomotive, 1904
P1284   7f Locomotive, 1905
P1285   8f Locomotive, 1906
P1286   9f Locomotive, 1909
P1287   10f Locomotive, 1910
P1295   10f Locomotive, 1905
P1288   20f Locomotive, 1920
P1289   30f Locomotive, 1928
P1290   40f Locomotive, 1930
P1291   50f Locomotive, 1935

P1292 60f Locomotive, 1949
P1293 100f Locomotive, 1939
P1294 300f Locomotive, 1951

Set of 19 £220 4·00

1950

P1318 11f Dispatch counter
P1319 12f Dispatch counter
P1320 13f Sorting compartment
P1321 15f Sorting compartment
P1322 16f Loading parcels
P1323 17f Dispatch counter
P1324 18f Loading parcels
P1325 20f Loading parcels

Set of 8 55·00 1·75

1951

P1375 25f Mercury .... 8·50 6·00

1953
Nos. P1318, P1321 *and* P1324 *surcharged*
P1448 13f on 15f Sorting compartment
P1449 17f on 11f Dispatch counter
P1450 20f on 18f Loading parcels

Set of 3 80·00 4·75

P1451 200f Electric train and Brussels skyline
(green)
P1452 200f Electric train and Brussels skyline
(green & brown)

Set of 2 £300 7·25

P1485 1f "Nord" Station
P1486 2f "Nord" Station

P1487 3f "Nord" Station
P1488 4f "Nord" Station
P1489 5f "Nord" Station
P1490 5f "Congress" Station
P1491 6f "Nord" Station
P1492 7f "Nord" Station
P1493 8f "Nord" Station
P1494 9f "Nord" Station
P1495 10f "Midi" Station
P1496 10f "Congress" Station
P1497 15f "Congress" Station
P1498 20f "Midi" Station
P1498a 20f "Congress" Station
P1499 30f "Midi" Station
P1500 40f "Midi" Station
P1501 50f "Midi" Station
P1501a 50f "Congress" Station
P1502 60f "Chapelle" Station
P1503 80f "Chapelle" Station
P1504 100f Central Station
P1505 200f Central Station
P1506 300f Central Station

Set of 24 £250 4·50

P1517 13f Electric train and "Nord" Station,
Brussels
P1518 18f Electric train and "Nord" Station,
Brussels
P1519 21f Electric train and "Nord" Station,
Brussels

Set of 3 29·00 90

1956
Nos. P1517/19 *surcharged*
P1585 14f on 13f Electric train and "Nord"
Station, Brussels
P1586 19f on 18f Electric train and "Nord"
Station, Brussels
P1587 22f on 21f Electric train and "Nord"
Station, Brussels

Set of 3 27·00 20

1957

P1600 14f Mercury and winged railway wheel
P1601 19f Mercury and winged railway wheel
P1602 22f Mercury and winged railway wheel

Set of 3 21·00 75

1959

Nos. P1601/2 surcharged

P1678 20f on 19f Mercury and winged railway wheel
P1679 20f on 22f Mercury and winged railway wheel

Set of 2 45·00   55

P1695 20f Brussels "Nord" Station
P1696 24f Brussels "Midi" Station
P1697 26f Antwerp Central Station
P1698 28f Ghent St. Pieter's Station

Set of 4 35·00   2·00

1960

P1722 20f International Railway Congress seal, diesel and electric locomotives
P1723 50f International Railway Congress seal, diesel and electric locomotives
P1724 60f International Railway Congress seal, diesel and electric locomotives
P1725 70f International Railway Congress seal, diesel and electric locomotives

Set of 4 £160   £130

1961

Nos. P1695/8 surcharged

P1787 24f on 20f Brussels "Nord" Station
P1788 26f on 24f Brussels "Midi" Station
P1789 28f on 26f Antwerp Central Station
P1790 35f on 28f Ghent St. Pieter's Station

Set of 4 60·00   1·00

1967

P2017 25f Arlon Station
P2018 30f Arlon Station
P2019 35f Arlon Station
P2020 40f Arlon Station

Set of 4 32·00   1·75

1968

P2047 1f Electric train Type "122"
P2048 2f Electric train Type "122"
P2049 3f Electric train Type "122"
P2050 4f Electric train Type "122"
P2051 5f Electric train Type "122"
P2052 6f Electric train Type "122"
P2053 7f Electric train Type "122"
P2054 8f Electric train Type "122"
P2055 9f Electric train Type "122"
P2056 10f Electric train Type "126"
P2057 20f Electric train Type "126"
P2058 30f Electric train Type "126"
P2059 40f Electric train Type "126"
P2060 50f Electric train Type "160"
P2061 60f Electric train Type "160"
P2062 70f Electric train Type "160"
P2063 80f Electric train Type "160"
P2063a 90f Electric train Type "160"
P2064 100f Diesel-electric train Type "205"
P2065 200f Diesel-electric train Type "205"
P2066 300f Diesel-electric train Type "205"
P2067 500f Diesel-electric train Type "210"

Set of 22 80·00   4·75

1970

Nos. P2017, P2019/20 surcharged

P2180 37f on 25f Arlon Station
P2181 48f on 35f Arlon Station
P2182 53f on 40f Arlon Station

Set of 3 60·00   9·00

1971

P2192 32f Ostend Station
P2193 37f Ostend Station
P2194 42f Ostend Station
P2195 44f Ostend Station
P2196 46f Ostend Station
P2197 50f Ostend Station
P2198 52f Ostend Station
P2199 54f Ostend Station
P2200 61f Ostend Station

Set of 9 29·00   18·00

1972

Nos. P2192/5 and P2198/200 surcharged

P2256 34f on 32f Ostend Station
P2257 40f on 37f Ostend Station
P2258 47f on 44f Ostend Station

P2259 53f on 42f Ostend Station
P2260 56f on 52f Ostend Station
P2261 59f on 54f Ostend Station
P2262 66f on 61f Ostend Station

Set of 7 17·00 5·00

1980

P2266 100f "UIC" (International Railways
Union) emblem within bogie wheels 13·00 2·50

P2615	1f Goods wagon Type "2216 A8"
P2616	2f Goods wagon Type "2216 A8"
P2617	3f Goods wagon Type "2216 A8"
P2618	4f Goods wagon Type "2216 A8"
P2619	5f Goods wagon Type "2216 A8"
P2620	6f Goods wagon Type "2216 A8"
P2621	7f Goods wagon Type "2216 A8"
P2622	8f Goods wagon Type "2216 A8"
P2623	9f Goods wagon Type "2216 A8"
P2624	10f Packet wagon Type "3614 A5"
P2625	20f Packet wagon Type "3614 A5"
P2626	30f Packet wagon Type "3614 A5"
P2627	40f Packet wagon Type "3614 A5"
P2628	50f Self-discharging wagon Type "1000 D"
P2629	60f Self-discharging wagon Type "1000 D"
P2630	70f Self-discharging wagon Type "1000 D"
P2631	80f Self-discharging wagon Type "1000 D"
P2632	90f Self-discharging wagon Type "1000 D"
P2633	100f Pneumatic discharging wagon Type "2000 G"
P2634	200f Pneumatic discharging wagon Type "2000 G"
P2635	300f Pneumatic discharging wagon Type "2000 G"
P2636	500f Pneumatic discharging wagon Type "2000 G"

Set of 22 50·00 3·75

1974

P2353 100f Global emblem of International
Symposium on Railway Cybernetics 12·00 2·00

1976

1985

P2431 20f Railway junction
P2432 50f Railway junction
P2433 100f Railway junction
P2434 150f Railway junction

Set of 4 16·00 6·00

P2824 250f Electric train entering station
P2825 500f Electric trains at station

Set of 2 25·00 15·00

1977

P2505 1000f Railway station at night .... 28·00 6·00

1987

P2923 10f Buildings and electric locomotive
P2924 20f Buildings and electric locomotive
P2925 50f Buildings and electric locomotive
P2926 100f Buildings and electric locomotive
P2927 150f Buildings and electric locomotive
Set of 5   10·00   6·00

RAILWAY PARCEL POSTAGE DUE STAMPS

1982

PD2703 10f Electric locomotive at station
PD2704 20f Electric locomotive at station
PD2705 50f Electric locomotive at station
PD2706 100f Electric locomotive at station
Set of 4   5·75   3·25

RAILWAY OFFICIAL STAMPS

1929

Stamps of 1922 *overprinted with Winged Railway Wheel*
O481 5c King Albert
O482 10c King Albert
O483 35c King Albert
O484 60c King Albert
O485 1f50 King Albert
O486 1f75 King Albert
Set of 6   22·00   15·00

STAMP MONTHLY

— finest and most informative magazine for all
collectors. Obtainable from your newsagent or by
postal subscription — details on request.

Stamps of 1929 *overprinted with Winged Railway Wheel*
O534 5c The Belgian Lion
O535 10c The Belgian Lion
O536 25c The Belgian Lion
O537 35c The Belgian Lion
O538 40c The Belgian Lion
O539 50c The Belgian Lion
O540 60c The Belgian Lion
O541 70c The Belgian Lion
O542 75c The Belgian Lion
Set of 9   15·00   8·00

1932

Stamp of 1932 *overprinted with Winged Railway Wheel*
O620 10c Reaper   60   50

1935

Stamps of 1932 *and* 1934 *overprinted with Winged Railway Wheel*
O677 35c Mercury
O678 70c King Leopold III
O679 75c King Albert
Set of 3   10·50   50

1936

Stamps of 1935 *and* 1936 *overprinted with Winged Railway Wheel*
O721 10c State Arms
O722 35c State Arms
O723 40c State Arms
O724 50c State Arms
O725 70c King Leopold III
O726 75c King Leopold III
Set of 6   4·00   1·00

1941

Stamps of 1936 *overprinted with* **B** *in oval frame*
O948 10c State Arms
O949 40c State Arms
O950 50c State Arms

O951 1f King Leopold III (face values in frame)
O952 1f King Leopold III (face values either side of head)
O953 2f25 King Leopold III (facing right)
O954 2f25 King Leopold III (facing left)
Set of 7 1·25 90

1942
Nos. O722 and O725/6 surcharged
O983 10c on 35c State Arms
O984 50c on 70c King Leopold III
O985 50c on 75c King Leopold III
Set of 3 45 30

1946

Design incorporating letter "B"
O1156 10c State Arms
O1157 20c State Arms
O1158 50c State Arms
O1159 65c State Arms
O1160 75c State Arms
O1161 90c State Arms
Set of 6 10·50 1·00

1948

Designs incorporating letter "B"
O1240 1f35 Woman making lace
O1241 1f75 Woman making lace
O1242 3f Antwerp Docks
O1243 3f15 Textile machinery
O1244 4f Textile machinery
Set of 5 50·00 25·00

1952

Design incorporating letter "B"
O1424 10c State Arms
O1425 20c State Arms
O1426 30c State Arms
O1427 40c State Arms
O1428 50c State Arms
O1429 60c State Arms
O1430 65c State Arms
O1431 80c State Arms
O1432 90c State Arms
O1433 1f State Arms
O1434 1f50 State Arms
O1434a 2f50 State Arms
Set of 12 35·00 22·00

1954

Design incorporating letter "B"
O1523 1f50 King Baudouin
O1524 2f King Baudouin (red)
O1525 2f King Baudouin (green)
O1526 2f50 King Baudouin
O1527 3f King Baudouin
O1528 3f50 King Baudouin
O1529 4f King Baudouin
O1530 6f King Baudouin
Set of 8 70·00 1·25

1971

Design incorporating letter "B"
O2224 3f King Baudouin
O2225 3f50 King Baudouin
O2226 4f King Baudouin
O2227 4f50 King Baudouin (purple)
O2228 4f50 King Baudouin (blue)
O2229a 5f King Baudouin
O2230 6f King Baudouin
O2231 6f50 King Baudouin
O2232 7f King Baudouin
O2233 8f King Baudouin
O2233a 9f King Baudouin
O2234 10f King Baudouin
O2235a 15f King Baudouin
O2236 25f King Baudouin
O2237 30f King Baudouin
Set of 15 7·00 2·50

1977

Design incorporating letter "B"
O2455 50c Belgian Lion
O2456 1f Belgian Lion
O2457 2f Belgian Lion
O2458 4f Belgian Lion
O2459 5f Belgian Lion
Set of 5 60 20

BELIZE

Central America
100 cents = 1 dollar

1979

481†	10c Railway tracks on dock	10	10
483†	45c Stann Creek Railway mail, 1910	45	45

1984

796†	75c British Honduras steam locomotive, 1910	55	65
MS798†	$3 Sydney Harbour Bridge (on Australia No.143)	2·10	2·50

BENIN

West Africa
100 centimes = 1 franc

1985

No. 342 of Dahomey surcharged **Republique Populaire du Benin 75f**

1006†	75f on 70f Loading mail on train	1·40	1·75

BERMUDA

North Atlantic Ocean
1949 12 pence = 1 shilling
20 shillings = 1 pound
1970 100 cents = 1 dollar

1949

As No. 114 of Antigua

130†	2½d Silhouette of steam locomotive	75	65

1987

535	15c Train in Front Street, Hamilton, 1940
536	40c Train crossing Springfield Trestle

537	50c "St. George Special" at Bailey's Bay Station		
538	$1.50 Boat train at St. George		
	Set of 4	4·25	4·50

BHUTAN

Central Asia
100 chetrum = 1 ngultrum

1971

Stamp from Appendix surcharged

264†	90ch on 2n50 Steam train	4·50	6·00

1974

284†	2ch Early and modern locomotives	5	5
289†	1n40 Early and modern locomotives (air)	1·00	1·00

1978

No. 289 surcharged

397†	25ch on 1n40 Early and modern locomotives	4·50	4·50

1984

531	50ch Sans Pareil, 1829
532	1n Planet, 1830
533	3n Experiment, 1832
534	4n Black Hawk, 1835
535	5n50 Jenny Lind, 1847
536	8n Semmering–Bavaria line engine, 1851
537	10n Great Northern No. 1 1870
538	25n German National "tinder" engine, 1880

	Set of 8	12·00	12·00

MS539   Four sheets: (a) 20n Crampton's
locomotive, 1846; (b) 20n *Erzsebet*, 1870; (c)
20n Sondermann freight locomotive, 1896; (d)
20n Darjeeling–Himalayan Railway .... 18·00   18·00

1987

695	50ch Canadian National Class "U1-f" steam locomotive No. 6060		
696	1n Via Rail "L.R.C." electric locomotive No. 6903		
697	2n Canadian National GM "GF30t" diesel locomotive No. 5341		
698	3n Canadian National steam locomotive No. 6157		
699	8n Canadian Pacific steam locomotive No. 2727		
700	10n Via Express diesel locomotive No. 6524		
701	15n Canadian National "Turbotrain"		
702	20n Canadian Pacific diesel-electric locomotive No. 1414		
	Set of 8	6·75	6·75

MS703   Two sheets (a) 25n Cab and tender of
Royal Hudson steam locomotive No. 2860; (b).
25n Cab and tender of Canadian National
steam locomotive No. 6402
Set of 2 *sheets*   5·00   5·00

1988

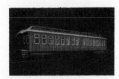

726†	50ch Pullman "Pioneer" sleeper, 1865 ..	5	5
727†	1n Stephenson's *Rocket*, 1829	8	5
735†	10n Trevithick's railway locomotive, 1804	80	75

MS736†   Four sheets (a) 25n *Mallard* steam
locomotive; (b) 25n French "TGV" express
train; (c) 25n Japanese Shinkansen "Tokaido"
bullet train (fourth sheet shows "Concorde"
aircraft)
Set of 4 *sheets*   10·00   10·00

Appendix
The following stamps have either been issued in excess of
postal needs, or have not been made available to the public in
reasonable quantities at face value. Miniature sheets,imperforate
stamps, etc. are excluded from this section.

1969
5000 *Years of Steel Industry. On steel foil.* Postage 45ch,
1n75, 2n.

1970
New U.P.U. Headquarters Building, Berne. Postage 3, 10, 20ch,
2n50.

BOHEMIA AND MORAVIA
Central Europe
100 haleru = 1 koruna

1939

No. 388 *of Czechoslovakia overprinted* **BOHMEN u MAHREN**
CECHY a MORAVA
7†   50h Steam train, armament factory, Pilsen   10   15

1940

34†	4k Steam train at iron works, Moravska Ostrava	15	12
53†	5k Electric train on bridge, Beching	12	8

1941

66†	1k20 Steam train at steel mill, Pilsen	25	30
67†	2k50 Steam train at steel mill, Pilsen	30	35

BOLIVIA
South America
1938 100 centavos = 1 boliviano
1963 100 centavos = 1 peso boliviano

1938

332†	45c Sucre-Camiri Railway map	1·75	70
345†	5b Steam locomotive (air)	4·00	50

COLLECT SHIPS ON STAMPS
The largest Stanley Gibbons thematic catalogue to date
– available at £10.95 (p. + p. £2) from:
Stanley Gibbons Publications Ltd, 5 Parkside,
Christchurch Road, Ringwood, Hants BH24 3SH.

1943

398†	1b25 Tracks at mine	1·25	70
400†	2b Mine wagons	1·50	1·10
402†	3b Tracks going into Pulacayo Mine	2·00	1·25

1944

430	10c Railway train (red)		
432	10c Railway train (blue)		
	Set of 2	1·50	30

1947

As Nos. 430 and 432, but with posthorn and envelope smaller

469	10c Railway train (red)		
470	10c Railway train (yellow)		
471	10c Railway train (green)		
472	10c Railway train (brown)		
	Set of 4	3·75	1·25

1957

651	50b Railway train		
652	350b Railway train		
653	1000b Railway train		
654	600b Railway train (air)		
655	700b Railway train		
656	900b Railway train		
	Set of 6	7·00	1·75

1960

Unissued stamp surcharged

701	1200b on 10b Locomotive	1·25	75

1973

935†	2p Railcar crossing bridge, Al Beni	1·50	50

1975

961†	1p Steam train in Oruro coat of arms	40	20

1977

1012	3p Miner and ore truck	2·25	80

1979

1042†	9p50 Train at Puerto Suarez iron ore deposits	2·25	75

1980

1048 3p Diesel locomotive 65 40

1984

No. 652 surcharged

1088† 200p on 350p Railway train . . . . 2·75 1·50

1988

1164 1b La Paz–Beni steam locomotive 85 60

BOSNIA AND HERZEGOVINA

South-east Europe
100 heller = 1 krone

1906

189† 5h Tracks in Naretva Pass 20 5

1910

No. 189 with date-label "1830–1910" at foot

346† 5h Tracks in Naretva Pass 35 5

1914

No. 189 surcharged **1914 7 Heller**

383† 7h on 5h Tracks in Naretva Pass 25 25

1915

No. 189 surcharged **1915 7 Heller**

385† 7h on 5h Tracks in Naretva Pass . . . . 8·00 8·00

BOTSWANA

Southern Africa
100 cents = 1 rand

1966

203† 5c Tracks at Lobatsi Abattoir 10 5

1970

261† 3c Tracks at Diamond Treatment Plant,
     Orapa 15 5

1974

318† 2c Diesel mail train 45 35

BRAZIL

South America
1916 1000 reis = 1 milreis
1942 100 centavos = 1 cruzeiro

1916

286 100r Tracks. Bay of Guajara, Belem . . . . . . 7·00 2·00

1920

| 317† | 10r Steam locomotive | 5 | 5 |
| 318† | 20r Steam locomotive | 5 | 5 |

1941

647†	10r Steam locomotive and tank wagons at oil wells	5	5
648†	20r Steam locomotive and tank wagons at oil wells	5	5
649†	50r Steam locomotive and tank wagons at oil wells	5	5
650†	100r Steam locomotive and tank wagons at oil wells	12	5

1947

As Nos. 647/50, but values in centavos

751†	2c Steam locomotive and tank wagons at oil wells	10	5
752†	5c Steam locomotive and tank wagons at oil wells	10	5
753†	10c Steam locomotive and tank wagons at oil wells	10	5

1954

| 884 | 40c *Baronesa* (first locomotive used in Brazil) | 80 | 40 |

1957

| 955 | 2cr50 Ingot wagons, Volta Redonda Steel Mill | 25 | 10 |

| 966 | 2cr50 Count of Pinhal and locomotive | 60 | 30 |

1958

| 974 | 2cr50 Early locomotive *Baronesa* and skyscraper | 60 | 20 |

1959

| 1001 | 2cr50 Map and railway line | 20 | 15 |

1960

| 1024 | 11cr50 Adel Pinto (engineer) | 15 | 8 |

| 1038 | 2cr50 Locomotive piston gear | 30 | 10 |

STAMP MONTHLY

— finest and most informative magazine for all collectors. Obtainable from your newsagent or by postal subscription — details on request.

1963

1093   8cr Viscount de Maua (founder of
Brazilian railways) 30   20

1964

1105†   30cr Tramway viaduct, Rio de Janeiro
(black and blue) .... 1·00   40
MS1109†   Two sheets. 30cr Tramway viaduct,
Rio de Janeiro (orange) (sheets contain five
other designs)
Set of 2 sheets   4·00   4·00

1966

1137   30cr Cross section of rail 25   10

1967

1159   50cr Railway bridge 75   15

1968

1241   5c Steam locomotive of 1868 .... 2·50   70

1969

1267†   20c Monument and railway bridge .... 1·25   40

1976

1629   1cr60 Metro train, Sao Paulo 35   15

1977

1665   1cr30 Locomotive leaving tunnel 30   10

1696†   1cr30 Train crossing bridge and
badges of Engineering Corps and
Railway Battalion 25   5

1978

Brasil 78 1,80

1735†	1cr80 Postal tramcar	60	60
1738†	7cr50 Travelling post office	1·00	60

1979

Brasil 79 2,50

1754	2cr50 Underground trains, Rio de Janeiro	40	10

XVIII CONGRESSO DA UNIÃO POSTAL UNIVERSAL
UPU
Brasil 79 2,50

1780†	2cr50 Envelope and diesel train	35	20

1980

Brasil 80 4,00

1810	4cr Coal trucks	25	15

Brasil 80 5,00

1873	5cr Carvalho Viaduct	35	15

ALBUM LISTS

Write for our latest list of albums and accessories. This will be sent on request.

1981

Brasil 81 7,00

1891	7cr Tram tracks, Rio de Janeiro	20	10

Brasil 81

1906	7cr Locomotive *Colonel Church* and map of Madeira–Mamore Railway	40	20

1982

Brasil 82 17,00

1942	17cr Henrique Lage (industrialist) and coal trucks	75	15

1983

Brasil 83 30,00

2020	30cr Baldwin "No. 1" locomotive, 1880		
2021	30cr Hohenzollern "No. 980", 1889		
2022	38cr Fowler "No. 1", 1871		
	Set of 3	65	35

1984

Brasil 84
65,00

2095	65cr Da Luz Station, Sao Paulo		
2096	65cr Japeri Station, Rio de Janeiro		
2097	80cr Sao Joao del Rei Station, Minas Gerais		
	Set of 3	65	25

1985

2128 200cr Electric trains and station plan 40 8

2210 500cr Diesel train on bridge 10 5

BRITISH GUIANA
South America
100 cents = 1 dollar

1949
As No. 114 of Antigua
324† 4c Silhouette of steam locomotive 20 15

1954

360† 24c Diesel locomotive and bauxite mine 80 5

BRITISH HONDURAS
Central America
100 cents = 1 dollar

1949
As No. 114 of Antigua
172† 4c Silhouette of steam locomotive 15 15

1971

321† 5c Quebec Railway Bridge 10 10

BRITISH VIRGIN ISLANDS
West Indies
12 pence = 1 shilling
20 shillings = 1 pound

1949
As No. 114 of Antigua
126† 2½d Silhouette of steam locomotive 15 15

BRUNEI
South-east Asia
100 cents = 1 dollar

1949
As No. 114 of Antigua
96† 8c Silhouette of steam locomotive 65 90

BULGARIA
South-east Europe
100 stotinki = 1 lev

1911

161† 3s Railway bridge, Tirnovo 60 10
164† 15s Tracks along River Isker (bistre) .... 4·50 20

1913
Nos. 161 and 164 overprinted with two words in Cyrillic and
1912–1913
176† 3s Railway bridge, Tirnovo 35 15
179† 15s Tracks along River Isker .... 1·10 30

1915
As No. 164, but colour changed
183† 15s Tracks along River Isker (olive) 50 15

1921
Design as No. 161
229† 50s Railway bridge, Tirnovo (orange) 40 10
230† 50s Railway bridge, Tirnovo (blue) ...... 5·00 1·60

1924
No. 230 surcharged
259† 3 lev on 50s Railway bridge, Tirnovo 60 25

1939

418 1 lev First Bulgarian locomotive
419 2 lev Modern express train

420 4 lev Train crossing viaduct
431 7 lev King Boris as engine driver

Set of 4   7·50   4·50

1940

438† 10 lev Mail train .... 1·25   50

1941

491† 14 lev Tram tracks at Palace of Justice   55   35

1946

585† 35 lev Red Cross train (red & black) .... 1·25   75
587† 100 lev Red Cross train (red & brown) .. 2·75 1·75

588† 4 lev Steam locomotive and Postal
       Savings emblem   15   10

1947

As Nos. 585 and 587, but colours changed
645i 35 lev Red Cross train (red & green) .... 1·25   75
645k 100 lev Red Cross train (red & blue) .... 2·75 1·75

1949

743† 5 lev Railway tunnel construction   50   20
744† 9 lev Steam locomotive .... 1·40   5

1950

771† 20 lev Strikers and train   60   30
772† 60 lev Train and two strikers .... 1·50   90

774† 2 lev Steam locomotive (black) .... 1·50   10
774a 2 lev Steam locomotive (brown) .... 1·50   10

1952

874† 44s Freight wagons at factory   80   40

1953

914† 8s Railway viaduct   20   20

1954

953 44s Steam locomotive (turquoise)
954 44s Steam locomotive (black)

Set of 2   2·50   40

1955

1010† 16s Danube Railway Bridge 15 5

1959

1139† 2 lev Striking railway workers .... 2·00 1·40

1962

1348† 2s Electric train 10 5

1964

1449 1s Stephenson's *Rocket*
1450 2s Steam locomotive
1451 3s Diesel locomotive
1452 5s Electric locomotive
1453 8s Steam train on bridge
1454 13s Diesel train emerging from tunnel
Set of 6 1·40 50

1965

1525 13s Electric locomotive 80 20

1572† 1s Railway bridge and tunnel, Tirnovo 5 5

1967

1756† 1s Railway bridge over River Yantra
and tunnel 5 5
1759† 5s Railway bridge over River Yantra
and tunnel (different) 20 10

1969

1874† 3s Steam locomotive 10 5

1970

2055† 2s "Third Class Carriage" (sculpture by
I. Funev) 15 5
2059† 28s "Engineer" (sculpture by I. Funev) 85 30

COLLECT BIRDS ON STAMPS
New second edition available at £8.50 (p. + p. £2) from:
Stanley Gibbons Publications Ltd, 5 Parkside,
Christchurch Road, Ringwood, Hants BH24 3SH.

1973

2254† 5s "Armed Train" (painting by B.
Angelushev) 40 15

1974

2327† 2s Salt wagons 5 5
2329† 28s "Friendship Train" .... 2·25 1·50

1976

2441 2s Modern articulated tram-car
2442 13s Early 20th-century tram-car
Set of 2 90 40

1977

2626 13s Diesel train on bridge 45 10

1978

2634† 35s Friendship Bridge 80 80

1979

MS2731 5s Monument in front of Sofia Central
Railway Station (sheet contains four other
designs) .... 1·75 1·75

1980

2877† 35s Children in railway coach 60 25

1983

3110 5s Trevithick's locomotive 1830
3111 13s Blenkinsop's rack locomotive *Prince
Royal*, 1810
3112 42s Hedley's *Puffing Billy*, 1812
3113 60s First German locomotive *Der Adler*,
1835
Set of 4 2·50 1·00

1984

3159 13s *Best Friend*, Charleston, U.S.A.,
1830
3160 25s *Saxonia*, Dresden, Germany, 1836

3161 30s *Lafayette*, U.S.A., 1837
3162 42s *Borsig*, Germany, 1841
3163 60s *Philadelphia*, U.S.A., 1843
　　　　　　　　　　　　 Set of 5 　 3·50 　 1·25

1986

3344 13s Electric locomotive .... 20 　 10

1987

3405 5s Nineteenth-century steam locomotive,
　　　 Ruse–Varna Railway .... 8 　 5

1988

3493 5s Steam locomotive *Yantra*, 1888
3494 13s Steam locomotive *Kh Botoev*, 1905
3495 25s Steam locomotive No. "807", 1918
3496 32s Steam locomotive, 1943
3497 42s Diesel locomotive, 1964
3498 60s Electric locomotive, 1979
　　　　　　　　　　　　 Set of 6 　 2·25 　 1·00

PARCEL POST STAMPS

1941

P495† 2 lev Loading mail coach .... 5 　 5
P502† 9 lev Loading mail coach .... 15 　 8
P513† 30 lev Loading mail coach .... 25 　 10

BURKINA FASO

West Africa
100 centimes = 1 franc

1985

809 50f Electric locomotive No. 105-30 and
　　　 tank wagon
810 75f Diesel shunter
811 80f Diesel passenger locomotive
812 100f Diesel railcar (air)
813 150f Diesel railcar No. 6093
814 200f Diesel railcar No. 105
815 250f Diesel locomotive pulling passenger
　　　 train
　　　　　　　　　　 Set of 7 　 4·50 　 3·50

839† 250f Diesel train .... 1·75 　 1·50

1986

848 90f Couple carrying rail
849 120f Laying tracks
850 185f Workers waving to passing train
851 500f "Inauguration of first German
　　　 Railway" (painting by Heim) (air)
　　　　　　　　　　 Set of 4 　 3·75 　 2·75
MS852 1000f German Experimental inter-city
　　　 train and diesel locomotive Series "290" ...... 4·50 　 3·75

BURMA

South-east Asia
100 pyas = 1 kyat

1977

272 15p Early steam locomotive
273 20p Early train and ox-cart
274 25p Railway station
275 50p Railway bridge
276 1k Diesel train emerging from tunnel
                              Set of 5   3·50   2·00

BURUNDI

Central Africa
100 centimes = 1 franc

1970

527† 6f50 Aerial view of "Expo '70", Osaka,
      showing monorail system   20   8

1974

978† 14f Part of mail coach   80   50
979† 14f Rest of mail coach and steam
      locomotive   80   50
986† 31f Part of mail coach . . . .   1·50   70
987† 31f Rest of mail coach and steam
      locomotive . . . .   1·50   70

1979

1350† 60f Mail coach and steam locomotive
       (on stamp Nos. 978/9) . . . .   1·50   90

1984

1439† 65f Mail coach and steam locomotive
       (on stamp Nos. 978/9) . . . .   1·25   70

CAICOS ISLANDS

West Indies
100 cents = 1 dollar

1984

64† 50c Mickey Mouse, Donald Duck and toy
     steam train   90   90

CAMBODIA

South-east Asia
1954 100 cents = 1 piastre
1955 100 cents = 1 riel

1954

41† 2p50 Steam locomotive . . . .   1·00   90
43† 4p Steam locomotive . . . .   1·50   1·25
45† 5p Steam locomotive . . . .   2·00   1·75
47† 10p Steam locomotive . . . .   2·50   2·25
48† 15p Steam locomotive . . . .   3·25   2·75

1969

252 3r Diesel train and route map of
    Phnom-Penh–Sihanoukville Railway
253 6r Phnom-Penh Station
254 8r Diesel locomotive and rural station
255 9r Steam locomotive at Sihanoukville
    Station

Set of 4   4·50   3·00

CAMEROUN
West Africa
100 centimes = 1 franc

1956

267† 15f Wouri Bridge 55   10

1959

274† 20f Goods wagons on dock 45   30

1961
Nos. 267 and 274 surcharged **REPUBLIQUE FEDERALE** and
new value
290† 3d on 15f Wouri Bridge 65   45
292† 6d on 20f Goods wagons on dock ...... 1·25   90

1965

376 12f Inscription recording laying of first rail
    on Mbanga–Kumba Railway
377 20f Diesel locomotive
Set of 2   1·75   1·10

1966

412† 50f Diesel locomotive and goods
    wagons ....   3·75   1·75

1967

452 20f Map of Africa, railway lines and
    signals
453 25f Map of Africa and diesel train
Set of 2   2·75   1·40

1968

491† 30f "Transcamerounais" express train
    leaving tunnel ....   2·00   65

520 50f Wouri Bridge   80   80

1969

538 30f Kumba Station
539 50f Diesel train on bridge
Set of 2   2·25   1·25

1974

717 5f Route map of Trans-Cameroun Railway
     and tracks
718 20f Laying track
719 40f Welding rails
720 100f Railway bridge over Djerem River
Set of 4   4·50   2·25

No. 717 surcharged **100f 10 DECEMBRE 1974**
736 100f on 5f Route map of Trans-Cameroun
     Railway and tracks .... 1·25   1·00

1982

943† 20f Railway tracks 35   25

CANADA

North America
100 cents = 1 dollar

1927

270† 12c Map of Canada showing railway
      lines .... 8·00   1·75

1928

282† 12c Quebec Railway Bridge .... 12·00   2·75
283† 20c Steam train and wheat fields .... 18·00   3·50

1930

295† 20c Steam train and grain elevators .... 13·00   20

1933

No. 295 *overprinted* **WORLD'S GRAIN EXHIBITION &
CONFERENCE REGINA 1933**
330 20c Steam train and grain elevators ...... 20·00   4·50

1946

406† $1 *Abegweit* (train ferry) .... 27·00   1·00

1951

436† 4c Mail trains, 1851 and 1951 35   10

1963

535 5c Sir Casimir Gzowski (engineer) 10   5

1966

572 5c Railway crossing sign 15 5

1967

606† 6c "Turbotrain" (red) 45 5
607† 6c "Turbotrain" (black) 25 5
609† 7c "Turbotrain" 30 5
589† 50c "Summers Stores" (grain elevators,
J. Ensor) .... 1·75 5

1970

673 6c Sir Donald Alexander Smith 10 5

1977

892† 12c Sir Sandford Fleming (engineer) 15 5

1979

962† 15c Toy train 15 5

STAMP MONTHLY
— finest and most informative magazine for all collectors. Obtainable from your newsagent or by postal subscription — details on request.

1980

987† 17c Tracks and grain elevators 15 15

1981

1022 17c Aaron R. Mosher (labour leader) and railway workers 15 15

1982

MS1047 30c Montreal tram; 30c Goods yard, Alberta (sheet also contains ten other 30c designs) .... 3·25 3·75

1071† $2 McAdam Railway Station, New Brunswick .... 1·90 1·60

1983

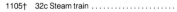

1105† 32c Steam train 25 25

1106   32c Type 0-4-0 *Dorchester* locomotive
1107   32c Type 4-4-0 *Toronto* locomotive
1108   37c Type 0-6-0 *Samson* locomotive
1109   64c Type 4-4-0 *Adam Brown* locomotive
  Set of 4   1·90   1·25

1984

MS1123   32c Diesel goods train at grain
elevators in painting "Saskatchewan" (J.P.
Lemieux) (sheet also contains eleven other
32c designs) ....   5·00   5·00

1132   32c Type 0-6-0 *Scotia* locomotive
1133   32c Type 4-4-0 *Countess of Dufferin*
   locomotive
1134   37c Type 2-6-0 GT Class "E3"
   locomotive
1135   64c Type 4-6-0 CP Class "D10a"
   locomotive
  Set of 4   2·75   1·75

1985

1185   34c Class "K2" steam locomotive
1186   34c Class "P2a" steam locomotive
1187   39c Class "O10a" steam locomotive
1188   68c Class "H4D" steam locomotive
  Set of 4   1·60   1·40

STANLEY GIBBONS
STAMP COLLECTING SERIES

Introductory booklets on *How to Start, How to Identify
Stamps* and *Collecting by Theme*. A series of well
illustrated guides at a low price.
  Write for details.

1986

1197†   68c Early electric tram and monrail
   train, Vancouver   70   75

1203†   34c Railway rotary snowplough   50   60

1222   34c John Molson (businessman) and
   early railway train   35   40

1223   34c Class "V-1-a" steam locomotive
1224   34c Class "T1a" diesel locomotive No.
   9000
1225   39c Class "U-2-a" steam locomotive
1226   68c Class "H1c" steam locomotive No.
   2850
  Set of 4   2·00   1·75

SPECIAL DELIVERY STAMPS

1927

S5   20c Mail trains, 1867 and 1927 ....   8·00   6·50

OFFICIAL STAMPS

1949
No. 406 overprinted **O.H.M.S.**
O9† $1 Abegweit (train ferry) .... 45·00 40·00

1950
No. 406 overprinted **G**
O28† $1 Abegweit (train ferry) .... 48·00 40·00

CANAL ZONE
Central America
1915 100 cents = 1 balboa
1924 100 cents = 1 dollar

1915
Nos. 166 and 180/2 of Panama overprinted **CANAL ZONE**
57† 5c Electric towing engine, Gatun locks .... 6·50 4·00
61† 24c Electric towing engine, Gatun locks 35·00 10·00
62† 50c Goods wagon, Balboa Docks £250 £150
63† 1b Electric towing engine, Pedro Miguel
     Locks £130 50

1928

109† 5c Side-dump wagons .... 1·25 60

1939

149† 1c Steam locomotive and side-dump
      wagons, Balboa 45 30
151† 3c Steam work train, Gaillard Cut 45 20
153† 6c Steam work train, Bas Obispo .... 2·40 1·40
155† 8c Steam work train, Gatun Lock .... 3·00 2·00
156† 10c Electric towing locomotive .... 3·00 1·75
157† 11c Steam locomotive and side-dump
      wagons .... 12·00 8·00
159† 14c Signal and railway bridge, Gamboa 12·00 8·00
160† 15c Steam train and railway bridge,
      Gamboa .... 15·00 12·50
161† 18c Steam railway cranes .... 12·00 12·00
162† 20c Electric towing locomotives .... 15·00 8·00
163† 25c Steam railway crane and pile-driver 15·00 15·00

1951

211 10c Steam work train .... 3·50 1·60

1955

212 3c Early train .... 2·25 90

1964

230† 30c Railway tracks .... 4·75 1·40

1978

251 15c Electric towing locomotive .... 1·25 30

OFFICIAL STAMPS

1941
No. 109 overprinted **OFFICIAL PANAMA CANAL**
O182† 5c Side-dump wagons .... – 24·00

POSTAGE DUE STAMPS

1929
No. 109 surcharged **POSTAGE DUE** and value
D120 1c on 5c Side-dump wagons
D121 2c on 5c Side-dump wagons
D122 5c on 5c Side-dump wagons
D123 10c on 5c Side-dump wagons
Set of 4 25·00 12·50

CAPE JUBY
North-west Africa
100 centimos = 1 peseta

1948
Nos. 307 and 316 of Spanish Morocco overprinted **CABO JUBY**
154† 2c Steam goods train 10 50
163† 2p50 Steam goods train .... 5·50 4·50

CAYMAN ISLANDS

West Indies
12 pence = 1 shilling
20 shillings = 1 pound

1949
As No. 114 of Antigua
131†   2½d Silhouette of steam locomotive   20   15

CENTRAL AFRICAN EMPIRE

Central Africa
100 centimes = 1 franc

1977
No. 360 of Central African Republic overprinted **EMPIRE CENTRAFRICAIN**
440†   100f Diesel locomotive ....   5·00   5·00

1978

557†   50f Steam locomotive ....   2·00   90

621†   100f Mail train ....   1·50   90

CENTRAL AFRICAN REPUBLIC

Central Africa
100 centimes = 1 franc

1963

47   20f Railcar
48   25f Diesel train
49   50f Diesel shunter
50   100f Diesel locomotive
                               Set of 4   6·50   7·00

1969

197   100f Toy steam locomotive ....   1·50   1·00

1974

360   100f Diesel locomotive ....   1·50   1·00

1979

671   60f Steam locomotive and U.S.A. stamp
672   100f Steam locomotive and French stamp
673   150f Steam locomotive and German
       stamp
674   250f Steam locomotive and British stamp
                               Set of 4   4·25   75
MS675   500f Steam locomotive and Central
      African Republic stamp ....   4·50   90

1982

832†   10f "Beyer-Garratt 1" locomotive   75   45

ALBUM LISTS
Write for our latest list of albums and accessories. This will be sent on request.

1984

1017   110f "CC 1500 ch" locomotive
1018   240f P.L.M. Series "210" locomotive, 1868
1019   350f Class "231–726" locomotive, 1937
1020   440f Pacific "S 3/6" locomotive, 1908
1021   500f Henschel "151 Series 45" locomotive, 1937
                       Set of 5   9·00   3·50

1985

Nos. 1019/20 overprinted **TSUKUBA EXPO '85** (No. 1084) or **MOPHILA '85 HAMBOURG** (No. 1086)
1084†   350f Class "231–726" locomotive, 1937   1·25   1·00
1086†   440f Pacific "S 3/6" locomotive, 1908 ..   1·50   1·25

1095†   100f Monorail train on 1964 Tokyo Olympic Games poster   80   55

1986

1238   40f Prussian Railways Class "DH2 Green Elephant" steam locomotive and Alfred de Glehn
1239   70f Rudolf Diesel and steam locomotive *Rheingold* No. 1829
1240   160f Electric locomotive Type "103 Rapide" and Carl Golsdorf
1241   300f Wilhelm Schmidt and Beyer-Garratt type steam locomotive
1242   400f De Bousquet and compound locomotive Class "3500" (air)
                       Set of 5   4·75   3·00
MS1243   500f Werner von Siemens and electric railcar ....   2·50   1·75

CEYLON

Indian Ocean
100 cents = 1 rupee

1935

378†   1r Goods wagons on dock   ....   5·50   5·00

1938

As No. 378, *but with portrait of King George VI*
395†   1r Goods wagons on dock   ....   3·75   45

1949

410   5c Steam train
411   15c Steam train
412   25c Diesel railcar
                       Set of 3   2·40   80

1957

442†   4c Steam locomotive   25   5
443†   10c Steam locomotive   30   5

1964

503   60c Trains of 1864 and 1964 (inscr in Sinhala and Tamil)
504   60c Trains of 1864 and 1964 (inscr in Sinhala and English)
                       Set of 2   2·25   20

CHAD

Central Africa
100 centimes = 1 franc

1974

411†   40f Electric train .... 1·50   1·00

1984

740†   50f *Lady*, tank locomotive, 1879 40   40

753   100f Locomotive *Nord*, 1885
754   150f Locomotive *Columbia*, 1888
755   250f Locomotive *Rete Mediterranea*, 1900
756   350f MAV "114" locomotive
                   Set of 4   5·75   2·50

1985

809†   250f Modern diesel freight train .... 1·40   1·00

COLLECT SHIPS ON STAMPS

The largest Stanley Gibbons thematic catalogue to date
– available at £10.95 (p. + p. £2) from:
Stanley Gibbons Publications Ltd, 5 Parkside,
Christchurch Road, Ringwood, Hants BH24 3SH.

Appendix
The following stamps have either been issued in excess of
postal needs, or have not been available to the public in
reasonable quantities at face value. Miniature sheets, imperforate
stamps, etc. are excluded from this section.

1973

Locomotives 10, 40, 50, 150, 200f.

CHAMBA

Indian sub-continent
12 pies = 1 anna
16 annas = 1 rupee

1938

No. 255 of India overprinted **CHAMBA STATE**
90†   4a Mail train .... 4·00   4·25

CHILE

South America
1938 100 centavos = 1 peso
1960 1000 milesimos = 100 centisimos = 1 escudo
1975 100 centavos = 1 peso

1938

270†   20c Hopper wagons at nitrate works 15   5
338j†   10p Steam train 75   8

1954

431   1p Early locomotive
432   10p Early locomotive (air)
                   Set of 2   75   75

1956

455†   5p Diesel locomotive and plane 15   5

1960

As No. 455, but face value in milesimos

524† 5m Diesel locomotive and plane 15 10

1978

802 25p Tram at Catholic University,
Valparaiso .... 1·50 60

1983

939 40p Incline Railway, Valparaiso 90 65

1984

954 9p Presidential Coach, 1911
955 9p Service car and tender
956 9p Type "80" steam locomotive, 1929
Set of 3 1·60 90

1987

1091 95p Kitson Meyer steam locomotive .... 1·00 45

1113 25p Santiago Underground train at
platform 20 10

1988

1161 60p Esslingen steam locomotive No.
3331 (75th anniversary of Arica–La
Paz Railway)
1162 60p North British steam locomotive No.
45 (centenary of Antofagasta–Bolivia
Railway)
Set of 2 95 50

OFFICIAL STAMPS

1940

No. 270 overprinted **OFICIAL**

O283† 20c Hopper wagons at nitrate works 2·00 75

1955

No. 338j overprinted **OFICIAL**

O443 10p Steam train .... 11·00 6·50

CHINA

Eastern Asia
100 cents = 1 dollar (yuan)

Chinese Empire

1901

British Railway Administration. Surcharged **B.R.A. 5 Five Cents**

BR133 5c on ½c Chinese dragon .... £125 65·00
"B.R.A." stamps were used for the collection of a late letter fee on letters posted in railway postal vans on the Peking–Shanhaikwan line.

Chinese Republic

1913

309†	½c Steam train on bridge	10	10
310†	1c Steam train on bridge	40	10
289a†	1½c Steam train on bridge	40	50
312†	2c Steam train on bridge	50	10
313†	3c Steam train on bridge	50	10
292†	4c Steam train on bridge (red)	70	10
314†	4c Steam train on bridge (grey)	4·25	20
315†	4c Steam train on bridge (olive)	50	10
293†	5c Steam train on bridge	70	10
294†	6c Steam train on bridge (grey)	1·00	45

317†	6c Steam train on bridge (red)	1·00	10
318†	6c Steam train on bridge (brown)	11·00	2·00
319†	7c Steam train on bridge	2·00	1·50
296†	8c Steam train on bridge	1·90	20
321†	10c Steam train on bridge	1·50	10

1920

Nos. 312, 313, 292, 294 surcharged with new values in English and Chinese characters

349	1c on 2c Steam train on bridge	2·50	1·00
361	2c on 3c Steam train on bridge	2·50	20
350	3c on 4c Steam train on bridge	3·25	90
351	5c on 6c Steam train on bridge	4·75	4·00

On Nos. 349/51 the English numeral is at the foot and on No. 361 in the centre.

1925

Nos. 312/15 surcharged with new values in English and Chinese characters

366	1c on 2c Steam train on bridge	50	10
367	1c on 3c Steam train on bridge	20	10
369	1c on 4c Steam train on bridge	60	10
370	3c on 4c Steam train on bridge	1·50	10

On Nos. 366/70 the English numeral is at the top.

1936

448†	2c Steam locomotive	60	40

1941

599	8c Steam train and mine truck	
600	21c Steam train and mine truck	
601	28c Steam train and mine truck	
602	33c Steam train and mine truck	
603	50c Steam train and mine truck	
604	$1 Steam train and mine truck	
	Set of 6	2·25 3·25

1947

985†	$100 Steam train	10	50

1949

Revenue stamps surcharged

1136	50c on $20 Steam train and signal		
1137	$1 on $15 Steam train and signal		
1127	$2 on $50 Steam train and signal		
1144	$3 on $50 Steam train and signal		
1138	$5 on $500 Steam train and signal		
1129	$10 on $30 Steam train and signal		
1140	$15 on $20 Steam train and signal		
1141	$25 on $20 Steam train and signal		
1145	$50 on $50 Steam train and signal		
1147	$50 on $300 Steam train and signal		
1130	$80 on $50 Steam train and signal		
1146	$100 on $50 Steam train and signal		
1124	$200 on $50 Steam train and signal		
1142	$200 on $500 Steam train and signal		
1125	$300 on $50 Steam train and signal		
1143	$500 on $15 Steam train and signal		
1134	$500 on $30 Steam train and signal		
1135	$1,000 on $50 Steam train and signal		
1148	$1,000 on $100 Steam train and signal		
1126	$1,500 on $50 Steam train and signal		
1151	$2,000 on $300 Steam train and signal		
	Set of 21	11·50	32·00

Surcharged as Nos. 1124/51, but key pattern inverted at top and bottom

1183	$50 on $10 Steam train and signal		
1184	$100 on $10 Steam train and signal		
1185	$500 on $10 Steam train and signal		
1186	$1,000 on $10 Steam train and signal		
1187	$5,000 on $20 Steam train and signal		
1188	$10,000 on $20 Steam train and signal		
1189	$50,000 on $20 Steam train and signal		
1190	$100,000 on $20 Steam train and signal		
1191	$500,000 on $20 Steam train and signal		
1192	$2,000,000 on $20 Steam train and signal		
1193	$5,000,000 on $20 Steam train and signal		
	Set of 11	£850	£250

No value indicated. The stamps were sold at the rate for the day for the service indicated

1211†	Steam locomotive (Ordinary Postage)	1·50	50

Gold Yuan currency revenue stamps overprinted for type of service

1232	$10 Steam train and signal (B)
1233	$30 Steam train and signal (A)
1234	$50 Steam train and signal (C)
1235	$100 Steam train and signal (D)
1236	$200 Steam train and signal (A)
1237	$500 Steam train and signal (A)

Set of 6   95·00   75·00

Overprint translation: (A) Domestic Letter Fee; (B) Express Letter Fee; (C) Registered Letter Fee; (D) Air Mail Fee.

Revenue stamps surcharged

1284	1c on $5,000 Steam train and signal
1285	4c on $100 Steam train and signal
1286	4c on $3,000 Steam train and signal
1287	10c on $50 Steam train and signal
1288	10c on $1,000 Steam train and signal
1289	20c on $1,000 Steam train and signal
1290	50c on $30 Steam train and signal
1291	50c on $50 Steam train and signal
1292	$1 on $50 Steam train and signal

Set of 9   24·00   16·50

Revenue stamps surcharged as Nos. 1284/92, but with key pattern at top and bottom inverted

1312	1c on $20 Steam train and signal
1313	10c on $20 Steam train and signal

Set of 2   32·00   34·00

MANCHURIA

Kirin and Heilunkiang

1927

用貼黑吉限

Nos. 309/21 of China overprinted

1†	½c Steam train on bridge	25	25
2†	1c Steam train on bridge	25	10
3†	1½c Steam train on bridge	75	75
4†	2c Steam train on bridge	50	40
5†	3c Steam train on bridge	60	60
6†	4c Steam train on bridge	50	10
7†	5c Steam train on bridge	75	30
8†	6c Steam train on bridge	75	50
9†	7c Steam train on bridge	1·75	1·75
10†	8c Steam train on bridge	1·50	1·50
11†	10c Steam train on bridge	1·75	10

SINKIANG

1915

Nos. 309/21 of China overprinted

47†	½c Steam train on bridge	25	25
48†	1c Steam train on bridge	40	10
49†	1½c Steam train on bridge	1·00	1·50
50†	2c Steam train on bridge	50	40
4†	3c Steam train on bridge	50	10
5†	4c Steam train on bridge	50	40
52†	4c Steam train on bridge (grey)	2·75	1·75
53†	4c Steam train on bridge (olive)	1·25	75
6†	5c Steam train on bridge	50	40
7†	6c Steam train on bridge (grey)	50	60
55†	6c Steam train on bridge (red)	1·50	1·00
56†	6c Steam train on bridge (brown)	12·00	13·00
8†	7c Steam train on bridge	1·00	1·50
9†	8c Steam train on bridge	1·50	1·25
10†	10c Steam train on bridge	1·50	25

1932

空航

Nos. 6 and 10 overprinted

83†	5c Steam train on bridge	£100	75·00
84†	10c Steam train on bridge	£100	65·00

1942

用貼省新限

Nos. 599/600 and 602/4 of China overprinted

221	8c Steam train and mine truck
215	21c Steam train and mine truck
216	28c Steam train and mine truck
223	33c Steam train and mine truck
218	50c Steam train and mine truck
225	$1 Steam train and mine truck

Set of 6   13·00   44·00

SZECHWAN

1933

用貼川四限

Nos. 310 and 316 of China overprinted

1†	1c Steam train on bridge	75	35
2†	5c Steam train on bridge	2·00	10

YUNNAN
1926

用貼省滇限

Nos. 309/21 of China overprinted

1†	½c Steam train on bridge	20	30
2†	1c Steam train on bridge	45	10
3†	1½c Steam train on bridge	70	1·00
4†	2c Steam train on bridge	65	40
5†	3c Steam train on bridge	65	40
6†	4c Steam train on bridge	65	10
7†	5c Steam train on bridge	70	35
8†	6c Steam train on bridge	1·75	1·00
9†	7c Steam train on bridge	2·00	2·25
10†	8c Steam train on bridge	2·00	1·50
11†	10c Steam train on bridge	1·75	10

Communist Regional Issues
CENTRAL CHINA
1949

Revenue stamps as 1949 issue of Chinese Republic surcharged

CC71	$3 on $30 Steam train and signal
CC72	$15 on $15 Steam train and signal
CC73	$30 on $50 Steam train and signal
CC74	$60 on $50 Steam train and signal
CC75	$130 on $15 Steam train and signal

Set of 5   7·00   10·50

Nos. 1151, 1124, 1142, 1147, 1131 and 1141 of Chinese Republic surcharged

CC79	$5 on $2,000 on $300 Steam train and signal
CC80	$10 on $200 on $50 Steam train and signal
CC81	$10 on $200 on $500 Steam train and signal
CC82	$30 on $50 on $300 Steam train and signal
CC83	$50 on $100 on $50 Steam train and signal
CC84	$100 on $25 on $20 Steam train and signal

Set of 6   12·00   15·00

EAST CHINA
1949

EC307A	$1 Steam train
EC308A	$2 Steam train
EC309A	$3 Steam train

EC310A	$5 Steam train
EC311A	$10 Steam train
EC312A	$13 Steam train
EC313A	$18 Steam train
EC314A	$21 Steam train
EC315A	$30 Steam train
EC316A	$50 Steam train
EC317A	$100 Steam train

Set of 11   9·00   14·50

Dated "1949.2.7"

EC320A	$1 Steam train
EC321A	$2 Steam train
EC322A	$3 Steam train
EC323A	$5 Steam train
EC324A	$10 Steam train
EC325A	$13 Steam train
EC326A	$18 Steam train
EC327A	$21 Steam train
EC328A	$30 Steam train
EC329A	$50 Steam train
EC330A	$100 Steam train

Set of 11   2·50   14·00

No. 1122 of Chinese Republic surcharged

EC351	$5 on 50c on $20 Steam train and signal
EC352	$10 on 50c on $20 Steam train and signal
EC353	$20 on 50c on $20 Steam train and signal
EC354	$20 on 50c on $20 Steam train and signal

Set of 4   21·00   22·00

As Nos. EC320/30, but dated "1949"

EC370	$10 Steam train
EC371	$15 Steam train
EC372	$30 Steam train
EC373	$50 Steam train
EC374	$60 Steam train
EC375	$100 Steam train
EC376	$1,600 Steam train
EC377	$2,000 Steam train

Set of 8   5·00   8·00

NORTH CHINA

PARCEL POST STAMPS

1949

NCP374	$500 Steam train
NCP375	$1,000 Steam train
NCP376	$2,000 Steam train

NCP377 $5,000 Steam train
NCP378 $10,000 Steam train
NCP379 $20,000 Steam train
NCP380 $50,000 Steam train

Set of 7   £400   £325

NORTH EAST CHINA

1947

NE38 $1 Railwaymen and steam locomotive
NE39 $2 Railwaymen and steam locomotive
NE40 $5 Railwaymen and steam locomotive
NE41 $10 Railwaymen and steam locomotive

Set of 4   4·25   9·00

1949

NE178 $5,000 Steam train at factory
NE179 $10,000 Steam train at factory
NE180 $50,000 Steam train at factory
NE181 $100,000 Steam train at factory

Set of 4   7·00   30·00

NE192 $1,500 Steam train at factory   20   1·75

No. NE192 *surcharged*
NE197† $5,000 on $1,500 Steam train at factory   30   2·50

1950

NE230 $2,500 Steam locomotive
NE231 $5,000 Steam locomotive

Set of 2   7·00   8·50

PARCEL POST STAMPS

1951

NEP247 $100,000 Steam locomotive
NEP248 $300,000 Steam locomotive
NEP249 $500,000 Steam locomotive
NEP250 $1,000,000 Steam locomotive

Set of 4   £350

PORT ARTHUR AND DAIREN

1949

54†   Train on dock ....   10·00   12·00

No. 54 surcharged
59† $100 on $10 Train on dock £250   £250
61† $500 on $10 Train on dock £750   £750

62    $10 "Labour" and steam locomotive ......   6·00   10·00

SOUTH WEST CHINA

1950

人
民　西
郵
政　南

No. 1211 *of Chinese Republic overprinted*
SW44†   (–) Steam locomotive ....   65·00   55·00

Chinese People's Republic

1949 100 cents = 1 yuan
1955 100 fen = 1 yuan

1950

中國人民郵政

No. 1211 *of Chinese Republic surcharged*

1424†	$500 on (–) Steam locomotive	10	15
1430†	$800 on (–) Steam locomotive	60	20
1426†	$1,000 on (–) Steam locomotive	10	10

1469	$400 Steam locomotive	
1470	$800 Steam locomotive	

Set of 2   6·50   5·00

中國人民郵政

壹佰圓

★★

Nos. EC370/1, EC373, EC376/7 *of East China surcharged*

1474	$50 on $10 Steam train
1475	$100 on $15 Steam train
1476	$300 on $50 Steam train
1477	$400 on $1,600 Steam train
1478	$400 on $2,000 Steam train

Set of 5   60   3·25

1951

中國人民郵政

貳拾伍圓 [25]

No. 1211 *of Chinese Republic surcharged*

1506†	$25 on (–) Steam locomotive	10	75

1952

1566†	$800 Chengtu Railway Viaduct	20	10

1954

1611†	$250 Steam train on bridge, Tienshui–Lanchow Railway	10	10
1614†	$800 Mine trucks, Fuhsin open cast mine	10	10

1955

1666†	8f Electric mine locomotive	25	10
1667†	8f Petroleum trucks and derricks	25	10
1669†	8f Steam train at factory	25	10
1677†	8f Steam train on dock	30	10

1957

1720	8f Yangtse River Railway Bridge		
1721	20f Aerial view of Yangtse River Railway Bridge		

Set of 2   65   20

1729†	35f Railway tracks	10·00	65

WHEN YOU BUY AN ALBUM LOOK FOR THE NAME "STANLEY GIBBONS"

It means Quality combined with Value for Money.

1958

1741† 16f Steam train on viaduct 30 10

1959

1850† 8f Goods wagons at steel mill 35 10
1851† 8f Steam locomotive and coal trucks 35 10
1853† 8f Steam locomotive on bridge 35 15

1868† 4f Electric train on bridge 30 15

1960

1932 8f Peking Railway Station
1933 10f Steam train arriving at station
　　　　　　　　　　　　　　　Set of 2　8·00　2·00

1961

1972 8f Chan Tien-yu (railway construction
　　　engineer)

1973 10f Train on Peking–Changchow Railway
　　　　　　　　　　　　　　Set of 2　2·00　30

1963

2135† 10f Railway tracks, Hwangshan 70 8

1964

2220† 20f Petroleum trucks .... 10·00 1·50

2232† 8f Petroleum trucks at chemical factory 25 10

1966

2304† 4f Mobile transformer .... 3·50 20

2313† 8f Train conductress 15 10

1967

2341†8f   Steam locomotive .... 4·25   2·25

1968

2392†   8f Railwayman holding lantern ("The
Red Lantern" opera) .... 3·00   1·75

1972

2478†   8f Railwayman holding lantern ("The
Red Lantern" opera) .... 1·25   1·00
2479†   8f Steam locomotive ("Red Detachment
of Women" ballet) 50   50

1973

2504†   8f Steam locomotive ("New Power in the
Mines" painting) 30   30

2535†   1y Steam and diesel trains .... 2·75   25

1975

2599†   8f Diesel train at steel mill 40   30

1976

2642†   8f Steam coal train 20   20
2647†   8f Diesel train on viaduct 20   20

2661†   8f Yangtse River Railway Bridge 40   30

2684†   10f Shaoshan Railway Station 35   15

1977

2697†   1f Diesel coal train 10   10
2699†   2f Loading diesel locomotive on ship .. 10   10

2700†	3f Diesel locomotive and lumber trucks	10	10
2710†	70f Diesel train on Yangtse Viaduct	55	35

2712†	8f Yangtse River Railway Bridge	40	15

2720†	10f Mongolian iron ore train	30	20

1978

2750†	8f Petroleum trucks at Tung Fang Hung Refinery, Peking	25	10

2787†	8f Goods wagons	10	10

2797†	8f Automated loading of burning coke	25	12
2801†	8f Loading steel train	25	12

2845†	10f Loading mine trucks	25	15
2846†	20f Electric mine train	40	20

1979

2909	8f "Shaoshan" type electric locomotive		
2910	8f Train on viaduct		
2911	8f Goods train crossing bridge		
	Set of 3	1·40	50

1980

2977†	8f Railway post office carriage	30	10

1981

3074†	8f Diesel train	20	10

1983

3235	8f Peking–Hankow Railway Workers Strike Memorial Tower, Jiangan		
3236	8f Memorial Tower, Zhengzhou		
	Set of 2	40	20

3282	8f Steam locomotive	15	10

Taiwan

100 cents = 1 yuan

1949

用貼灣臺限

No. 1211 *of Chinese Republic overprinted*
86† (–) Steam locomotive 75 20

1954

180 40c Silo Bridge over River Cho-Shui-chi
181 $1.60 Silo Bridge over River-Cho-Shui-chi
182 $3.60 Silo Bridge over River Cho-Shui-chi
183 $5 Silo Bridge over River Cho-Shui-chi
Set of 4 55·00 3·50

1956

角貳

0.20

No. 1211 *of Chinese Republic surcharged*
224† 20c on (–) Steam locomotive 50 10
304† 20c on (–) Steam locomotive 25 10
On No. 304 the Chinese characters are below the figures.

225 40c Steam train and map of China
226 $1 Steam train and map of China
227 $1.60 Steam train and map of China
228 $2 Steam train and map of China
Set of 4 3·00 1·00

233 40c Earliest and latest locomotives
234 $2 Earliest and latest locomotives
235 $8 Earliest and latest locomotives
Set of 3 6·75 85

1961

403 80c Jeme Tien-yao (railway engineer) and
steam locomotive
404 $2 Jeme Tien-yao (railway engineer) and
steam locomotive
Set of 2 1·75 45

1967

601† $5 Diesel train .... 1·25 15

1968

674† $2.50 Steam locomotive .... 1·00 30

1972

908† $5 Diesel railcar under bridge 75 30

1974

1021† $1 Tunnel, Taiwan North Link Railway 15 10
1023† $2.50 Electric train and signal bridge 25 10

1976

1099† $8 Diesel locomotive 50 15

As Nos. 1021/3, but Chinese inscription in double-lined characters. Figures of value solid.
1122a† $1 Tunnel, Taiwan North Link Railway 15 10
1122b† $2 Electric train and signal bridge 15 10

1125† $10 Chiang Kai-shek and Dr Sun
Yat-sen in railway carriage 60 25

1977

1137 $2 Steam goods train
1138 $10 Steam goods train
Set of 2 70 30

As Nos. 1122a/b, but redrawn with double-lined figures of value
1145† $1 Tunnel, Taiwan North Link Railway 10 10
1146† $2 Electric train and signal bridge 15 10

No. 1146 overprinted 1977 and five vertical lines of Chinese characters
1168† $2 Electric train and signal bridge 12 5

1980

1316† $2 Electric train, T.R.A. Trunk Line 10 10
1325† $2 Diesel train leaving tunnel on Taiwan
North Link Line 10 10

1981

1361 $2 Electric and first steam locomotives
1362 $14 Side view of steam and electric
locomotives
Set of 2 65 50

1397† $3 Diesel locomotive 15 10

1985

1623† Diesel locomotive 10 10

1986

1695† $2 Diesel locomotive 15 5

1989

1857 $3 Taipeh Underground train in tunnel
1858 $16 Taipeh Underground train in cutting
Set of 2 70 35

POSTAGE DUE STAMPS

1953

Revenue stamps as 1949 *issue of Chinese Republic surcharged*
D151   10c on $50 Steam train and signal
D152   20c on $100 Steam train and signal
D153   40c on $20 Steam train and signal
D154   80c on $500 Steam train and signal
D155   100c on $30 Steam train and signal
                          Set of 5   36·00   22·00

CHRISTMAS ISLAND

Indian Ocean
100 cents = 1 dollar

1963

11†   2c Map showing railway lines   40   15
15†   8c Phosphate train   ....   1·60   35

1972

37   1c Map showing railway lines
38   2c Map showing railway lines
39   3c Map showing railway lines
40   4c Map showing railway lines
41   5c Map showing railway lines
42   6c Map showing railway lines
43   7c Map showing railway lines
44   8c Map showing railway lines
45   9c Map showing railway lines
46   10c Map showing railway lines
47   20c Map showing railway lines
48   25c Map showing railway lines
49   30c Map showing railway lines
50   35c Map showing railway lines
51   50c Map showing railway lines
52   $1 Map showing railway lines
                          Set of 16   10·00   8·50

1973

57   7c Map showing railway lines
58   25c Map showing railway lines
                          Set of 2   3·50   1·75

1979

114†   20c Map showing railway lines (on
         stamp No. 11)   25   30

1981

137†   28c Loading phosphate trucks   25   25
138†   40c Diesel locomotive and phosphate
         train   40   40

1988

256†   55c Phosphate mine trucks, 1910   50   55
257†   70c Steam locomotive No. 1, 1914   65   70

COLOMBIA

South America
100 centavos = 1 peso

1917

400† 40c La Sabana Railway Station .... 9·00 2·50

1939

541† 40c La Sabana Railway Station .... 18·00 8·00

1959

992† 25c Railway train .... 1·25 75

1962

1109† 10c Monserrate cable and funicular
railway 15 15

1129 10c Railway map of Colombia Atlantic
Railway
1130 5c 1854 and 1961 locomotives (air)

1131 10c Railway map of Colombia Atlantic
Railway
1132 1p Magdalena Railway Bridge
1133 5p Magdalena Railway Bridge

Set of 5 9·00 2·50

1974

1367 1p10 La Quiebra Tunnel, Antioquia
Railway 30 10

ACKNOWLEDGEMENT OF RECEIPT STAMPS

1917

AR371† 4c La Sabana Railway Station .... 7·50 6·50

OFFICIAL STAMPS

1937

No. 400 overprinted **OFICIAL**
O503† 40c La Sabana Railway Station ...... 13·00 8·50

COMORO ISLANDS

Indian Ocean
100 centimes = 1 franc

1976

186† 50f Children in locomotive and tender
(on United Nations No. 162) 75 40

1977

221 20f French locomotive, 1837
222 25f Brazilian steam locomotive (19th century)
223 50f Trans-Siberian Express, 1905
224 75f "Southern Belle" pullman express, 1910-1925
225 200f "Pacific" locomotive, 1930 (air)
226 500f "Rheingold Express", 1933
　　　　　　　　　Set of 6　　7·50　　2·00
MS227 500f Locomotive *Nord Express*, 1925　4·00　1·50

1978

300† 20f Locomotive *Der Adler* . . . . 　80　　50

1979

372† 100f Early locomotive and toy train . . . . . . 　1·25　　60

STAMP MONTHLY
— finest and most informative magazine for all collectors. Obtainable from your newsagent or by postal subscription — details on request.

1982

496† 75f "Sleeping Porter" (painting Norman Rockwell) . . . . 　1·25　　85

Appendix
The following stamps have either been issued in excess of postal needs, or have not been made available to the public in reasonable quantities at face value. Miniature sheets, imperforate stamps, etc. are excluded in this section.

1976

American Revolution 500f.

CONGO (BRAZZAVILLE)

Central Africa
100 centimes = 1 franc

1966

106 60f Pointe-Noire Railway Station . . . . 　1·25　　75

1968

149 45f Train crossing Mayombe Viaduct . . . . 　1·25　　40

1969

169 50f Mindouli Railway Viaduct (on Middle
Congo No. 76) .... 1·40 1·00

175 100f Doll and toy steam locomotive ...... 1·75 60

188 40f Train entering Mbamba Tunnel
189 60f Train crossing the Mayombe
Set of 2 3·75 90

1970

222 25f Laying cable
223 30f Diesel locomotive and cable-laying
gang
Set of 2 2·75 1·00

246 40f "Mikado 141" steam locomotive, 1932
247 60f Type "130 + 032" steam locomotive,
1947

248 75f Alsthom "BB 1100" engine, 1962
249 85f C.E.M. C.A.F.L. "BB BB 302" diesel,
1969
Set of 4 10·00 6·00

1971

Nos. 222/3 surcharged **REPUBLIQUE POPULAIRE DU CONGO
INAUGURATION DE LA LIAISON COAXIALE 18-11-71** and new
value
325 30f on 25f Laying cable
326 40f on 30f Diesel locomotive and
cable-laying gang
Set of 2 2·00 60

1973

371 30f Golwe steam locomotive, 1935
372 40f Diesel-electric locomotive, 1935
373 75f Whitcomb diesel-electric locomotive,
1946
374 85f "CC/200" diesel-electric locomotive,
1973
Set of 4 9·00 5·00

1974

428 75f George Stephenson with early and
modern locomotives .... 1·00 60

1975

450 50f Paris–Brussels Railway Line, 1890
451 75f Santa Fe Line
Set of 2 2·25 1·00

453† 50f Steam train on trestle 90 50

1979

669† 150f U.P.U. emblem and locomotive .... 1·50 1·00

670 65f Sir Rowland Hill and diesel locomotive
671 100f Steam locomotive
672 200f Diesel locomotive
673 300f Steam locomotive

Set of 4 4·25 50
MS674 500f French "TGV" train .... 3·50 60

1980

783 75f New railway bridge 45 25

COLLECT MAMMALS ON STAMPS

A Stanley Gibbons thematic catalogue on this popular subject. Copies available at £7.50 (p. + p. £2) from: Stanley Gibbons Publications Ltd, 5 Parkside, Christchurch Road, Ringwood, Hants BH24 3SH.

1982

846 100f "Inter-city 125" Train
847 150f Shinkansen train, Japan
848 200f Advanced Passenger Train, Great Britain
849 300f TGV 001 locomotive

Set of 4 4·25 2·00

1984

950 10f Loulombo Station
951 25f Chinese railway workers camp, Les Bandas
952 125f "50" forming bridge and tunnel, and diesel train
953 200f Railway Headquarters building

Set of 4 3·25 1·40

954 100f "CC203" diesel locomotive and log trucks
955 150f "BB103" diesel train
956 300f "BB-BB301" diesel locomotive and log trucks
957 500f "BB420" Diesel train L'Eclair

Set of 4 6·25 4·50

POSTAGE DUE STAMPS

1961

D27† 10f Steam locomotive, 1932 .... 60 40
D28† 10f Diesel locomotive 60 40

COOK ISLANDS

South Pacific
100 cents = 1 dollar

1979

636† 30c Railway train 35 25

1980

No. 636 overprinted **ZEAPEX STAMP EXHIBITION AUCKLAND**
1980
690† 30c Railway train 30 30

1985

1022 20c "The Kingston Flyer" (New Zealand)
1023 55c Class "640" locomotive (Italy)
1024 65c "Gotthard" type locomotive
    (Switzerland)
1025 75c Union Pacific locomotive No. 6900
    (U.S.A.)
1026 95c "Super Continental" type locomotive
    (Canada)
1027 $1.25 "TGV" type train (France)
1028 $2.20 "The Flying Scotsman" (Great
    Britain)
1029 $3.40 "The Orient Express"
                Set of 8 10·00 7·00

COSTA RICA

Central America
100 centimos = 1 colon

1901

48† 1col Steam train on Birris Bridge .... 32·00 7·50

1912

Telegraph stamps surcharged **CORREOS DOS CENTIMOS 2**
102 2c on 5c Steam train
109 2c on 10c Steam train
104 2c on 50c Steam train
105 2c on 1col Steam train
112 2c on 2col Steam train
107 2c on 5col Steam train
108 2c on 10col Steam train
                Set of 7 75·00 50·00

1929

Telegraph stamps as 1912 issue surcharged **CORREOS** *and*
value
171 5c on 2col Steam train
173 13c on 40c Steam train
                Set of 2 50 40

1930

Telegraph stamps as 1912 issue overprinted or surcharged
Correo Aereo
182† 5c on 10c Steam train 20 10
183† 20c on 50c Steam train 20 15
184† 40c on 50c Steam train 40 15
185† 1col Steam train .... 1·50 40

1932

Telegraph stamp as 1912 issue overprinted with wings inscribed
CORREO CR AEREO
193 40c Steam train .... 2·50 60

1945

Telegraph stamps as 1912 issue overprinted **CORREO AEREO**
1945
402 40c Steam train
403 50c Steam train
404 1col Steam train
                Set of 3 1·40 75

1947

461 35c Steam locomotive .... 2·50 90

1957

548† 5c Map of Costa Rica showing railway
lines 5 5

1959

570† 20c Tracks on Puntarenas Quay 50 10
574† 1col Electric train .... 1·60 40

1963

669† 10col Mule drawn mail van .... 7·50 4·00

1980

1206† 2col10 Rio Frio Railway Bridge .... 2·25 90

1981

1225† 2col10 Ass-drawn mail van, 1857 ...... 2·50 1·50

1982

1272† 3col Electric railway line to Atlantic
coast .... 2·00 75

OFFICIAL STAMPS

1901

No. 48 overprinted **OFICIAL**
O59† 1col Steam train on Birris Bridge ...... 32·00 22·00

CROATIA

South-east Europe
100 banicas = 1 kuna

1941

32† 25b Tracks and tunnel, Mt. Ozalj 5 5

1944

136† 12k50 + 6k Side-dump trucks 8 15

COLLECT MAMMALS ON STAMPS
A Stanley Gibbons thematic catalogue on this popular
subject. Copies available at £7.50 (p. + p. £2) from:
Stanley Gibbons Publications Ltd, 5 Parkside,
Christchurch Road, Ringwood, Hants BH24 3SH.

CUBA

West Indies
100 centavos = 1 peso

1928

357† 8c Railway station, Havana .... 2·00 1·00
361† 30c Goods wagons at sugar refinery .... 3·50 75

1936

404† 5c Steam locomotive, Matanzas .... 1·25 20
412† 50c Steam locomotive and goods
wagons, Fort San Severino (air) ...... 7·00 2·00

1937

424† 5c Goods wagons at sugar refinery ...... 1·10 20

Surcharged **1837 1937 PRIMER CENTENARIO FERROCARRIL
EN CUBA** and value either side of an early engine and coach
425 10c on 25c Coat of arms .... 4·50 75

1950

544 1c Balanzategui, Pausa and railway crash
545 2c Balanzategui, Pausa and railway crash
546 5c Balanzategui, Pausa and railway crash
Set of 3 3·00 1·25

1954

701† 15c Train load of sugar .... 1·75 50
702† 20c Sugar cane wagons 80 10
705† 40c Tracks on dock .... 2·50 75

1960

925† 8c Derailed goods wagons, Battle of
Santa Clara .... 1·40 40

1965

1313† 4c "TEM-4" diesel locomotive .... 1·40 30
1314† 7c "BB.69,000" diesel locomotive ...... 1·40 30

1967

1547† 5c Train at factory ("Dawn of the Five
Year Plan" painting by Romas) 85 25

1970

1778† 10c Ox-cart and diesel locomotive .... 1·50 30

1971

1865†   3c "Little Train" (children's drawing by Yuri Ruiz)   25   15

1974

2088†   13c Derailed goods wagons. Battle of Santa Clara (on stamp No. 925) ......   1·40   40

1975

2242   1c *La Junta*, Cuba's first locomotive, 1837
2243   3c Steam locomotive *M.M. Prieto*, 1910
2244   5c Russian "TEM-4" diesel locomotive
2245   13c Hungarian "DVM-9" diesel locomotive
2246   30c Russian "M-62K" diesel locomotive
              Set of 5   2·40   60

1980

2663   1c Inspection locomotive
2664   2c Inspection locomotive, Chaparra Sugar Company
2665   7c Steam storage locomotive

2666   10c Four-coupled double-ended locomotive
2667   13c Four-coupled locomotive
2668   30c Oil combustion locomotive, 1909
              Set of 6   1·75   50

MS2681   50c Steam locomotive, 1839 ....   1·50   1·50

1981

2704   3c Toy steam train   20   10

2726†   1c Horse-drawn tram   5   5

1982

2865   5c Miniature steam train and boating lake, Lenin Park, Havana   15   8

1983

2971† 20c Railway tracks, Santa Clara 75 35

1984

3015 1c Steam locomotive
3016 4c Steam locomotive No. 73
3017 5c Steam locomotive
3018 10c Steam locomotive
3019 30c Steam locomotive No. 350
3020 50c Steam locomotive No. 495

Set of 6 3·00 1·25

MS3054 1p Locomotive No. 498 . . . . 3·00 3·00

1985

3082 20c Small steam locomotive (on stamp
No. 493 of Argentine Republic) 65 25

1986

3173 1c *Stourbridge Lion* (U.S.A.), 1829
3174 4c *Rocket* (Great Britain), 1829

3175 5c First Russian locomotive, 1845
3176 8c Sequin's locomotive (France), 1830
3177 30c First Canadian locomotive, 1836
3178 50c Belgium Grand Central Railway
steam locomotive, 1872

Set of 6 1·90 80
MS3179 1p *La Junta* (Cuba), 1837 . . . . 2·10 1·75

1987

3296 3c Balanzategui, Pausa and railway
crash (on stamp No. 545)
3297 5c "BB 69.000" diesel locomotive (on
stamp No. 1314)
3298 10c *La Junta*, Cuba's first locomotive,
1837 (on stamp No. 2242)
3299 20c Steam locomotive *M.M. Prieto*, 1910
(on stamp No. 2243)
3300 35c Four-coupled double-ended
locomotive (on stamp No. 2666)
3301 40c Four-coupled locomotive (on stamp
No. 2667)

Set of 6 1·90 1·40
MS3302 Two sheets. 1p 1937 **PRIMER
CENTENARIO FERROCARRIL EN CUBA.**
10c surcharge (No. 428) (other sheet shows
Nos. 3296/301 imperforate)

Set of 2 sheets 3·75 2·00

1988

3346 20c Early Cuban steam locomotive
pulling passenger train 30 25

SPECIAL DELIVERY STAMPS

1945

E485 10c Steam locomotive . . . . 2·00 40

CYPRUS

Mediterranean
1949 40 paras = 1 piastre
180 piastres = 1 pound
1955 1000 milliemes = 1 pound

1949

As No. 114 of Antigua
168† 1½pi Silhouette of steam locomotive 50 55

1955

176† 10m Mine truck, copper pyrites mine 25 5

1960

KYΠPIAKH
ΔHMOKPATIA
KIBRIS
CUMHURIYETI

No. 176 overprinted "CYPRUS REPUBLIC" in Greek and Turkish
191† 10m Mine truck, copper pyrites mine 30 5

Turkish Cypriot Posts

100 kurus = 1 lira

1986

202 50li Locomotive No. 11 and Trakhoni
station
203 100li Locomotive No. 1
Set of 2 95 80

CZECHOSLOVAKIA ARMY IN SIBERIA

Eastern Asia
100 kopeks = 1 rouble

1919

2† 50k Armoured train Orik (imperf) .... 8·75 12·50
5† 50k Armoured train Orik (perf) .... 8·25 8·25

CZECHOSLOVAKIA

Central Europe
100 haleru = 1 koruna

1926

258† 40h Railway bridge, Orava Castle 50 10
273b† 3k Railway bridge, Orava Castle 75 10

1938

388† 50h Steam train, armament factory,
Pilsen 10 8

1949

545† 3k Mail-coach and steam train .... 2·40 1·75

1950

588† 2k Dump truck and steam shovel .... 2·00 75

603 1k50 Steam train on viaduct
604 3k Steam train on viaduct
Set of 2 1·75 1·00

1952

677† 1k50 Steam locomotive and electric welding 30 25

726† 2k Tracks, Ostrava Mine 10 8
727† 3k Tracks and mechanical excavator 15 5

732 1k50 Goods wagon on dock 20 10

1953

767† 2k Tracks and welder 15 8
768† 3k Steam train at Gottwald Foundry, Kuncice 15 8

806† 60h Steam locomotive 60 20

1954

824† 1k60 Mine trucks .... 2·25 10
826† 2k40 Woman engine-driver .... 2·75 10

1955

903† 20h Railway viaduct 25 20
904† 30h Steam train crossing bridge 15 10
905† 60h Railway tunnel 20 5

1956

911† 60h Goods wagons 15 5

946 10h Steam locomotive *Zbraslav*, 1846
947 30h Steam locomotive *Kladno*, 1855
948 40h Steam locomotive RADY "534.0", 1945
949 45h Steam locomotive RADY "556.0", 1952
950 60h Steam locomotive RADY "477.0", 1955
951 1k Electric locomotive "E499.0", 1954
Set of 6 20·00 10·00

1957

984† 60h F. J. Gerstner (engineer) 25 8

ALBUM LISTS

Write for our latest list of albums and accessories. This will be sent on request.

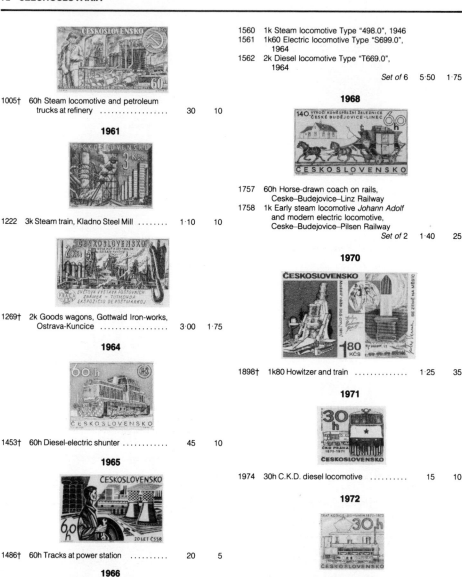

1005† 60h Steam locomotive and petroleum trucks at refinery 30 10

1961

1222 3k Steam train, Kladno Steel Mill .... 1·10 10

1269† 2k Goods wagons, Gottwald Iron-works, Ostrava-Kuncice .... 3·00 1·75

1964

1453† 60h Diesel-electric shunter 45 10

1965

1486† 60h Tracks at power station 20 5

1966

1557 20h Steam locomotive *Ajax*, 1841
1558 30h Steam locomotive *Karlstejn*, 1865
1559 60h Steam locomotive Type "423.0", 1946

1560 1k Steam locomotive Type "498.0", 1946
1561 1k60 Electric locomotive Type "S699.0", 1964
1562 2k Diesel locomotive Type "T669.0", 1964
Set of 6   5·50   1·75

1968

1757 60h Horse-drawn coach on rails, Ceske–Budejovice–Linz Railway
1758 1k Early steam locomotive *Johann Adolf* and modern electric locomotive, Ceske–Budejovice–Pilsen Railway
Set of 2   1·40   25

1970

1898† 1k80 Howitzer and train .... 1·25 35

1971

1974 30h C.K.D. diesel locomotive 15 10

1972

2025 30h Steam and electric locomotives, Kosice–Bohumin Railway 20 8

2051† 1k Steam locomotive and pendant in line-work 60 15

1973

2130† 1k40 Railway bridge, Orava Castle 30 5

1974

2186† 60h Early railway carriage 35 5

1975

2249† 1k Underground Railway, Prague 55 10

1976

2286† 60h Trams at Manes Hall, Prague 40 10
2288† 2k Tram at Powder Tower, Prague 90 20

1978

2408† 40h Railway Bridge, Prague 35 10

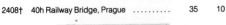

2420† 60h Gottwald Bridge, Prague 40 10

1979

2449† 30h "Soyuz 28" on launch truck 12 12

1982

2618 6k Locomotives of 1922 and 1982 ...... 2·50 2·00

2643† 4k Railway Bridge over Danube,
Bratislava .... 1·25 1·00

1984

2754† 2k Diesel locomotive and container
trucks 90 30

1985

2801† 1k Train and map of Prague
underground railway 40 10

WHEN YOU BUY AN ALBUM LOOK
FOR THE NAME "STANLEY GIBBONS"
It means Quality combined with Value for Money.

1986

2818	4k Steam locomotive *Kladno*, 1855	85	30

2850	50h Type "Kt8" articulated tram of 1920		
2851	1k Series "E458.1" electric shunting engine and 1882-1913 steam locomotive		
2852	3k Series "T466.2" diesel locomotive and 1900-24 steam locomotive		
2853	5k Series "M152.0" railcar and 1930-35 railbus		
	Set of 4	2·75	75

1987

2882†	4k Tank locomotive *Archduke Charles*, 1907	95	35
2883†	4k Prague tram, 1900	95	35

2891†	1k Cranes with egg on railway points (book illustration by Frederic Clement)	40	15

DAHOMEY

West Africa
100 centimes = 1 franc

1906

18†	1c General Faidherbe (builder of Dakar–St. Louis Railway)	30	30

19†	2c General Faidherbe (builder of Dakar–St. Louis Railway)	30	30
20†	4c General Faidherbe (builder of Dakar–St. Louis Railway)	70	60
21†	5c General Faidherbe (builder of Dakar–St. Louis Railway)	4·00	60
22†	10c General Faidherbe (builder of Dakar–St. Louis Railway)	5·50	75

1968

342†	70f Loading mail on train	1·90	80

1970

402†	5f Japanese "Hikari" electric train on bridge	15	10

1974

553†	125f French mobile post office van, 1860	2·00	75

557	35f 2-3-2 locomotive, 1911		
558	40f 0-3-0 goods locomotive, 1877		
559	100f "Crampton" locomotive, 1849		
560	200f "Stephenson" locomotive, 1846		
	Set of 4	4·75	2·00

POSTAGE DUE STAMPS

1967

D313† 5f Modern railcar 25 20

DANZIG

Baltic
100 pfennig = 1 mark

1920

Nos. 113/15 of Germany overprinted **DANZIG** *horizontally*
8† 1m Tram, General Post Office, Berlin 50 40
9† 1m25 Tram, General Post Office, Berlin .. 50 40
10† 1m50 Tram, General Post Office, Berlin .. 70 65

DENMARK

Northern Europe
100 ore = 1 krone

1947

351† 20ore + 5ore Bombed railway 60 60

353 15ore First Danish locomotive *Odin*
354 20ore Steam train
355 40ore Diesel train *Lyntog*
Set of 3 1·75 80

1955

No. 351 surcharged
400† 30ore + 5ore on 20ore + 5ore Bombed
railway .... 1·25 1·25

1963

452 15ore Rail and sea symbols of
Denmark–Germany Railway 20 10

1972

540 70ore Early locomotive, ship and
passengers 40 10

1976

626† 100ore Interior of Central Railway
Station, Copenhagen 50 10

1983

767† 2k50 Elderly people on train 50 10

1986

824† 2k80 Hoje Tastrup Railway Station and
diesel locomotive 75 15

1987

851 280ore Steam locomotive and mail
wagon, 1912 .... 75 10

DJIBOUTI REPUBLIC

East Africa
100 centimes = 1 franc

1977

No. 682 of French Territory of the Afars and the Issas overprinted
REPUBLIQUE DE DJIBOUTI

705† 75f Volta and electric train . . . . 2·50   2·50

1979

749 40f Alsthom "BB 1201" locomotive
750 55f Locomotive No. 231
751 60f Locomotive No. 130
752 75f Diesel locomotive "CC 2001"
                         Set of 4   2·00   1·00

764† 80f Diesel train . . . . 1·40   1·00

1980

779† 100f Lion Club banner and steam
    locomotive . . . . 1·25   30

1981

804 100f Diesel train . . . . 1·50   90

812 40f German "231" and American "RC4"
    locomotives
813 55f George Stephenson, *Rocket* and
    Djibouti locomotive
814 65f French and Japanese high speed
    trains
                         Set of 3   1·90   75

1982

855† 55f Diesel train . . . . 1·25   40

1985

951 55f Steam locomotive No. 29, Addis
    Ababa–Djibouti Railway
952 75f German locomotive *Der Adler*, 1835
                       Set of 2   1·50   1·25

DOMINICA

West Indies
100 cents = 1 dollar

1949

As No. 114 of Antigua
114† 5c Silhouette of locomotive 15 15

1976

534† 1c Tracks at launch centre 5 5
535† 2c Railway wagons 5 5

1984

Commonwealth of DOMINICA
60¢
CHRISTMAS 1984

929† 60c Donald Duck as Father Christmas
riding toy steam train 70 40

1987

Commonwealth of
DOMINICA 15¢
MAGLEV-MLU 001
Fastest Rail Speed With Passenger

1086† 15c MAGLEV-MLU 001 (fastest
passenger train), 1979 .... 12 10
1088† 35c First elevated railway, New York,
1868 .... 20 20
1089† 45c Tom Thumb (first U.S. passenger
locomotive), 1830 .... 25 25
1092† $1 First cable cars, San Francisco,
1873 .... 50 50
1093† $3 "Orient Express", 1883 .... 1·50 1·50

Commonwealth of DOMINICA
25¢
MICKEY MOUSE
60th ANNIVERSARY
DISNEYLAND
HORSE-DRAWN TROLLEY

1101† 25c Goofy driving horse tram,
Disneyland 15 15
1102† 45c Donald Duck in Roger E. Broggie,
Walt Disney World 25 25
1103† 60c Goofy, Mickey Mouse, Donald
Duck and Chip n'Dale aboard Big
Thunder Mountain train, Disney World 30 30
1104† 90c Mickey Mouse in Walter E. Disney,
Disneyland 45 45
1105† $1 Mickey and Minnie Mouse, Goofy,
Donald and Daisy Duck in monorail,
Walt Disney World 50 50
1106† $3 Dumbo flying over Casey Jr. .... 1·50 1·50
1107† $4 Daisy Duck and Minnie Mouse in
Lilly Belle, Walt Disney World .... 1·90 1·90
MS1108† Two sheets (a) $5 Seven Dwarfs in
Rainbow Caverns Mine train, Disneyland; (b)
$5 Donald Duck and Chip n'Dale on toy train
(from film Out of Scale)
Set of 2 sheets 4·50 5·00

1988

Nos. 1092/3 overprinted showing various exhibition emblems
1126 $1 First cable cars, San Francisco, 1873
(overprinted **FINLANDIA 88**)
1127 $3 "Orient Express", 1883 (overprinted
INDEPENDENCE 40)
Set of 2 1·60 1·90

Commonwealth
of DOMINICA

1193† 60c Winnie the Pooh in shop window
with toy steam locomotive 25 30

STANLEY GIBBONS
STAMP COLLECTING SERIES

Introductory booklets on How to Start, How to Identify
Stamps and Collecting by Theme. A series of well
illustrated guides at a low price.
Write for details.

DOMINICAN REPUBLIC

West Indies
100 centavos = 1 peso

1902

131† 50c Steam train 50   1·00

1942

477   3c Steam train
478   15c Steam train

Set of 2   12·00   5·00

1974

1197†   2c Steam train 30   45

EAST GERMANY

See under Germany

ECUADOR

South America
100 centavos = 1 sucre

1908

331†   1c Steam locomotive 40   30

1924

Tobacco Tax stamps overprinted CASA–CORREOS
407†   1c Steam locomotive 35   15

1926

Overprinted QUITO 1926 ESMERALDAS and railway train
418   1c President Roca
419   2c President Dr. Noboa
420   3c Robles
421   4c Vivero
422   5c Pres. Gen. Urvina
423   10c Pres. Dr. Garcia Moreno

Set of 6   27·00   19·00

1928

Surcharged Frril. Norte Julio 8 de 1928 Est. Cayambe and value
431   10c on 30c Letamendi
432   50c on 70c Roca
433   1s on 80c Rocafuerte

Set of 3   35·00   45·00

Consular Service stamps surcharged Postal – Frril. Norte Est.
OTAVALO and value
450   5c on 20c Coat of Arms
451   10c on 20c Coat of Arms
452   20c on 1s Coat of Arms
453   50c on 1s Coat of Arms
454   1s on 1s Coat of Arms
455   5s on 2s Coat of Arms
456   10s on 2s Coat of Arms

Set of 7   22·00   14·00

1930

478†   16c Steam train .... 1·25   30

1933

No. 478 surcharged
489†   10c on 16c Steam train 45   10

1936

Tobacco Tax stamps as 1924 issue

(a) Surcharged Seguro Social del Campesino 3 ctvs
525   3c on 1c Steam locomotive

(b) Surcharged SEGURO SOCIAL DEL CAMPESINO 3 ctvs
526   3c on 1c Steam locomotive

(c) Overprinted POSTAL
527   1c Steam locomotive

Set of 3   75   40

Tobacco Tax stamp as 1924 *issue surcharged* **TIMBRE PATRIOTICO DIEZ CENTAVOS**

541	10c on 1c Steam locomotive	35	10

1938

580†	50c Winged railway wheel	20	8
581†	1s Steam train on bridge	40	8

1939

Tobacco Tax stamp as 1924 *issue surcharged* **POSTAL ADICIONAL CINCO CENTAVOS**

623	5c on 1c Steam locomotive	25	10

1940

Tobacco Tax stamp as 1924 *issue surcharged* **CASAS DE CORREOS Y TELEGRAFOS CINCO CENTAVOS**

624	5c on 1c Steam locomotive	25	10

Tobacco Tax stamp as 1924 *issue surcharged* **TIMBRE PATRIOTICO VEINTE CENTAVOS**

625b	20c on 1c Steam locomotive	1·75	40

1943

656	20c Tram, Guayaquil (red)		
656a	20c Tram, Guayaquil (blue)		
	Set of 2	1·50	10

660†	20c Devil's Nose Zigzag, Guayaquil–Quito Railway	15	10
664†	1s Devil's Nose Zigzag, Guayaquil–Quito Railway (air)	75	50

Nos. 580/1 *overprinted* **AEREO LOOR A. BOLIVIA JUNIO 11 – 1943**

675†	50c Winged railway wheel	40	40
676†	1s Steam train on bridge	1·00	60

Nos. 580/1 *overprinted* **AEREO LOOR AL PARAGUAY JULIO 5 – 1943**

678†	50c Winged railway wheel	40	40
679†	1s Steam train on bridge	1·00	60

Nos. 580/1 *overprinted* **AEREO LOOR A VENEZUELA JULIO 23 – 1943**

681†	50c Winged railway wheel	40	40
682†	1s Steam train on bridge	1·00	60

1957

MS1091a 20c Railway viaduct; 20c Railway bridge; 20c Ibana railway bridge; 20c Crane loading goods wagon; 20c Railway tracks
MS1091b 30c Railway tracks; 30c San Lorenzo railway bridge; 30c Railway bridge; 30c Alstom diesel locomotive, 1956; 30c Railway tunnel.

Set of 2 sheets	7·00	7·00

1958

1109	30c Steam locomotive		
1110	50c Diesel-electric train		
1111	5s Four founders of the Guayaquil–Quito Railway		
	Set of 3	1·75	1·25

1960

1175†	2s Ambato Railway Bridge	60	12

1985

(illustration half-size)

MS1938† 30s Sugar cane wagons at Valdez Sugar Refinery .... 4·50 4·50

1986

2000† 5s National Railway Emblems 20 5

OFFICIAL STAMPS

1946

Tobacco Tax stamp as 1924 issue overprinted
CORRESPONDENCIA OFICIAL
O803 1s Steam locomotive .... 1·00 15

EGYPT
North Africa
1000 milliemes = 1 pound

1933

189 5m 2-4-0 locomotive, 1852
190 13m 2-2-2 locomotive, 1859
191 15m 2-2-2 locomotive, 1862
192 20m 4-4-2 locomotive, 1932
Set of 4 29·00 27·00

1957

521 10m Early locomotive and modern
  express train 45 15

528 10m Railway lines on map of Gaza 75 75

1959

595† 10m Diesel-electric train 40 25
MS601† 50m Diesel train .... 5·50 7·00

1961

660† 10m Diesel-electric train 20 10

1963

743† 40m Luxor Railway Station 70 60

1964

794 10m Diesel train and Afro-Asian map 25 10

1971

1103† 85m Pont Limont Railway Station, Cairo 1·00 50

1977

1327 20m Old and modern trains 55 20

1979

1396	20m Railway bridge	30	10

1987

1674	5p Underground train in station, Cairo	30	15

1989

1720	5p Cairo Underground train and route map	5	5

EGYPTIAN OCCUPATION OF PALESTINE

Western Asia
1000 milliemes = 1 pound

1957

As No. 528 of Egypt overprinted **PALESTINE** in English and Arabic

87	10m Railway lines on map of Gaza	1·75	3·00

COLLECT MAMMALS ON STAMPS

A Stanley Gibbons thematic catalogue on this popular subject. Copies available at £7.50 (p. + p. £2) from: Stanley Gibbons Publications Ltd, 5 Parkside, Christchurch Road, Ringwood, Hants BH24 3SH.

EL SALVADOR

Central America
1891 8 reales = 100 centavos = 1 peso
1912 100 centavos = 1 colon

1891

39	1c Steam locomotive and San Miguel Volcano		
40	2c Steam locomotive and San Miguel Volcano		
41	3c Steam locomotive and San Miguel Volcano		
42	5c Steam locomotive and San Miguel Volcano		
43	10c Steam locomotive and San Miguel Volcano		
44	11c Steam locomotive and San Miguel Volcano		
45	20c Steam locomotive and San Miguel Volcano		
46	25c Steam locomotive and San Miguel Volcano		
47	50c Steam locomotive and San Miguel Volcano		
48	1p Steam locomotive and San Miguel Volcano		
	Set of 10	1·40	7·50

No. 40 surcharged **1 centavo**

49	1c on 2c Steam locomotive and San Miguel Volcano	2·00	3·00

No. 40 surcharged **UN CENTAVO**

50	1c on 2c Steam locomotive and San Miguel Volcano	1·75	2·50

No. 41 surcharged **5 CENTAVOS**

51	5c on 3c Steam locomotive and San Miguel Volcano	6·00	4·50

1896

160†	3c Steam train (orange)	15	15

1897

No. 160 in new colour

222	3c Steam train (brown)	15	15

1916

683†	1c Tram tracks, National Theatre	25	10
684†	2c Tram tracks, National Theatre	25	10
685†	5c Tram tracks, National Theatre	25	10
686†	6c Tram tracks, National Theatre	30	15
687†	10c Tram tracks, National Theatre	30	15
688†	12c Tram tracks, National Theatre	2·75	75
689†	17c Tram tracks, National Theatre	50	20
690†	25c Tram tracks, National Theatre	75	40
691†	29c Tram tracks, National Theatre	5·00	1·25
692†	50c Tram tracks, National Theatre	1·75	1·00

1917

No. O697 surcharged **CORRIENTE Un Centavo**

704†	1c on 6c Tram tracks, National Theatre	3·00	3·00

Nos. O696/7 overprinted **CORRIENTE**

705†	5c Tram tracks, National Theatre	4·00	4·00
706†	6c Tram tracks, National Theatre	6·50	6·50

1919

Nos. 686/92 surcharged with new values and squares, circles or bars

710†	1c on 6c Tram tracks, National Theatre	3·00	3·00
711†	1c on 12c Tram tracks, National Theatre	2·50	2·50
712†	1c on 17c Tram tracks, National Theatre	2·50	2·50
713†	2c on 10c Tram tracks, National Theatre	2·50	2·50
714†	5c on 50c Tram tracks, National Theatre	2·50	2·50
715†	6c on 25c Tram tracks, National Theatre	2·50	2·50
716†	15c on 29c Tram tracks, National Theatre	1·75	1·75
717†	26c on 29c Tram tracks, National Theatre	3·50	3·50
719†	35c on 50c Tram tracks, National Theatre	3·50	3·50

No. O699 surcharged **1 CENTAVO 1** *and black squares*

721	1c on 12c Tram tracks, National Theatre	2·50	2·50

1924

754†	6c Railway bridge over River Lempa	50	10

1930

766 1c Presidents of El Salvador and Guatemala (Inauguration of rail link)

767 3c Presidents of El Salvador and Guatemala
768 5c Presidents of El Salvador and Guatemala
769 10c Presidents of El Salvador and Guatemala

Set of 4   4·75   4·00

1932

No. 754 overprinted **1932**

800†	6c Railway bridge over River Lempa	90	15

1935

864†	2c Steam train on dock, Cutuco	20	10

1938

No. 864 surcharged

881†	1c on 2c Steam train on dock, Cutuco	20	10

OFFICIAL STAMPS

1896

No. 160 overprinted **FRANQUEO OFICIAL** *in oval*

O184†	3c Steam train (orange)	25	

No. 160 overprinted **CORREOS DE EL SALVADOR DE OFICIO** *in circle and band*

O208†	3c Steam train (orange)	20·00	

1897

No. 222 overprinted **FRANQUEO OFICIAL** *in oval*

O234†	3c Steam train (brown)	35	

No. 222 overprinted **CORREOS DE EL SALVADOR DE OFICIO** *in circle and band*

O246†	3c Steam train (brown)	20·00	20·00

1916

Nos. 683/92 overprinted **OFICIAL**

O694	1c Tram tracks, National Theatre
O695	2c Tram tracks, National Theatre
O696	5c Tram tracks, National Theatre
O697	6c Tram tracks, National Theatre
O698	10c Tram tracks, National Theatre
O699	12c Tram tracks, National Theatre
O700	17c Tram tracks, National Theatre
O701	25c Tram tracks, National Theatre
O702	29c Tram tracks, National Theatre
O703	50c Tram tracks, National Theatre

Set of 10   6·50   9·00

1925

No. 754 overprinted **OFICIAL**

O765†	6c Railway bridge over River Lempa	7·00	5·75

ALBUM LISTS

Write for our latest list of albums and accessories. This will be sent on request.

EQUATORIAL GUINEA

West Africa
1972 100 centimos = 1 peseta
1973 100 centimos = 1 ekuele (plural = bikuele)

Appendix
The following stamps have been either been issued in excess of postal needs, or have not been available to the public in reasonable quantities at face value. Miniature sheets, imperforate stamps, etc. are excluded from this section.

1972
Japanese Railway Centenary. Various steam locomotives.
Postage 1, 3, 5, 8, 10p; Air 15, 25p.

1974
Universal Postal Union Centenary (1st issue). Postage 80c.
Universal Postal Union Centenary (2nd issue). Postage 2e25.

ERITREA

North-east Africa
100 centesimi = 1 lira

1930

157†	1li Tracks on Massawa dock		30	40
158†	2li Steam train on bridge		3·50	3·50

1936

239†	50c Tracks, Massawa–Asmara Railway		25	20
244†	2li Tracks, Massawa–Asmara Railway	..	65	45

ETHIOPIA

North-east Africa
1931 16 guerche = 1 menelik dollar
1946 100 cents = 1 Ethiopian dollar
1978 100 cents = 1 birr

1931

304†	½g Railway Bridge over River Awash	....	40	40

1936
No. 304 surcharged with value and Amharic inscription

319†	2c on ½g Railway Bridge over River Awash		75	50

1955

456†	50c Diesel train on bridge		3·25	1·00

1965

617†	30c Diesel locomotive		70	20
618†	35c Railway Station, Addis Ababa		70	25
621†	50c Blue Nile Railway Bridge (air)		70	40

1967

661	15c Diesel train and route map of Djibouti–Addis Ababa Line	
662	30c Diesel train and route map of Djibouti–Addis Ababa Line	
663	50c Diesel train and route map of Djibouti–Addis Ababa Line	

Set of 3   2·75   1·50

1972
Nos. 617/18 overprinted **U.N. SECURITY COUNCIL FIRST MEETING IN AFRICA 1972** *in English and Amharic*

806†	30c Diesel locomotive		1·75	1·50
807†	35c Railway Station, Addis Ababa		1·75	85

1979

1123†	25c Diesel train		60	25

1983

1266† 1b River bridge and railway tunnel .... 1·50 1·00

FALKLAND ISLANDS

South Atlantic
1949 12 pence = 1 shilling
20 shillings = 1 pound
1971 100 pence = 1 pound

1949

As No. 114 of Antigua
168† 1d Silhouette of steam locomotive ...... 1·50 75

1985

497 7p Technical drawing of "Wren" Class
    locomotive
498 22p Sail-propelled trolley
499 27p "Wren" Class locomotive at work
500 54p "Falkland Islands Express"
    passenger train
                            Set of 4 2·25 2·40

FALKLAND ISLANDS DEPENDENCIES

South Atlantic
12 pence = 1 shilling
20 shillings = 1 pound

1949

As No. 114 of Antigua
G21† 1d Silhouette of steam locomotive ...... 2·00 1·25

FERNANDO POO

Off West Africa
100 centimos = 1 peseta

1962

252† 35c Diesel train 25 25

FIJI

South Pacific
1949 12 pence = 1 shilling
20 shillings = 1 pound
1969 100 cents = 1 dollar

1949

As No. 114 of Antigua
272† 2d Silhouette of steam locomotive 55 25

1954

290† 1s6d Sugar cane train .... 12·00 1·00

1976

526 4c Steam locomotive No. 21
527 15c Diesel locomotive No. 8
528 20c Diesel locomotive No. 1
529 30c Free passenger train
                            Set of 4 2·50 1·25

FINLAND

Northern Europe
100 pennia = 1 markka

1938

329† 3½m Helsinki G.P.O. and Railway Station 5·00 5·50

1939

334 4m Helsinki G.P.O. and Railway Station .. 40 25

1942

As 1939 issue
382 7m Helsinki Railway Station
383 9m Helsinki Railway Station
384 20m Helsinki Railway Station
                            Set of 3 2·00 15

1944

392† 50p + 25p Red Cross train 40 40

1955

538 25m Tower of Helsinki Railway Station .... 13·00 15·00

1957

578 20m Steam train 80 40

1962

634 10m First locomotive *Ilmarinen*
635 30m Class "Hr 1" steam locomotive
636 40m Class "Hr 12" diesel locomotive
                     Set of 3   5·50   1·50

1963

672† 1m30 Helsinki Railway Station .... 1·00 10

COLLECT BIRDS ON STAMPS
New second edition available at £8.50 (p. + p. £2) from:
Stanley Gibbons Publications Ltd, 5 Parkside,
Christchurch Road, Ringwood, Hants BH24 3SH.

1976

904 80p Diesel train 60 10

1978

931 1m Steam tank locomotive on wharf,
      Kotka 55 10

1979

945 1m10 Tram on Helsinki street 50 10

1982

1018 1m20 Electric train and electric tram 50 10

1987

1116† 1m70 Diesel train 60 10

MS1122 1m70 Locomotive *Lemminkainen*,
1862; 1m70 Mail van No. 9935, 1871; 1m70
Mail van No. 9991, 1899; 2m30 Locomotive
No. 57, 1874 .... 4·00 4·75

1988

SUOMI FINLAND 2,40

1151† 2m40 Horse-drawn tram, 1890 .... 80 30

1989

1,90 SUOMI FINLAND

1181 1m90 Railway bridge, Savonlinna 50 10

FRANCE

Western Europe
100 centimes = 1 franc

1936

534 85c Mendon Railway Bridge, Paris
535 1f50 Mendon Railway Bridge, Paris
536 2f25 Mendon Railway Bridge, Paris
537 2f50 Mendon Railway Bridge, Paris
538 3f Mendon Railway Bridge, Paris
539 3f50 Mendon Railway Bridge, Paris
540 50f Mendon Railway Bridge, Paris

Set of 7 £750 £225

541 50f Mendon Railway Bridge, Paris £600 £225

1937

572 30c Electric train
573 1f50 Streamlined steam locomotive
Set of 2 9·50 4·00

1939

635 70c + 50c Steam locomotive .... 4·75 4·00

1944

821 1f50 Mobile Post Office van, 1844 .... 20 50

830 4f + 6f Engine-driver in modern cab and
old locomotive .... 1·25 1·40

1949

1056† 200f Railway bridge, Bordeaux .... 9·50 45
1057† 300f Tracks into Lyons .... 13·00 8·00

1951

1107 12f + 3f Travelling Post Office sorting
van .... 2·50 2·75

1952

1149 15f Garabit Railway Viaduct 55 40

1955

1243† 25f Electric locomotive at factory ...... 3·00 1·75

1249 12f Electric train, Valenciennes–Thionville
Line .... 1·25 1·10

1960

1466† 85c Chaumont Railway Viaduct .... 2·00 10

1966

1723 60c Globe and railway tracks 50 30

1967

1737† 30c + 10c Steam train 50 40

1761† 1f50 Morlaix Railway Viaduct 80 25

1970

1865 80c Hovertrain *Orleans* 1-80 .... 40 25

1971

1907 95c Austerlitz Railway Station, Paris 80 60

1972

1949 90c Japanese "Hikari" electric train 40 25

1974

2055 60c Turbotrain "TGV001" .... 1·00 40

1975

2084 1f Underground train, Paris .... 1·00 25

1977

2152†   2f10 Railway tracks, Franche-Comte   ..   75   35

2185   1f10 Paris Metro construction   40   25

1978

2284   1f20 Railway Carriage and Armistice Monument, Rethondes   50   15

1981

2392†   1f20 + 30c Louis Armand (railway engineer)   60   50

1984

2641   2f10 "TGV" mail train   75   25

1986

2707†   2f20 + 50c Marc Seguin (locomotive engineer)   85   85

2746   2f20 Steam locomotive, Mulhouse Technical Museum   40   10

2747   3f70 Quai d'Orsay Museum facade (formerly railway station)   65   20

1987

2748   2f50 Underground train in tunnel and Fulgence Bienvenue (designer of Paris Metro)   45   15

1988

2829†   3f60 Two-car electric train   70   20

FRENCH EQUATORIAL AFRICA

Central Africa
100 centimes = 1 franc

1936

Nos. 69/76 *of Middle Congo overprinted* **AFRIQUE ÉQUATORIALE FRANCAISE**

1†	1c Steam train on Mindouli Viaduct	10	50
2†	2c Steam train on Mindouli Viaduct	10	50
3†	4c Steam train on Mindouli Viaduct	40	75
4†	5c Steam train on Mindouli Viaduct	55	65
5†	10c Steam train on Mindouli Viaduct	80	65
6†	15c Steam train on Mindouli Viaduct	1·25	80
7†	20c Steam train on Mindouli Viaduct	1·25	80
8†	25c Steam train on Mindouli Viaduct	2·75	1·50

1937

34†	1c Steam train on Mayumba Viaduct	10	50
35†	2c Steam train on Mayumba Viaduct	10	50
36†	3c Steam train on Mayumba Viaduct	10	50
37†	4c Steam train on Mayumba Viaduct	10	40
38†	5c Steam train on Mayumba Viaduct	10	75

1940

Nos. 34/6 *and* 38 *overprinted* **AFRIQUE FRANCAISE LIBRE**

109†	1c Steam train on Mayumba Viaduct	35	1·00
110†	2c Steam train on Mayumba Viaduct	45	1·00
111†	3c Steam train on Mayumba Viaduct	45	1·00
112†	5c Steam train on Mayumba Viaduct	45	75

No. 3 *overprinted* **LIBRE**

118	4c Steam train on Mindouli Viaduct	5·00	5·00

No. 71 *of Middle Congo overprinted* **AFRIQUE FRANCAISE LIBRE**

163	4c Steam train on Mindouli Viaduct	20·00	20·00

1957

287	15f General Louis Faidherbe	1·25	75

FRENCH GUINEA

West Africa
100 centimes = 1 franc

1906

As Nos. 18/22 *of Dahomey*

33†	1c General Faidherbe (builder of Dakar– St. Louis Railway)	35	35
34†	2c General Faidherbe (builder of Dakar– St. Louis Railway)	40	40
35†	4c General Faidherbe (builder of Dakar– St. Louis Railway)	50	50
36†	5c General Faidherbe (builder of Dakar– St. Louis Railway)	2·00	90
37†	10c General Faidherbe (builder of Dakar– St. Louis Railway)	5·50	90

FRENCH MOROCCO

North-west Africa
100 centimes = 1 franc

1947

317	4f50 + 5f50 Phosphate ore trucks	65	80

FRENCH SOMALI COAST

East Africa
100 centimes = 1 franc

1915

182†	1f Railway bridge at Holl-Holli	75	35
226†	1f10 Railway bridge at Holl-Holli	3·50	3·50
227†	1f25 Railway bridge at Holl-Holli	5·50	4·00
228†	1f50 Railway bridge at Holl-Holli	70	40
229†	1f75 Railway bridge at Holl-Holli	3·00	2·00
183†	2f Railway bridge at Holl-Holli	1·75	90
230†	3f Railway bridge at Holl-Holli	7·50	3·50
184†	5f Railway bridge at Holl-Holli	2·75	1·25

1923

Nos 182 *and* 184 *surcharged*

204†	25c on 5f Railway bridge at Holl-Holli	40	35
209†	1f25 on 1f Railway bridge at Holl-Holli	45	40
210†	1f50 on 1f Railway bridge at Holl-Holli	60	50
211†	3f on 5f Railway bridge at Holl-Holli	2·25	2·50
212†	10f on 5f Railway bridge at Holl-Holli	3·50	4·00
213†	20f on 5f Railway bridge at Holl-Holli	6·50	7·50

1942
Nos. 228/9 overprinted **FRANCE LIBRE**

331†	1f50 Railway bridge at Holl-Holli	80	1·00
334†	1f75 Railway bridge at Holl-Holli	3·50	4·00

1943

361	5c Steam locomotive
362	10c Steam locomotive
363	25c Steam locomotive
364	30c Steam locomotive
365	40c Steam locomotive
366	80c Steam locomotive
367	1f Steam locomotive
368	1f50 Steam locomotive
369	2f Steam locomotive
370	2f50 Steam locomotive
371	4f Steam locomotive
372	5f Steam locomotive
373	10f Steam locomotive
374	20f Steam locomotive

Set of 14   3·50   4·00

1945
Nos. 361, 363 and 370 surcharged

378	50c on 5c Steam locomotive
379	60c on 5c Steam locomotive
380	70c on 5c Steam locomotive
381	1f20 on 5c Steam locomotive
382	2f40 on 25c Steam locomotive
383	3f on 25c Steam locomotive
384	4f50 on 25c Steam locomotive
385	15f on 2f50 Steam locomotive

Set of 8   1·75   1·75

1956

430†	500f Aerial map of Djibouti showing railway lines	48·00	35·00

431†	15f Goods wagons on dock, Djibouti	1·00	40

FRENCH SOUTHERN AND ANTARCTIC TERRITORIES

Antarctica and nearby islands
100 centimes = 1 franc

1984

193	4f70 Tracks on dock, Port Jeanne d'Arc	1·25	1·25

FRENCH TERRITORY OF THE AFARS AND THE ISSAS

East Africa
100 centimes = 1 franc

1973

584†	30f Diesel railcar	5·50	3·25

1977

682†	75f Volta and electric train	5·25	3·75

FRENCH WEST AFRICA

West Africa
100 centimes = 1 franc

1947

50†   15f Renault railcar   75   10

1951

73†   20f Railway coaches and wagons under
Abidjan Bridge   70   30

1955

87†   3f Diesel locomotive, Mossi Railway   90   35

1957
As No. 287 of French Equatorial Africa
95   15f General Louis Faidherbe   80   80

FUJEIRA

Arabian Peninsula
100 dirhams = 1 riyal

Appendix
The following stamps have either been issued in excess of
postal needs, or have not been available to the public in
reasonable quantities at face value. Miniature sheets, imperforate
stamps, etc. are excluded from this section.

1969
Famous Railway Locomotives. Postage 15, 25, 50, 75d, 1r, Air 2,
3, 5r.

1971
History of Railways. 10, 20, 70d, 2, 3r.

GABON

West Africa
100 centimes = 1 franc

1966

265   50f Diesel locomotive ....   1·90   65

1967

284   30f Diesel railcar   60   40

1968

339†   30f Railway spur, Port Owendo   50   20

1973

479   100f Diesel locomotive on "stamp"   ......   1·40   60

1975

(*illustration half-size*)

544 20f Marc Seguin locomotive, 1829
545 25f Locomotive *Iron Duke*, 1847
546 40f Locomotive *Thomas Rogers*, 1895
547 50f Russian locomotive Type "LA272",
1934

Set of 4   2·75   2·50

550 50f Diesel locomotive 60   35

1978

REPUBLIQUE GABONAISE

641 500f Diesel train .... 5·75   4·00

681 60f Diesel train on bridge and route map
of Trans-Gabon Railway 60   30

1981

767 75f Japanese "D-51" locomotive and
French "TGV001"
768 100f Baltimore & Ohio "Mallet 7100" and
Prussian State Railway "T–3"
locomotives
769 350f George Stephenson's *Rocket* and
"BB Alsthom" diesel locomotive

Set of 3   4·50   2·25

*Miniature sheet containing Nos. 767/9, but colours changed,
overprinted* **26 fevrier 1981–Record du monde de vitesse 380
km a l'heure**
MS771   75f As No. 767; 100f As No. 768; 350f
As No. 769 .... 4·00   4·00

1983

835 75f Presidents Bongo and Mitterand,
route map of Trans-Gabon Railway and
diesel train 65   30

1984

903†   165f Trans-Gabon train .... 1·25   70

1985

932†   150f Diesel train, satellite and dish aerial   1·25   50

1986

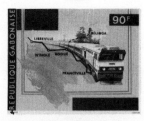

964   90f Diesel train and route map of
Owendo–Franceville Trans-Gabon
Railway   65   35

GAMBIA
West Africa
1949 12 pence = 1 shilling
20 shillings = 1 pound
1971 100 bututs = 1 dalasy

1949
As No. 114 of Antigua
166†   1½d Silhouette of steam locomotive   20   25

1987

752   60b Morty and Ferdie examining
Trevithick's locomotive, 1804
753   75b Clarabelle Cow in "Empire State
Express", 1893
754   1d Donald Duck inspecting Stephenson's
Rocket, 1829
755   1d25 Piglet and Winnie the Pooh with
Santa Fe Railway locomotive, 1920
756   2d Donald and Daisy Duck with
Pennsylvania Railway Class "GG-1",
1933
757   5d Mickey Mouse in Stourbridge Lion,
1829
758   10d Goofy in Best Friend of Charleston,
1830
759   12d Brer Bear and Brer Rabbit with Union
Pacific No. M10001, 1934
Set of 8   5·50   6·00
MS760   Two sheets (a) 15d Chip n'Dale in The
General, 1855; (b) 15d Donald Duck and
Mickey Mouse in modern French "TGV" train
Set of 2 sheets   4·75   5·00

COLLECT SHIPS ON STAMPS
The largest Stanley Gibbons thematic catalogue to date
– available at £10.95 (p. + p. £2) from:
Stanley Gibbons Publications Ltd, 5 Parkside,
Christchurch Road, Ringwood, Hants BH24 3SH.

1988

808†   50b Stephenson's Locomotion (first
permanent public railway), 1825   8   10
810†   1d Sprague's Premiere (first operational
electric railway), 1888   15   20

GERMANY
Central Europe, divided after the Second World War into West
Germany, West Berlin and East Germany
1902 100 pfennig = 1 mark
1928 100 pfennig = 1 reichsmark

1902

113†   1m Tram, General Post Office, Berlin   1·50   40

1916
As 1902 issue
114†   1m25 Tram, General Post Office, Berlin   1·00   25
115†   1m50 Tram, General Post Office, Berlin   15   25

1921

186†   100pf Mine truck   5   10
163†   120pf Mine truck   5   10

1923

249†   5m Mine truck   5   6·50
252†   20m Mine truck   5   10
254†   30m Mine truck   5   25
256†   50m Mine truck   25   45·00

No. 249 surcharged **100m Rhein=Ruhr=Hilfe**
257†   5m + 100m Mine truck   5   4·00

1935

577 6pf *Der Adler* (first German locomotive)
578 12pf Steam train
579 25pf Diesel train "The Flying Hamburger"
580 40pf Streamlined steam train
                              Set of 4   19.00   1.75

1937

645† 15pf + 10pf Train ferry *Schwerin* . . . .   5·50   3·00
646† 25pf + 15pf Tracks on dock . . . .   9·00   3·00

1941

755† 25pf Leipzig Railway Station   65   65

1943

827† 25pf + 15pf Railway tracks   45   60

1944

871† 24pf + 10pf Railway gun   40   45

OFFICIAL STAMPS

1923

Nos. 252 *and* 254 *overprinted* **Dienstmarke**
O274† 20m Mine trucks   5   3·75
O275† 30m Mine trucks   5   14·00

Allied Occupation—French Zone

BADEN
1945 100 pfennig = 1 reichsmark
1948 100 pfennig = 1 deutsche mark

1947

FB12† 84pf Hollental Railway Bridge (green)   10   50

1948

As No. FB12, *but face value in* "D.PF"
FB26 84dpf Hollental Railway Bridge (red)   6·50   2·50

Design as No. FB12 *with* "pf" *omitted*
FB37† 90pf Hollental Railway Bridge . . . .   50·00   65·00

West Germany

100 pfennig = 1 deutsche mark

1953

1093† 4pf Train, semaphore and hand signal   6·00   4·25

1955

1145 20pf Railway signal . . . .   8·00   50

COLLECT SHIPS ON STAMPS
The largest Stanley Gibbons thematic catalogue to date – available at £10.95 (p. + p. £2) from:
Stanley Gibbons Publications Ltd, 5 Parkside, Christchurch Road, Ringwood, Hants BH24 3SH.

1957

1192† 40pf + 10pf Mine truck .... 13·00 15·00

1958

1203 10pf Rudolf Diesel (engineer) and first oil
engine 25 20

1960

1259 10pf Locomotive *Der Adler*, 1835 ...... 20 15

1963

1313 20pf Denmark–Germany Railway map
and flags 20 15

1965

1389† 5pf Railway crossing sign 5 5
1393† 40pf Old steam engine and modern
electric locomotive 20 15

1966

1433 30pf W. von Siemens (electrical
engineer) 20 15

1969

1506† 10pf + 5pf Steam locomotive, 1835
(pewter model) 15 10

1975

1729 30pf + 15pf Class "218" diesel
locomotive
1730 40pf + 20pf Electric locomotive Series
"103"
1731 50pf + 25pf Electric motor-train Series
"403"
1732 70pf + 35pf "Transrapid" hovertrain
(model)

Set of 4 4·00 4·25

1740† 10pf Rail motor-train 5 5
1754c† 300pf Electromagnetic monorail ...... 1·75 75

1976

1774 50pf Wuppertal monorail train 40 15

1977

1825† 50pf Electric train 45 5

1979

1895 60pf First electric railway, 1879 .... 45 15

1985

2112 80pf "Inauguration of First German
Railway" (painting by Heim) 5 12

1987

2199 80pf Loading and unloading mail train,
1897 .... 55 12

1989

2285 170pf Friedrich List (economist) and
19th-century train .... 1·00 50

West Berlin

100 pfennig = 1 deutsche mark

1952

B97† 20pf W. von Siemens (electrical
engineer) .... 1·75 40

1954

B122 20pf Blacksmith forging rail .... 6·00 1·25

1957

B156† 7pf Tracks on model of Hansa district 20 20

1969

B339† 10pf + 5pf Railway carriage, 1835
(pewter model) 15 15

1971

B381 5pf Local steam train, 1925
B382 10pf Electric tram, 1890
B383 20pf Horse-drawn tram-car, 1880
B384 30pf City train, 1933
B385 50pf Electric tram-car, 1950
B386 1dm Underground train, 1971
Set of 6 4·00 4·50

1975

B472 30pf + 15pf Steam locomotive *Drache*
B473 40pf + 20pf Tank locomotive Series "89"
B474 50pf + 25pf Steam locomotive Series "050"
B475 70pf + 35pf Steam locomotive Series "010"

Set of 4   3·25   3·50

As Nos. 1740 and 1754c of West Germany additionally inscribed "BERLIN"
B479† 10pf Rail motor-train 5   5
B490c† 300pf Electromagnetic monorail ...... 1·75   75

1988

B810 10pf First train on Berlin–Potsdam line leaving Potsdam Station, 1838 8   5

East Germany
100 pfennig = 1 mark

1952

E60† 12pf + 3pf Side-dump trucks 30   30

1953

E130† 25pf Railway engineer (design in dots) 2·50 1·50
E315† 25pf Railway engineer (design in lines) 8   15

E138† 24pf Ore trucks 80   50

1956

E255 20pf Tracks at Leipzig Fair
E256 35pf Tracks at Leipzig Fair

Set of 2   60   40

E260† 10pf Tram, Dresden 25   15

1957

E296† 25pf Electric locomotive 15   10

E305† 10pf Coal trucks 5   5
E306† 20pf Electric train 5   5

1958

E388† 10pf Leipzig Railway Station 5   5

E397† 20pf Modern postal sorting train 10   5

1960

E522† 25pf 19th-century railway mail-coach .. 80 80

E536 10pf "Young Socialist Express"
(double-decker train)
E537 20pf Train-ferry *Sassnitz*
E538 25pf Locomotive *Der Adler* of 1835 and
modern diesel locomotive No. V180
Set of 3 3·00 3·25

1962

E638† 20pf Railway-station hotel, Rostock 5 5

E655 5pf Diesel locomotive 15 10

1963

E697† 10pf Diesel railcar 50 10

E720 20pf Fork-lift truck loading mail train 20 10

1964

E790† 10pf Goods wagon on dock 15 10

1968

E1069† 10pf Diesel locomotive 15 10

E1120 10pf Model trains 15 10

1969

E1167† 20pf Railway crossing sign 5 5

1970

E1310† 20pf Railway policeman 10 5

1972

E1509† 35pf Red Cross carriage 25 25

1973

E1576	5pf Electric locomotive		
E1577	10pf Refrigerator wagon		
E1578	20pf Long-distance coach		
E1579	25pf Tank wagon		
E1580	35pf Double-deck coach		
E1581	85pf Tourist coach		
	Set of 6	3·00	3·00

1976

E1878†	10pf Railway bridge, Templin Lake	5	5
E1879†	15pf Adlergestell Railway Bridge, Berlin	10	5
E1880†	20pf Elbe River Railway Bridge, Rosslau	15	5
E1881†	25pf Goltzschtal Railway Viaduct	15	5

1974

| E1669† | 15pf Railway lines on map .... | 10 | 5 |

| E1689† | 10pf Mobile railway crane .... | 15 | 10 |

| E1701† | 20pf Old and new locomotives ...... | 30 | 15 |

1975

| E1797† | 35pf Railway crossing sign .... | 20 | 10 |

1977

| E1969† | 5pf Steam locomotive *Muldenthal*, 1861 .... | 15 | 5 |
| E1970† | 10pf Dresden tram, 1896 .... | 15 | 5 |

1978

| E2016† | 25pf Railway mail carriage, 1896 .... | 60 | 60 |
| E2017† | 35pf Railway mail carriage, 1978 .... | 80 | 80 |

| E2043† | 35pf Diesel locomotive and container wagons .... | 35 | 15 |

COLLECT SHIPS ON STAMPS

The largest Stanley Gibbons thematic catalogue to date – available at £10.95 (p. + p. £2) from:
Stanley Gibbons Publications Ltd, 5 Parkside, Christchurch Road, Ringwood, Hants BH24 3SH.

1979

E2124 5pf "MXA" electric locomotive
E2125 10pf Self-discharging wagon
E2126 20pf Diesel locomotive "BR110"
E2127 35pf Railway car transporter
                      Set of 4   2·50   2·00

E2139 20pf Train ferry *Rostock*
E2140 35pf Train ferry *Rugen*
                      Set of 2   1·25   1·00

1980

E2277 20pf Radebeul–Radeburg
       narrow-gauge locomotive
E2278 25pf Bad Doberan–Ostseebad
       Kuhlungsborn narrow-gauge
       locomotive
E2279 25pf Radebeul–Radeburg passenger
       carriage
E2280 35pf Bad Doberan–Ostseebad
       Kuhlungsborn passenger carriage
                      Set of 4   3·50   2·10

E2281† 10pf Toy steam locomotive, 1850   45   45

1981

E2342 5pf Freital–Kurort Kipsdorf
       narrow-gauge locomotive
E2343 5pf Putbus–Gohren narrow-gauge
       locomotive
E2344 15pf Freital–Kurort Kipsdorf luggage
       van
E2345 20pf Putbus–Gohren passenger
       carriage
                      Set of 4   2·00   1·50

1983

E2509 15pf Wernigerode–Nordhausen
       narrow-gauge locomotive
E2510 20pf Wernigerode–Nordhausen
       passenger carriage
E2511 20pf Zittau–Kurort Oybib/Kurort
       Jonsdorf narrow-gauge locomotive
E2512 50pf Zittau–Kurort Oybib/Kurort
       Jonsdorf luggage van
                      Set of 4   3·75   3·25

1984

E2576 30pf Cranzahl–Kurort Oberwiesenthal
       narrow-gauge steam locomotive
E2577 40pf Selketalbahn narrow-gauge steam
       locomotive
E2578 60pf Selketalbhan passenger coach
E2579 80pf Cranzahl–Kurort Oberwiesenthal
       passenger coach
                      Set of 4   2·00   1·00

1985

E2677 20pf Signal box
E2678 25pf A. Schubert (engineer), steam
locomotive *Saxonia*, 1838, and
electric locomotive Type "BR250"
E2679 50pf Electrification of railway
E2680 85pf Leipzig Central Station
Set of 4   1·75   80

1986

E2725 10pf Horsedrawn tram, Dresden, 1886
E2726 20pf Tram, Leipzig, 1896
E2727 40pf Tram, Berlin, 1919
E2728 70pf Tram, Halle, 1928
Set of 4   1·25   65

E2761 50pf Double-deck train ferry loading
ramps
E2762 50pf Two-deck railway ferry,
Mukran–Klaipeda
Set of 2   80   50

1988

E2908† 90pf Train on Rugendamm
Drawbridge   50   45

1989

E2939 15pf Friedrich List (economist)
E2940 20pf Dresdner Station, Leipzig, 1839
E2941 50pf Leipziger Station, Dresden, 1839
Set of 3   45   35

GHANA

West Africa
1957 12 pence = 1 shilling
20 shillings = 1 pound
1965 100 pesewas = 1 cedi
1967 100 new pesewas = 1 cedi
1972 100 pesewas = 1 cedi

1957

No. 158 *of Gold Coast overprinted* GHANA INDEPENDENCE 6th
MARCH 1957
175† 3d Steam locomotive and ore trucks   10   5

1959

219† 4d Ore trucks at diamond mine   40   5

1963

324 1d Steam and diesel locomotives
325 6d Steam and diesel locomotives
326 1s3d Steam and diesel locomotives
327 2s6d Steam and diesel locomotives
Set of 4   3·50   2·75

1965

No. 219 *surcharged* Ghana New Currency 19th July 1965 *and
value*
384† 4p on 4d Ore trucks at diamond mine   12   5

1967

No. 219 *surcharged with value in new pesewas*
446† 3½np on 4d Ore trucks at diamond mine   20   5

1978

868 11p Mail van
869 39p Pay and bank car
870 60p Steam locomotive
871 1c Diesel locomotive

Set of 4   5·00   2·75

1988

1231† 15c Repairing railway line   8   10
1233† 100c Miners with ore truck   50   55

GIBRALTAR

South-west Europe
1949 12 pence = 1 shilling
20 shillings = 1 pound
1971 100 pence = 1 pound

1949

As No. 114 of Antigua
136† 2d Silhouette of steam locomotive ......   1·75   1·00

1989

607† 25p Toy train   50   55

GILBERT AND ELLICE ISLANDS

Pacific Ocean
12 pence = 1 shilling
20 shillings = 1 pound

1949

As No. 114 of Antigua
59† 1d Silhouette of steam locomotive   45   35

GOLD COAST

West Africa
12 pence = 1 shilling
20 shillings = 1 pound

1948

140† 3d Steam locomotive and ore trucks   1·25   15

1949

As No. 114 of Antigua
149† 2d Silhouette of steam locomotive   30   40

1952

As No. 140 but with portrait of Queen Elizabeth II
158† 3d Steam locomotive and ore truck   35   5

GREAT BRITAIN

Western Europe
1964 12 pence = 1 shilling
20 shillings = 1 pound
1971 100 pence = 1 pound

1964

660† 6d Firth of Forth Railway Bridge   35   40

1967

715† 9d Goods wagons at dock   8   10

1968

777† 1s6d Boy with toy steam train   25   15

1975

984 7p Stephenson's *Locomotion*, 1825
985 8p Steam locomotive *Abbotsford*, 1876
986 10p Steam locomotive *Caerphilly Castle*, 1923
987 12p High Speed Train, 1975

Set of 4 1·40 1·60

1980

1113 12p *Rocket* at Moorish Arch, Liverpool
1114 12p First and second class carriages at Olive Mount
1115 12p Third Class carriage and sheep truck passing Chat Moss
1116 12p Flat truck carrying horse-drawn carriages and horse-box near Bridgewater Canal
1117 12p Truck and mailcoach at Manchester

Set of 5 1·10 1·10

1985

1272 17p "The Flying Scotsman"
1273 22p "The Golden Arrow"
1274 29p "The Cheltenham Flyer"
1275 31p "The Royal Scot"
1276 34p "The Cornish Riviera"

Set of 5 5·00 5·00

1988

1392† 18p Steam locomotive *Mallard* and mailbags on pick-up arms 50 50
1394† 31p Glasgow tram No. 1173 .... 90 1·00

1399† 34p Sydney Harbour Bridge .... 80 1·00

1989

1436† 19p Toy train 30 35

GREECE
South-east Europe
100 lepta = 1 drachma

1927

410† 5 le Steam train on bridge, Corinth Canal 35 5
415† 50 le Steam train on bridge, Corinth Canal .... 1·75 5
416† 80 le Steam train on bridge, Corinth Canal .... 1·75 30

1958

784† 10d Tram tracks, Piraeus .... 5·00 15
788† 30d Tram, Volos .... 1·40 60

STAMP MONTHLY
— finest and most informative magazine for all collectors. Obtainable from your newsagent or by postal subscription — details on request.

1977

1368 7d Steam locomotive wheel in emblem   30   25

1396† 11d Steam locomotive wheel in emblem
(on stamp No. 1368)   25   20

1978

1412† 7d Steam mail train   35   25

1979

1458† 2d Steam and diesel locomotives   30   10

1984

1665 15d Pelion steam train
1666 20d Steam goods train on Papadia
Bridge
1667 30d Piraeus–Peloponnese steam train
1668 50d Calavryta cogwheel railway steam
train
                                    Set of 4   2·75   1·60

1985

1691† 50d Tram, Salonika, 1912 ....   1·25   55

1988

1790† 150d Modern express and commuter
trains ....   1·25   60

CHARITY TAX STAMPS

1937

✚

ΠΡΟΝΟΙΑ

No. 415 *overprinted*
C500† 50 le Steam train on bridge, Corinth
Canal   40   5

1941

Κ.Π.
λεπτῶν
50

No. 410 *surcharged*
C561 50 le on 5 le Steam train on bridge,
Corinth Canal   12   12

1942

☦
ΦΥΜ· Τ.Τ.Τ.
10 ⊜ ΔΡ.

No. 410 *surcharged*
C591 10d on 5 le Steam train on bridge,
Corinth Canal   10   5

GRENADA

West Indies
100 cents = 1 dollar

1949

As No. 114 of Antigua

168†	5c Silhouette of steam locomotive	15	10

1970

392†	2c Monorail train Expo '70, Japan	5	5
396†	50c Cable car, San Francisco Pavilion, Expo '70	40	20

409†	15c Steam locomotive	15	10
410†	25c Diesel locomotive	20	10

1974

628†	½c Early American steam train	5	5
635†	$1 Mail train of the future	1·40	1·00

1981

1166†	90c Diesel locomotive (on stamp No. 410)	70	50
MS1168†	$5 Early American steam train (on stamp No. 628)	2·40	2·50

1982

1212	30c "Orient Express"		
1213	60c "Trans-Siberian Express"		
1214	70c "Golden Arrow"		
1215	90c "Flying Scotsman"		
1216	$1 German Federal Railways		
1217	$3 German National Railways		
	Set of 6	4·25	2·75
MS1218	$5 "20th Century Limited"	3·00	3·50

1984

1357†	$1.10 "Puffing Billy" steam train on trestle, Victoria, Australia	1·00	1·00
MS1359†	$5 Melbourne tram	3·75	4·50

1360	30c *Locomotion* (1825)		
1361	40c *Novelty* (1829)		
1362	60c *Washington Farmer* (1836)		
1363	70c French "Crampton" type (1859)		
1364	90c Dutch State Railways (1873)		
1365	$1.10 *Champion* (1882)		
1366	$2 Webb Compound type (1893)		
1367	$4 Berlin "No. 74" (1900)		
	Set of 8	7·50	7·00
MS1368	Two sheets (a) $5 Crampton *Phoenix* (1863); (b) $5 Mikado type (1897)		
	Set of 2 sheets	8·00	8·50

STANLEY GIBBONS
STAMP COLLECTING SERIES

Introductory booklets on *How to Start, How to Identify Stamps* and *Collecting by Theme*. A series of well illustrated guides at a low price.
Write for details.

1986

GRENADA $3⁰⁰

CHRISTMAS
TRAIN RIDE

1545† $3 Mickey Mouse, Donald Duck and
nephew riding toy train .... 1·50 1·60

1987

60c GRENADA

Trans-Siberian Railway   Longest Railway Line

1629† 60c Steam locomotive on Trans-
Siberian Railway 25 30

1711† $3 James Watt and drawing of steam
engine theory .... 1·40 1·50
No. 1711 is inscribed "RUDOLF DIESEL" in error.

1989

GRENADA

CANADA ATLANTIC RAILWAY
No. 2 1889
1889 CANADA

$2

1941 $2 Canada Atlantic Railway locomotive
No. 2, 1889
1942 $2 Virginia and Truckee Railroad "J. W.
Bowker" type locomotive, 1875

1943 $2 Philadelphia and Reading Railway
locomotive *Ariel*, 1872
1944 $2 Chicago and Rock Island Railroad
"America" type locomotive, 1867
1945 $2 Lehigh Valley Railroad Consolidation
locomotive No. 63, 1866
1946 $2 Great Western Railway locomotive
Scotia, 1860
1947 $2 Grand Trunk Railway "Birkenhead"
Class locomotive, 1854
1948 $2 Camden and Amboy Railway
locomotive *Monster*, 1837
1949 $2 Baltimore and Ohio Railway
"Grasshopper" Class locomotive, 1834
1950 $2 Baltimore and Ohio Railway
locomotive *Tom Thumb*, 1829
1951 $2 United Railways of Yucatan
locomotive *Yucatan*, 1925
1952 $2 Canadian National Railways Class
"T2" locomotive, 1924
1953 $2 St. Louis–San Francisco Railroad
"Light Mikado" class locomotive, 1919
1954 $2 Atlantic Coast Line Railroad "Light
Pacific" class locomotive, 1919
1955 $2 Edaville Railroad locomotive No. 7,
1913
1956 $2 Denver and Rio Grande Western
Railroad Class "K27" locomotive, 1903
1957 $2 Pennsylvania Railroad Class "E-2"
locomotive No. 7002, 1902
1958 $2 Pennsylvania Railroad Class "H6"
locomotive, 1899
1959 $2 Mohawk and Hudson Railroad
locomotive *De Witt Clinton*, 1831
1960 $2 St. Clair Tunnel Company locomotive
No. 598, 1891
1961 $2 Chesapeake and Ohio Railroad Class
"M-1" steam turbine electric locomotive,
No. 500, 1947
1962 $2 Rutland Railroad locomotive No. 93,
1946
1963 $2 Pennsylvania Railroad Class "T1"
locomotive, 1942
1964 $2 Chesapeake and Ohio Railroad Class
"H-8" locomotive, 1942
1965 $2 Atchison, Topeka and Santa Fe
Railway Model "FT" diesel locomotive,
1941
1966 $2 Gulf, Mobile and Ohio Railroad
Models "S-1" and "S-2" diesel
locomotive, 1940
1967 $2 New York, New Haven and Hartford
Railroad Class "15" locomotive, 1937
1968 $2 Seaboard Air Line Railroad Class "R"
locomotive, 1966
1969 $2 Newfoundland Railway Class "R-2"
locomotive, 1930
1970 $2 Canadian National Railway diesel
locomotive No. 9000, 1928

Set of 30   22·00   23·00

GRENADINES OF GRENADA

West Indies
100 cents = 1 dollar

1974

As Nos. 628 and 635 of Grenada

28†	$1 Early American steam train	40	40
MS29	$1 Bellman and antenna; $2 18th-century postman and mail train of the future	1·00	1·50

1979

334† $2 Diesel mail train 75 50

362† $2.50 Train driver Donald Duck .... 1·60 1·00

1980

No. 334 overprinted **LONDON 1980**

394† $2 Diesel mail train 90 65

1982

479† 40c Streamlined steam locomotive 30 20
MS482† $5 Advanced Passenger Train and
steam mail train .... 3·00 3·25

517 10c "Santa Fe"
518 40c "Mistral"
519 70c "Rheingold"
520 $1 "ET 403"
521 $1.10 Steam locomotive Mallard
522 $2 "Tokaido"
Set of 6 3·50 2·00
MS523 $5 "Settebello" .... 2·75 3·00

1984

627 20c Colonel Steven's model (1825)
628 50c Royal George (1827)
629 60c Stourbridge Lion (1829)
630 70c Liverpool (1830)
631 90c South Carolina (1832)
632 $1.10 Monster (1836)
633 $2 Lafayette (1837)
634 $4 Lion (1838)
Set of 8 7·00 7·00
MS635 Two sheets (a) $5 Sequin's locomotive
(1829); (b) $5 Der Adler (1835)
Set of 2 sheets 7·00 8·00

1987

878† 70c Jenny Lind (first mass produced
locomotive class), 1847 .... 30 35
880† $1.50 Steam locomotive, Metropolitan
Railway, London, 1863 .... 70 75

907† $3 Ruldolf Diesel and diesel engine .... 1·40 1·50
No. 907 is inscribed "JAMES WATT" in error.

1988

MS1087† Two sheets(b) $7 Mickey Mouse as
Father Christmas and Donald Duck in carnival
train (other sheet shows Peter Pan)
Set of 2 sheets 6·00 6·25

GRENADINES OF ST. VINCENT

West Indies
100 cents = 1 dollar

1985

1984

271/272   5c Class "D13" locomotive, U.S.A.
(1892)
273/274   10c High Speed Train "125", Great
Britain (1980)
275/276   15c Class "T9" locomotive, Great Britain
(1899)
277/278   35c Locomotive *Claud Hamilton*, Great
Britain (1900)
279/280   45c Class "J" locomotive, U.S.A. (1941)
281/282   60c Class "D16" locomotive, U.S.A.
(1895)
283/284 $1 Locomotive *Lode Star*, Great Britain
(1907)
285/286 $2.50 Locomotive *Blue Peter*, Great
Britain (1948)
Set of 16   4·50   4·50
The first stamp in each pair shows technical drawings and the
second the locomotive at work.

311/312   1c Class "C62" locomotive, Japan
(1948)
313/314   5c Class "V" locomotive, Great Britain
(1903)
315/316   20c Locomotive *Catch-Me-Who-Can*,
Great Britain (1808)
317/318   35c Class "E10" locomotive, Japan
(1948)
319/320   60c Locomotive *J.B. Earle*, Great Britain
(1904)
321/322 $1 Locomotive *Lyn*, Great Britain (1898)
323/324 $1.50 Locomotive *Talyllyn*, Great Britain
(1865)
325/326 $3 Locomotive *Cardean*, Great Britain
(1906)
Set of 16   5·50   5·50
The first stamp in each pair shows technical drawings and the
second the locomotive at work.

STAMP MONTHLY
— finest and most informative magazine for all
collectors. Obtainable from your newsagent or by
postal subscription — details on request.

351/352   1c P.L.M. "Grosse C" Locomotive,
France (1898)
353/354   15c Class "C12" locomotive, Japan
(1932)
355/356   75c Class "D50" locomotive, Japan
(1923)
357/358 $3 Locomotive *Fire Fly*, Great Britain
(1840)
Set of 8   3·25   3·25
The first stamp in each pair shows technical drawings and the
second the locomotive at work.

390/391   10c Class "581" 12-car train, Japan
(1968)
392/393   40c Class "231-132BT" locomotive,
Algeria (1936)
394/395   50c Class "S" locomotive *Slieve Gullion*,
Great Britain (1913)
396/397 $2.50 Class "Beattie" well tank
locomotive, Great Britain (1874)
Set of 8   2·75   3·00
The first stamp in each pair shows technical drawings and the
second the locomotive at work.

412/413   35c Locomotive *Coronation*, Great
Britain (1937)
414/415   70c Class "E18" locomotive, Germany
(1935)
416/417 $1.20 Hayes type locomotive, U.S.A.
(1854)
418/419 $2 Class "2120" locomotive, Japan
(1890)
Set of 8   4·25   4·75
The first stamp in each pair shows technical drawings and the
second the locomotive at work.

1986

443/444   15c Class "T15" locomotive, Germany (1897)
445/446   45c Class "13" locomotive, Great Britain (1900)
447/448   60c Locomotive *Halesworth*, Great Britain (1879)
449/450   75c Class "Problem" locomotive, Great Britain (1859)
451/452 $1 Class "Western" diesel locomotive, Great Britain (1961)
453/454 $1.50 Drummond's *Bug* locomotive, Great Britain (1899)
455/456 $2 Class "Clan" locomotive, Great Britain (1951)
457/458 $3 Class "1800" locomotive, Japan (1884)

           Set of 16   7·00   8·00

The first stamp in each pair shows technical drawings and the second the locomotive at work.

1987

504/505   10c Class "1001" locomotive No. 1275, Great Britain (1874)
506/507   40c Class "4P Garratt" locomotive, Great Britain (1927)
508/509   50c Locomotive *Papyrus*, Great Britain (1929)
510/511   60c Class "VI" locomotive, Great Britain (1930)
512/513   75c Class "40" diesel locomotive No. D200, Great Britain (1958)
514/515 $1 Class "42 Warship" diesel locomotive, Great Britain (1958)
516/517 $1.25 Class "P-69" locomotive, U.S.A. (1902)
518/519 $1.50 Class "60-3 Shay" locomotive No. 15, U.S.A. (1913)

           Set of 16   5·00   5·75

The first stamp in each pair shows technical drawings and the second the locomotive at work.

520/521   10c Class "142" diesel locomotive, East Germany (1977)

522/523   40c Class "120" electric locomotive, West Germany (1979)
524/525   50c Class "X" diesel locomotive, Australia (1954)
526/527   60c Class "59" diesel locomotive, Great Britain (1986)
528/529   75c New York Elevated Railroad locomotive *Spuyten Duyvel*, U.S.A. (1875)
530/531 $1 Camden & Amboy Railroad locomotive *Stevens* (later *John Bull*), U.S.A. (1831)
532/533 $1.50 "Royal Hudson" Class "H1-d" locomotive No. 2850, Canada (1938)
534/535 $2 "Pioneer Zephyr" 3-car diesel set, U.S.A. (1934)

           Set of 16   5·75   6·25

The first stamp in each pair shows technical drawings and the second the locomotive at work.

1989

592†   2c Mickey and Minnie Mouse on Indian steam train   5   5

APPENDIX

The following stamps have either been issued in excess of postal needs, or have not been made available to the public in reasonable quantities at face value. Miniature sheets, imperforate stamps, etc., are excluded from this section.

Bequia

1984

Railway Locomotives (1st series). Two designs for each value, the first showing technical drawings and the second the locomotive at work. 1, 5, 10, 25, 35, 45c, $1.50, $2, each × 2.

Railway Locomotives (2nd series). Two designs for each value, the first showing technical drawings and the second the locomotive at work. 1, 5, 10, 35, 75c. $1, $2.50, $3, each × 2.

1985

Railway Locomotives (3rd series). Two designs for each value, the first showing technical drawings and the second the locomotive at work. 25, 55, 60c, $2, each × 2.

Railway Locomotives (4th series). Two designs for each value, the first showing technical drawings and the second the locomotive at work. 25, 55, 60, 75c, $1, $2.50, each × 2.

1986

Railway Engineers and Locomotives. $1, $2.50, $3, $4.

1987

Railway Locomotives (5th series). Two designs for each value, the first showing technical drawings and the second the locomotive at work. 15, 25, 40, 50, 60, 75c., $1, $2, each × 2.

Union Island

1984

Railway Locomotives (1st series). Two designs for each value, the first showing technical drawings and the second the locomotive at work. 5, 60c, $1, $2, each × 2.

Railway Locomotives (2nd series). Two designs for each value, the first showing technical drawings and the second the locomotive at work. 5, 10, 20, 25, 75c, $1, $2.50, $3, each × 2.

1985

Railway Locomotives (3rd series). Two designs for each value, the first showing technical drawings and the second the locomotive at work. 5, 50, 60c, $2, each × 2.

1986

Railway Locomotives (4th series). Two designs for each value, the first showing technical drawing and the second the locomotive at work. 15, 30, 45, 60, 75c, $1.50, $2.50, $3, each × 2.

Railway Locomotives (5th series). Two designs for each value, the first showing technical drawings and the second the locomotive at work. 15, 45, 60, 75c, $1, $1.50, $2, $3, each × 2.

1987

Railway Locomotives (6th series). Two designs for each value, the first showing technical drawings and the second the locomotive at work. 15, 25, 40, 50, 60, 75c, $1, $2, each × 2.

Railway Locomotives. (7th series). Two designs for each value, the first showing technical drawings and the second the locomotive at work, 15, 20, 30, 45, 50, 75c, $1, $1.50, each × 2.

GUATEMALA

Central America
1886 100 centavos = 8 reales = 1 peso
1927 100 centavos de quetzal = 1 quetzal

1886

Correos Nacionales

150 c. 150 c.

Guatemala.

150 c. 150 c.

150 Ctavos.

Railway Bond Receipt stamps surcharged

26	25c on 1p President J. Rufino Barios			
27	50c on 1p President J. Rufino Barios			
28	75c on 1p President J. Rufino Barios			
29	100c on 1p President J. Rufino Barios			
30	150c on 1p President J. Rufino Barios			
		Set of 5	3·50	3·50

43a	1c Steam locomotive (blue)	1·75	15
44	2c Steam locomotive (brown)	2·50	20

46	5c Steam locomotive (violet)	3·50	20
47	6c Steam locomotive (mauve)	5·00	40
48	10c Steam locomotive (red)	4·00	20
49	20c Steam locomotive (green)	7·50	50
50	25c Steam locomotive (orange)	12·00	1·75
37	50c Steam locomotive	20·00	6·50
38	75c Steam locomotive	18·00	5·00
39	100c Steam locomotive	25·00	16·00
40	150c Steam locomotive	32·00	22·00
41	200c Steam locomotive	22·00	16·00

No. 44 surcharged **PROVISIONAL. 1886. 1 UN CENTAVO**

42	1c on 2c Steam locomotive	4·50	7·00

1894

Nos. 38/41 and 44 surcharged **1894**, *bar and value*

55	1c on 2c Steam locomotive	1·25	1·25
51	2c on 100c Steam locomotive	6·50	5·00
57	6c on 150c Steam locomotive	12·00	6·00
53	10c on 75c Steam locomotive	9·50	6·00
54	10c on 200c Steam locomotive	5·00	3·50

1895

No. 46 surcharged **1895 1 CENTAVO** *and bar*

59	1c on 5c Steam locomotive	75	60

1897

62	1c Steam locomotive, portrait and arms
63	2c Steam locomotive, portrait and arms
64	6c Steam locomotive, portrait and arms
65	10c Steam locomotive, portrait and arms
66	12c Steam locomotive, portrait and arms
67	18c Steam locomotive, portrait and arms
68	20c Steam locomotive, portrait and arms
69	25c Steam locomotive, portrait and arms
70	50c Steam locomotive, portrait and arms
71	75c Steam locomotive, portrait and arms
72	100c Steam locomotive, portrait and arms
73	150c Steam locomotive, portrait and arms
74	200c Steam locomotive, portrait and arms
75	500c Steam locomotive, portrait and arms
	Set of 14 £160 £160

No. 66 surcharged **UN CENTAVO 1898**

76	1c on 12c Steam locomotive, portrait and arms	1·10	1·10

1898

Nos. 37/41, 46, 48/50 surcharged **1898**, *bar and value*

77	1c on 5c Steam locomotive
78	1c on 25c Steam locomotive
79	1c on 50c Steam locomotive
80	1c on 75c Steam locomotive
81	6c on 5c Steam locomotive
82	6c on 10c Steam locomotive
83	6c on 20c Steam locomotive
84	6c on 100c Steam locomotive
85	6c on 150c Steam locomotive
86	6c on 200c Steam locomotive
87	10c on 20c Steam locomotive
	Set of 11 50·00 45·00

Fiscal stamp overprinted **CORREOS NACIONALES** *or surch* **2 CENTAVOS** *also*

88	1c Steam locomotive	1·50	1·50
89	2c on 1c Steam locomotive	2·50	2·50

1899
No. 46 surcharged **Un 1 Centavo 1899**

99	1c on 5c Steam locomotive	60	50

1900
No. 48 surcharged **1900 1 CENTAVO**

100	1c on 10c Steam locomotive	70	70

As 1886 issue, but colours changed

101	1c Steam locomotive (green)
102	2c Steam locomotive (red)
103	5c Steam locomotive (blue)
104	6c Steam locomotive (green)
105	10c Steam locomotive (brown)
106	20c Steam locomotive (mauve)
107	20c Steam locomotive (brown)
108	25c Steam locomotive (yellow)
109	25c Steam locomotive (green)

Set of 9 40·00 55·00

1901
Nos. 49/50 surcharged **1901 a**nd value

110	1c on 20c Steam locomotive (green)
111	1c on 25c Steam locomotive (orange)
112	2c on 20c Steam locomotive (green)

Set of 3 3·50 3·50

1902
As Nos. 88/9 surcharged **CORREOS NACIONALES 1902** *and value in figures and words*

113	1c on 1c Steam locomotive
114	2c on 1c Steam locomotive

Set of 2 3·25 3·25

1903
Nos. 38, 40/1, 101/2, 104/5 surcharged **1903 25 CENTAVOS**

127	25c on 1c Steam locomotive (green)
128	25c on 2c Steam locomotive (red)
129	25c on 6c Steam locomotive (green)
130	25c on 10c Steam locomotive (brown)
131	25c on 75c Steam locomotive
132	25c on 150c Steam locomotive
133	25c on 200c Steam locomotive

Set of 7 70·00 45·00

WHEN YOU BUY AN ALBUM LOOK FOR THE NAME "STANLEY GIBBONS"
It means Quality combined with Value for Money.

1919

159†	30c Steam train	2·50	75
171†	15p Railway bridge, Guatemala City (red and black)	23·00	12·50

1920
No. 159 surcharged **1920 2 centavos**

163†	2c on 30c Steam train	45	45

1922
No. 171 surcharged **1922** *and value*

181†	12½c on 15p Railway bridge, Guatemala City	75	65
194†	25c on 15p Railway bridge, Guatemala City	2·00	2·00

1924
As No. 171, but colour changed and imprinted "PERKINS BACON & CO. LD. LONDRES" *at foot*

210†	15p Railway bridge, Guatemala City (black)	5·50	3·50

1926
As No. 171, but imprinted "WATERLOW & SONS LIMITED. LONDRES" *at foot*

222†	15p Railway bridge, Guatemala City (black)	4·75	2·75

1929
Surcharged **SERVICIO POSTAL AEREO ANO DE 1928** *and new value*

239	3c on 15p Railway bridge, Guatemala City (No. 222)
240	5c on 15p Railway bridge, Guatemala City (No. 222)
240a	5c on 15p Railway bridge, Guatemala City (No. 210)
241	15c on 15p Railway bridge, Guatemala City (No. 222)
242	20c on 15p Railway bridge, Guatemala City (No. 222)

Set of 5 10·00 11·00

Surcharged **FERROCARRIL ORIENTAL 1929** *and new value*

244	3c on 3p Arms
245	5c on 3p Arms

Set of 2 4·75 6·00

1930
No. 222 surcharged **FERROCARRIL DE LOS ALTOS Inaugurado en 1929** *and new value*

246	1c on 15p Railway bridge, Guatemala City (black)
247	2c on 15p Railway bridge, Guatemala City (black)
248	3c on 15p Railway bridge, Guatemala City (black)
249	5c on 15p Railway bridge, Guatemala City (black)
250	15c on 15p Railway bridge, Guatemala City (black)

Set of 5 6·50 10·00

251　2c Dam providing railway electric power
252　3c Los Altos Railway tracks
253　5c Quetzaltenango Railway Station
Set of 3　7·00　7·00

No. 222 surcharged **SERVICIO AEREO INTERIOR 1930** and value
259†　10c on 15p Railway bridge, Guatemala
City (black) .... 3·00　3·00

1932
No. 222 surcharged **SERVICIO AEREO INTERIOR 1932** and value
270†　10c on 15p Railway bridge, Guatemala
City .... 12·00　8·00
271†　15c on 15p Railway bridge, Guatemala
City .... 17·00　12·00

1935

285†　3c Arms and steam locomotive .... 2·00　1·50
291†　10c Steam locomotive on dock, Port
Barrios (air) .... 3·50　3·25

310†　5c Railway Station, Barrios Plaza (blue)　50　20
310a†　5c Railway Station, Barrios Plaza
(orange).......................... 35　20
315　30c Railway tracks, Port Barrios (green)　5·00　3·50
315a†　30c Railway track, Port Barrios (red) ....　1·50　20
316†　50c Railway tracks, San Jose (red) ....　13·00　13·00
316a†　50c Railway tracks, San Jose (violet) ..　10·00　10·00

1937

364†　50c Railway Station, Barrios Plaza ...... 14·00　14·00

1939

395†　25c Barrios Railway Station .... 80　20

1971

909　2c Steam locomotive on bridge
910　10c Steam locomtoive on bridge
911　50c Steam locomotive on bridge
912　1q Steam locomotive on bridge
Set of 4　14·00　8·00

1983

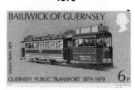

1217　10c First steam train crossing Puente de
las Vacas Bridge
1218　25c General Barrios, diesel and steam
locomotives
1219　30c Diesel goods train crossing Lake
Amatitlan Dam
Set of 3　3·50　3·50

GUERNSEY
Western Europe
100 pence = 1 pound

1979

BAILIWICK OF GUERNSEY

203†　6p Steam tram, 1879 .... 15　15
204†　8p Electric tram, 1896 .... 20　20

1989

467† 37p Boat train on Weymouth Quay 75 80

POSTAGE DUE STAMPS

1982

D33† 4p Tram, St Peter Port 8 10

GUINEA

West Africa
1974 100 caury = 1 syli
1986 100 centimes = 1 franc

1974

844† 6s Bauxite train 65 40
845† 10s Ore train at bauxite mine 90 50

860† 7s50 Monorail train 85 30

COLLECT BIRDS ON STAMPS

New second edition available at £8.50 (p. + p. £2) from:
Stanley Gibbons Publications Ltd, 5 Parkside,
Christchurch Road, Ringwood, Hants BH24 3SH.

1976

890† 9s Woman railway shunter .... 1·60 50

1980

1022† 5s Steam train 40 15

1984

1139† 15s Beyer-Garratt steam locomotive .... 1·25 80
MS1142† 30s Series "B" steam locomotive .... 2·25 1·60

1985

1212 7s Class "8F" steam locomotive
1213 15s German Class "Bo-Bo/5500 CH"
     series III electric locomotive
1214 25s Pacific steam locomotive No. 270
1215 35s German electric commuter train
     Series "420" (air)
                                    Set of 4   5·50   3·25
MS1216 50s German "ICE" high speed train   3·75   2·50

1986

Nos. 1212/15 *surcharged in francs*
1237 2f on 7s Class "8F" steam locomotive
1238 25f on 15 German Class "Bo-Bo/5500
     CH" series III electric locomotive

1239 50f on 25s Pacific steam locomotive No. 270

1240 90f on 35s German electric commuter train Series "420" (air)

Set of 4	1·25	40

MS1241 500f on 50s German "ICE" high speed train .... 3·25 1·60

1252 20f Dietrich Autorail railcar
1253 100f German "Type 13" steam locomotive No. 7906
1254 300f German steam locomotive No. 01220
1255 400f Guinea Autorail ABH 3 Type "5020" train (air)

Set of 4	4·25	1·90

MS1256 600f Locomotive *Der Adler* and Guinea Renault Autorail ABH 3 train .... 3·50 1·60

GUINEA-BISSAU

West Africa
100 centavos = 1 peso

1977

522† 35p German locomotive *Der Adler* ...... 2·75 1·50

1980

618† 25p Early and modern locomotives and child with toy train .... 1·40 50

1984

904 5p White Mountain Central Railway locomotive, 1926
905 8p Portuguese locomotive, 1886
906 15p Single-rail suspended railcar, 1901
907 20p Peruvian mountain rack-railway locomotive
908 24p Rack-railway locomotive, Achensee, Austria
909 30p Vitznau–Rigi railway steam locomotive
910 35p Vitznau–Rigi railway locomotive, 1873

Set of 7	1·75	30

1986

978† 15p Frankfurt am Main railway station, Germany, 1914 .... 5 5

GUYANA

South America
100 cents = 1 dollar

1966

No. 360 of British Guiana overprinted **GUYANA INDEPENDENCE 1966**
401† 24c Diesel locomotive and bauxite mine 35 20

1982

No. 401 additionally surcharged **H.R.H. Prince William 21st June 1982 $2.20**
987† $2.20 on 24c Diesel locomotive and bauxite mine .... 1·75 1·75

1983

No. 401 additionally surcharged **Commonwealth Day 14 March 1983** *and new value*
1067† $1.30 on 24c Diesel locomotive and bauxite mine 75 55
1068† $2.40 on 24c Diesel locomotive and bauxite mine .... 1·40 1·25

1987

2194 $1.20 Steam locomotive *Alexandra* (green)
2195 $1.20 Front view of diesel locomotive (green)
2196 $1.20 Steam locomotive with searchlight (green)
2197 $1.20 Side view of diesel locomotive (green)
2198 $1.20 Steam locomotive *Alexandra* (purple)
2199 $1.20 Front view of diesel locomotive (purple)
2200 $1.20 Steam locomotive with searchlight (purple)
2201 $1.20 Side view of diesel locomotive (purple)
2202 $3.20 Steam locomotive *Alexandra*
2203 $3.20 Front view of diesel locomotive
2204 $3.20 Steam locomotive with searchlight
2205 $3.20 Side view of diesel locomotive
2206 $3.20 Molasses warehouses and early locomotive
2207 $3.30 Front view of diesel locomotive
2208 $3.30 Steam locomotive *Alexandra*
2209 $3.30 Side view of diesel locomotive
2210 $3.30 Steam locomotive with searchlight
2211 $3.30 Diesel locomotive and passenger train
2212 $10 Cattle train
2213 $12 Molasses train

       Set of 20 7·50 8·50

1988
Nos. 2194/201 *overprinted*
2346 $1.20 Steam locomotive *Alexandra* (green) (optd **BEWARE OF ANIMALS**)
2347 $1.20 Front view of diesel locomotive (green) (optd **BEWARE OF CHILDREN**)
2348 $1.20 Steam locomotive with searchlight (green) (optd **DRIVE SAFELY**)
2349 $1.20 Side view of diesel locomotive (green) (optd **DO NOT DRINK AND DRIVE**)
2350 $1.20 Steam locomotive *Alexandra* (purple) (optd **BEWARE OF ANIMALS**)
2351 $1.20 Front view of diesel locomotive (purple) (optd **BEWARE OF CHILDREN**)
2352 $1.20 Steam locomotive with searchlight (purple) (optd **DRIVE SAFELY**)
2353 $1.20 Side view of diesel locomotive (purple) (optd **DO NOT DRINK AND DRIVE**)

       Set of 8 1·10 1·40

GWALIOR
Indian sub-continent
12 pies = 1 anna
16 annas = 1 rupee

1938
No. 255 *of India overprinted* **GWALIOR** *in English and Hindi*
110† 4a Mail train .... 14·00 1·25

HAITI
West Indies
100 centimes = 1 gourde

1906

139† 3c Tram tracks, Iron Market, Port-au-Prince (brown) .... 1·00 20
140† 3c Tram tracks, Iron Market, Port-au-Prince (orange) .... 3·50 3·50
144† 8c Tram tracks in front of Catholic College, Port-au-Prince (red) .... 2·50 85
169† 8c Tram tracks in front of Catholic College, Port-au-Prince (green) ...... 13·00 8·50

1914
Overprinted **GL O.Z. 7 FEV 1914** *in frame*
185† 3c Tram tracks, Iron Market, Port-au-Prince (No. 139) .... 1·60 55
186† 3c Tram tracks, Iron Market, Port-au-Prince (No. 140) 75 75
189† 8c Tram tracks in front of Catholic College, Port-au-Prince (No. 144) .... 3·50 2·25
201† 8c Tram tracks in front of Catholic College, Port-au-Prince (No. 169) .... 4·50 4·50

1917
Surcharged **GOURDE** *and new value in frame*
251† 2c on 3c Tram tracks, Iron Market, Port-au-Prince (No. 139) 65 50
252† 2c on 3c Tram tracks, Iron Market, Port-au-Prince (No. 140) 75 60
253† 2c on 8c Tram tracks in front of Catholic College, Port-au-Prince (No. 144) 50 35
255† 2c on 8c Tram tracks in front of Catholic College, Port-au-Prince (No. 169) 90 90

1919
Surcharged with new values in frame
269† 2c on 8c Tram tracks in front of Catholic College, Port-au-Prince (No. 189) 60 40
270† 2c on 8c Tram tracks in front of Catholic College, Port-au-Prince (No. 201) 60 40
277† 3c on 3c Tram tracks, Iron Market, Port-au-Prince (No. 185) 70 50
279† 5c on 3c Tram tracks, Iron Market, Port-au-Prince (No. 185) 70 40
280† 5c on 3c Tram tracks, Iron Market, Port-au-Prince (No. 186) .... 1·40 1·75

1920

294†	3c Steam train	3·00	2·00
295†	5c Steam train	1·00	10

HONDURAS

Central America
1898 100 centavos = 1 peso
1933 100 centavos = 1 lempira

1898

108	1c Steam train	
109	2c Steam train	
110	5c Steam train	
111	6c Steam train	
112	10c Steam train	
113	20c Steam train	
114	50c Steam train	
115	1p Steam train	
	Set of 8 4·50	6·25

1915

186†	1c Ulua Railway Bridge	20	10
187†	2c Ulua Railway Bridge	30	10
190†	10c Ulua Railway Bridge	60	30
191†	20c Ulua Railway Bridge	1·75	1·75

1925
Nos. 190/1 *overprinted* **AEREO CORREO**

229†	10c Ulua Railway Bridge	£225	£225
231†	20c Ulua Railway Bridge	£160	£160

Nos. 186, 190/1 *surcharged* **AEREO CORREO** *and new value*

235†	25c on 1c Ulua Railway Bridge	£110	£110
236c†	25c on 10c Ulua Railway Bridge	£4300	
237†	25c on 20c Ulua Railway Bridge	£225	£225

1926
No. 187 *overprinted* **HABILITADO 1926**

242†	2c Ulua Railway Bridge	50	75

1927
No. 191 *surcharged* **vale 6ct. 1927** *and bar*

245†	6c on 20c Ulua Railway Bridge	1·50	1·50

1930
No. 186 *overprinted* **Habilitado julio-1930**

305†	1c Ulua Railway Bridge	75	75

1931
No. O209 *surcharged* **Servicio aereo interior Vale 15cts Octubre 1931**

344a	15c on 20c Ulua Railway Bridge	7·50	7·50

1935

372†	20c Mayol Railway Bridge	80	40

1966

686†	5c Steam locomotive	2·50	75

OFFICIAL STAMP

1898
Nos. 110 *and* 112/15 *overprinted* **OFICIAL**

O116	5c Steam train	
O117	10c Steam train	
O118	20c Steam train	
O119	50c Steam train	
O120	1p Steam train	
	Set of 5 1·60	

1915
Nos. 186/7 *and* 190/1 *overprinted* **OFICIAL**

O204†	1c Ulua Railway Bridge	50	1·00
O205†	2c Ulua Railway Bridge	50	1·00
O208†	10c Ulua Railway Bridge	1·60	1·60
O209†	20c Ulua Railway Bridge	1·60	1·60

1933
No. O208 *surcharged* **Aereo Oficial Vale L. 0.70 1933**

O375	70c on 10c Ulua Railway Bridge	12·50	12·50

STANLEY GIBBONS
STAMP COLLECTING SERIES

Introductory booklets on *How to Start, How to Identify Stamps* and *Collecting by Theme*. A series of well illustrated guides at a low price.
Write for details.

HONG KONG

South-east coast of China
100 cents = 1 dollar

1949

As No. 114 of Antigua

173†	10c Silhouette of steam locomotive	85	25

1977

364†	20c Tram cars	25	5
366†	$1.30 Peak Railway car	90	1·00

1979

384	20c Diagrammatic view of railway station		
385	$1.30 Diagrammatic view of car		
386	$2 Plan showing route of Mass Transit Railway		
	Set of 3	1·10	1·10

1983

443†	$1 Clock Tower of Kowloon–Canton Railway Station, Tsam Sha Tsui	55	55

1985

469†	$1.30 Double-deck trams outside Old Supreme Court Building	50	55

1986

517†	50c Mass Transit train	25	15

1988

577	50c Lower Terminal and tram, Peak Tramway		
578	$1.30 Tram on incline		
579	$1.70 Tram near Peak Tower Upper Terminal		
580	$5.00 Tram		
	Set of 4	1·25	1·40

HUNGARY

Central Europe
1941 100 filler = 1 pengo
1946 100 filler = 1 forint

1941

703†	10f Count Szechenyi	8	5
704†	16f Count Szechenyi	12	8
707†	40f Steam locomotive	45	12

1945

845†	2p Winged Wheel (emblem of railway workers)	3·75	3·75

1946

957 10,000ap "Heves" Class steam
locomotive
958 20,000ap Class "424" steam locomotive
959 30,000ap Electric locomotive
960 40,000ap Arpad railcar

Set of 4 16·00 14·00

1948

1030† 5fi George Stephenson 25 20
1035† 30fi Kalman Kando .... 1·25 60

1949

1078 50fi Steam locomotive .... 3·50 3·00

1950

1082† 8fi Electric mine train 25 5
1089† 2fo Steam locomotive on bridge ...... 1·00 8
1091† 2fo Steam train at factory .... 2·25 15
1092† 3fo Steam locomotive .... 2·50 20

1132† 20fi Petofi Railway Bridge 5 5
1134† 70fi Steam train at Diosgyor steel-mill 20 5
1138† 3fo Steam train .... 2·50 40
1139† 5fo Steam train at Matyas Hakosi
steel-mill .... 1·25 45

1951

1178† 50fi Train on Budapest Pioneer
Railway 45 20

1180b† 10fi Szekesfehervar Railway Station 50 5
1181† 20fi Ganz Wagon Works 50 5
1183† 40fi Central Railway Station, Budapest 70 5
1184a† 70fi Goods wagons at grain elevator 1·00 5

1952

1247 60fi Steam train and railwayman
1248 1fo Track-laying machine

Set of 2 2·25 50

1953

1267 60fi Constructing Underground tunnel,
Budapest
1268 1fo Budapest Underground Railway map
and station

Set of 2 1·75 40

1300† 30fi Goods wagons at factory, Maly 75 5
1304† 70fi Goods wagons at blast furnace,
Diosgyor .... 1·75 5

WHEN YOU BUY AN ALBUM LOOK FOR THE NAME "STANLEY GIBBONS"

It means Quality combined with Value for Money.

1955

| 1407† | 60fi Steam train at blast furnace | 30 | 10 |

| 1419† | 40fi Railway guard | 90 | 5 |
| 1426† | 1fo40 Tram and conductor | 60 | 5 |

As No. 1139, but printed on aluminium-surfaced paper
| 1437 | 5fo Steam train at Matyas Rakosi Steel Mill | 7·50 | 7·50 |

| 1441† | 40fi "Hargita" diesel multiple unit | 40 | 10 |
| 1445† | 1fo20 Class "303" steam locomotive | 1·40 | 50 |

1957

No. 1419 surcharged with shield, cross and premium
| 1472† | 40fi + 40fi Railway guard | 35 | 30 |

1958

| 1535† | 1fo Steam locomotive | 35 | 20 |

1959

1564†	20fi Early steam locomotive *Deru*	35	5
1565†	30fi Ganz diesel railcar	35	8
1566†	40fi Early railway semaphore signal	45	10

1961

| 1740† | 40fi Steam locomotive | 15 | 5 |

| 1751† | 60fi George Stephenson | 15 | 5 |
| 1752† | 1fo Winged railway wheel | 20 | 10 |

1962

| 1795 | 1fo Railway signals | 25 | 10 |

1963

| 1890† | 1fo20 Diesel mail train and Mongolian stamp | 50 | 10 |

1900†	20fi Tram car	10	5
1902†	40fi Budapest West Station	10	5
1903†	50fi Railway petroleum truck	20	5
1904†	60fi Budapest South Station	10	5
1905†	70fi Railway T.P.O. coach	25	5
1911†	1fo70 Diesel multi-unit train	65	5
1914†	2fo60 Signal, signal box and train	90	10
1917†	5fo Railway fork-lift truck	85	5

1964

2024† 20fi Trams on Arpad Bridge, Budapest ... 10 ... 5
2025† 30fi Trams on Margaret Bridge,
Budapest .... 10 ... 5
2027† 1fo Trams on Elizabeth Bridge,
Budapest .... 45 ... 5
2028† 1fo50 Tracks on Freedom Bridge,
Budapest .... 65 ... 15
2029† 2fo Trams on Petofi Bridge, Budapest ... 90 ... 25
2030† 2fo50 Diesel railcar on South Bridge,
Budapest .... 1·75 ... 1·00

1966

2162† 2fo Count Szechenyi .... 30 ... 10

2182 1fo Steam locomotive *Deru*
2183 2fo Electric locomotive and South
Station, Budapest
Set of 2 ... 1·40 ... 50

2226† 20fi Helsinki Railway Station, Finland .. 5 ... 5

1967

2273 1fo Diesel train .... 25 ... 5

1968

2335 2fo Kalman Kando, Class "V43" electric
locomotive and map .... 60 ... 10

2345 2fo Diesel train .... 35 ... 5

2370 2fo Type "424" steam locomotive ...... 1·25 ... 25

2379† 4fo Diesel train .... 1·25 ... 60

1970

2514† 2fo + 1fo Elizabeth Bridge, Budapest ... 40 ... 55

COLLECT SHIPS ON STAMPS

The largest Stanley Gibbons thematic catalogue to date
– available at £10.95 (p. + p. £2) from:
Stanley Gibbons Publications Ltd, 5 Parkside,
Christchurch Road, Ringwood, Hants BH24 3SH.

2517 1fo Underground train at station,
Budapest 40 5

1971

2603 1fo Locomotive *Bets* and route map,
1846 .... 65 10

1972

2647 40fi Hungarian Class "303" steam
locomotive, 1950
2648 60fi Prussian Class "P6" steam
locomotive, 1902
2649 80fi Italian Mediterranean Class "380"
steam locomotive, 1894
2650 1fo Russian Class "P36" steam
locomotive, 1950
2651 1fo20 Japanese Heisler steam
locomotive
2652 2fo Scottish Caledonian 0-4-4T steam
locomotive, 1873
2653 4fo Austrian Class "166" steam
locomotive, 1882
2654 5fo French Crampton *Le Continent*
steam locomotive, 1852
Set of 8 5·25 2·40

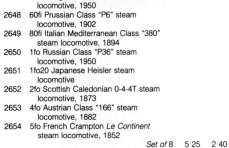

2717 1fo Diesel train and U.I.C. emblem 65 15

2720† 1fo Diesel train 15 5
2722† 2fo Elizabeth Bridge, Budapest 30 5

1974

2882† 2fo Diesel mail train 60 10

MS2894 2fo50 × 4 designs of Budapest Rack
Railway: Passenger train, 1874; Goods train,
1874; Passenger train 1929; Passenger train,
1973 .... 3·25 3·25

1975

2943 3fo Elizabeth Bridge, Budapest .... 1·25 50

2946† 40fi "Railway Rebuilding" 25 5
2949† 4fo Small train .... 1·10 20

2961† 3fo Count Szechenyi 50 20

1977

3092† 1fo Budapest Eastern Railway Station 25 5

2964 1fo Electric locomotive and transformer 65 10

1976

3013 1fo Count Szechenyi on banknote 35 10

1978

3196 1fo Diesel MK45 locomotive, Budapest
Pioneer Railway 30 5

3210 1fo Diesel train 35 5

3039 1fo Pioneer Railway guard 25 5

1979

3237 40fi Stephenson's *Rocket*
3238 60fi Siemens and Halske electric
locomotive, 1879
3069 40fi "Sigi" steam locomotive, 1875
3070 60fi Locomotive No. 17, 1885
3071 1fo "Ganz" railbus, 1925
3072 2fo "Hanomag" steam locomotive, 1920
3073 3fo "Ganz" railcar, 1926
3074 4fo "Ganz" express railcar, 1934
3075 5fo "Raba" railcar, 1971
3239 1fo Early American locomotive *Pioneer*
3240 2fo Hungarian "MAVle" pulling "Orient
Express"
3241 3fo "Trans-Siberian Express"
3242 4fo Japanese "Hikari Express"
3243 5fo German "Transrapid 05"
        Set of 7 4·25 1·75
MS3244 20fo European railway map .... 8·00 8·00

       Set of 7 4·75 1·25

MS3271 5fo × 4 designs of Gyor–Sopron–Ebenfurt Railway: Light passenger locomotive; Locomotive Series "424"; Goods locomotive Series "520"; Diesel locomotives Type "M41" .... 5·00 5·00

1981

3387 2fo Stephenson and *Locomotion* 80 25

1982

3459 2fo Underground train at station 60 20

1984

3576† 1fo Atrium Hyatt Hotel and trams,
　　　Budapest 20 10
3578† 4fo Forum Hotel and tram, Budapest .. 60 30
3581† 8fo Gellert Hotel and tram, Budapest .. 1·25 50

COLLECT MAMMALS ON STAMPS
A Stanley Gibbons thematic catalogue on this popular subject. Copies available at £7.50 (p. + p. £2) from: Stanley Gibbons Publications Ltd, 5 Parkside, Christchurch Road, Ringwood, Hants BH24 3SH.

1985

3609† 1fo Baja Railway Bridge 20 10
MS3615† 20fo Elizabeth Bridge, Budapest .... 3·50 3·50

3633† 2fo High speed railway, "Expo '85", Tsukuba 50 20

MS3657 20fo Elizabeth Bridge, Budapest .... 5·50 6·00

3696 2fo Buda Castle Cable Railway 50 25

1987

3790 4fo Old and new railway emblems and Railway Officers' Training Institute 50 25

1988

3857† 2fo Toy steam train, Toy Museum,
        Kecskemet 55   30

MS3871† 10fo East Railway Station, Budapest 2·75 3·00

POSTAGE DUE STAMPS

1973

D2852† 2fo Diesel mail train .... 1·10   15

1987

D3813† 8fo Railway mail carriage 90   45

INDIA

Southern Asia
1937 12 pies = 1 anna
16 annas = 1 rupee
1964 100 paisa = 1 rupee

1937

255† 4a Mail train .... 7·50   5

1953

343   2a Locomotives of 1853 and 1953 30   5

1954

350† 4a Steam train .... 1·75 15

1955

362† 8a Chittarajan Locomotive Works ...... 3·25   5

1965

Value expressed as "0.10"
509† 10p Electric locomotive 25   5

1972

657   20p Signal Box panel 40   25

1974

As No. 509, but value expressed as "10"
727† 10p Electric locomotive 20   5

1976

798   25p L.N. Mishra, Minister of Railways   15   20

806   25p Diesel locomotive, 1963
807   50p Steam locomotive, 1895
808   1r Steam locomotive, 1963
809   2r Steam locomotive, 1853
                                   Set of 4   5·50   3·50

1977

862†   3r Mail van on Ballard Pier, Bombay   . . . .   1·40   2·00

1982

1069   2r85 Darjeeling Himalayan Railway   55   55

1070   50p Vintage rail coach and silhouette of
        steam locomotive   10   15

1987

1237   1r South Eastern Railway emblem
1238   1r50 Metre-gauge tank locomotive No.
        691, 1887
1239   2r Electric train on viaduct, 1987
1240   4r Steam locomotive, c.1900
                                   Set of 4   95   1·10

1988

1317   1r Victoria Terminus Station, Bombay   8   10

1342†   6r50 Travelling post office handstamp
        of Allahabad-Cawnpore Railway,
        1864   50   55

INDIAN FORCES IN INDO-CHINA

South-east Asia
100 paisa = 1 rupee

1968

No. 509 of India overprinted **ICC** in English and Devanagari for
use in Laos and Vietnam

N53   10p Electric locomotive   30   30

COLLECT BIRDS ON STAMPS

New second edition available at £8.50 (p. + p. £2) from:
Stanley Gibbons Publications Ltd, 5 Parkside,
Christchurch Road, Ringwood, Hants BH24 3SH.

INDO-CHINA

South-east Asia
100 cents = 1 piastre

1938

247	5c Steam locomotive, Trans-Indo-China Railway	
248	6c Steam locomotive, Trans-Indo-China Railway	
249	18c Steam locomotive, Trans-Indo-China Railway	
250	37c Steam locomotive, Trans-Indo-China Railway	

Set of 4   4·50   1·25

1943

314†	1c Steam locomotive	30	50
323†	15c Steam locomotive	50	50

INDONESIA

South-east Asia
100 sen = 1 rupiah

Republic in Java and Madura

1946

J60†	40s Goods wagons on quay, Tandjong Priok	40	50

1948

J70	50s Steam locomotive
J71	100s Steam locomotive

Set of 2   16·00   20·00

POSTAGE DUE STAMPS

1948

Nos. J70/1 overprinted **DENDA** or surcharged also

JD72	50s Steam locomotive
JD73	100s Steam locomotive
JD75	1r on 50s Steam locomotive
JD76	1r on 100s Steam locomotive

Set of 4   —   50·00

United States of Indonesia

1959

815†	20s Cogwheel and diesel train	10	10
817†	75s Cogwheel and diesel train	10	10
818†	1r15 Diesel train	15	10

1960

831†	10s Steam locomotive and sugar cane trucks	10	10

1964

1002†	4r Toy diesel train	10	10
1005†	10r Diesel train	10	10

1965

No. 1005 surcharged **'65 Sen** as revalued currency

1074†	(10)s on 10r diesel train	25	10

1968

1193	20r Trains of 1867 and 1967		
1194	30r Trains of 1867 and 1967		

Set of 2   1·50   75

1975

852†	10d Vereshk Railway Bridge (mauve)	75	10
853†	10d Vereshk Railway Bridge (green)	15	10
856†	25d Steam train on Karj Bridge (red)	3·00	10
857†	25d Steam train on Karj Bridge (violet)	45	10

1397†	120r Petroleum trucks at storage farm	75	55

1949

905†	50d Goods wagons on dock, Bandar Shahpur	1·60	30
907†	2r50 Steam train on Vereshk Railway Bridge	7·50	45
908†	5r Railway line on map of Iran	7·50	1·00

1977

1482	50r Train and flags	50	25

1957

1115	2r50 Track and signal
1116	5r Diesel train and map
1117	10r Steam express train and mosque

Set of 3 20·00 9·00

IRAN

Western Asia
100 dinars = 1 rial

1935

736†	1r Railway bridge over River Karun	14·00	2·75

1942

850†	5d Railway bridge over River Karun (violet)	75	10
851†	5d Railway bridge over River Karun (orange)	15	10

1958

1149	6r Steam train on viaduct
1150	8r Steam express train and route-map of Teheran–Tabriz Railway

Set of 2 24·00 8·00

1968

1563†   10r Steam train   45   20

1971

IRAN - TURKEY RAILWAY LINK Sept. 1971

1678   2r Ghatur Railway Bridge   75   10

1973

1773   10r Railway tracks encircling globe   75   20

1974

1897†   10d Ghatur Railway Bridge (orange & brown)   10   5

1975

As No. 1897, but colours changed

1940†   10d Ghatur Railway bridge (purple & green)   10   5

1976

2002   8r Mohammed Riza Pahlavi, Riza Shah Pahlavi and steam train   50   50

1978

2078†   5r Shah and Crown Prince at inauguration of Trans-Iranian Railway   50   30

1988

2461   20r Miners pushing coal truck   35   30

1989

2509†   20r Diesel locomotive and passenger train   35   30

IRAQ

Western Asia
1000 fils = 1 dinar

1949

336†   50f Aeroplane over Dhiyala Railway Bridge ....   1·10   50
337†   100f Aeroplane over Dhiyala Railway Bridge ....   2·50   75

1967

759 5f Track plan for Um Qasr Port
760 10f Railway wagons on quay
761 15f Railway wagons on quay
762 40f Track plan for Um Qasr Port
Set of 4   2·40   1·10

1972

1073 25f International Railway Union emblem
1074 45f International Railway Union emblem
Set of 2   3·50   1·10

1975

1206 25f Diesel train
1207 30f Diesel locomotive
1208 35f Steam tank locomotive and train
1209 50f German steam locomotive
Set of 4   7·25   7·25

IRELAND

Western Europe
100 pence = 1 pound

1981

498 30p "Railway Embankment" (W. J. Leech)   60   50

1984

577 23p Locomotive *Princess*, Dublin and
Kingstown Railway
578 26p Locomotive *Macha*, Great Southern
Railway
579 29p Locomotive *Kestrel*, Great Northern
Railway
580 44p Two-car electric unit, Coras lompair
Eireann
Set of 4   2·50   2·10

1987

658 24p Cork electric tram
659 28p Dublin standard tram
660 30p Howth (G.N.R.) tram
661 46p Galway horse tram
Set of 4   2·00   2·10

ISLE OF MAN

Western Europe
100 pence = 1 pound

1973

17† 3p Tram, Douglas Promenade   10   10
22† 5½p Tram, Douglas Promenade   25   25

35 2½p Steam locomotive *Sutherland*
36 3p Steam locomotive *Caledonia*
37 7½p Steam locomotive *Kissack*
38 9p Steam locomotive *Pender*
Set of 4   3·00   3·00

1975

60† 5½p Terminal Tower, Railway Station,
Cleveland, Ohio 15 10

1976

80† 5½p First horse tram, 1876 .... 10 12
81† 7p "Toast-rack", 1890 .... 15 15
83† 13p Royal tram, 1972 .... 50 45

1979

149† 11p Horse-drawn tram, Douglas
Promenade 30 30

1984

276† 28p Early Australian steam train 90 90

1988

365 1p Horse tram terminus, Douglas Bay
Tramway
366 2p Snaefell Mountain Railway

367 3p Marine Drive Tramway
368 5p Douglas Head Incline Railway
369 10p Manx Electric Railway train at
Maughold Head
370 13p Douglas Cable Tramway
371 14p Manx Northern Railway No. 4
Caledonia at Gob-y-Deigan
372 15p Laxey Mine Railway Lewin locomotive
Ant
373 16p Port Erin Breakwater Tramway
locomotive *Henry B. Loch*
374 17p Ramsey Harbour Tramway
375 18p Locomotive No. 7 *Tynwald* on
Foxdale line
376 19p Baldwin Reservoir Tramway steam
locomotive *Injebreck*
377 20p I.M.R. No. 13 *Kissack* near St. Johns
378 25p I.M.R. No. 12 *Hutchinson* leaving
Douglas
379 50p Groudle Glen Railway locomotive
Polar Bear
380 £1 I.M.R. No. 11 *Maitland* pulling Royal
Train, 1963
                                Set of 16   5·25   6·00

ISRAEL

Western Asia
1951 1000 prutot = 1 pound
1960 100 agorot = 1 pound
1980 100 agorot = 1 shekel

1951

54 50pr Dump truck
                        (*without tab*)   25   15
                        (*with tab*)   17·00   11·00

1966

350† 40a Postman and steam locomotive
                        (*without tab*)   25   10
                        (*with tab*)   35   15

1970

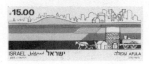

441 80a Camel and diesel train, Dimona–Oron
Railway

(without tab)	70	30
(with tab)	1·50	90

1977

685 65a "Mogul" 2-6-0 steam locomotive
686 £1.50 0-6-0 steam locomotive
687 £2 4-6-0 "P" class steam locomotive
688 £2.50 Diesel locomotive

Set of 4 (without tabs)	50	45
Set of 4 (with tabs)	1·00	60

1983

911 15s Steam locomotive

(without tab)	25	15
(with tab)	35	30

ITALY

Southern Europe
100 centesimi = 1 lira

1939

550 20c Steam locomotive *Bayard*, 1839, and
1939 railcar
551 50c Steam locomotive *Bayard*, 1839, and
1939 railcar
552 1li25 Steam locomotive *Bayard*, 1839, and
1939 railcar

Set of 3	75	80

1949

715 50li Globes and diesel railcar . . . . 16·00 3·00

1954

871 25li Train on bridge 50 5

1956

931 25li Coach and steam train leaving
Simplon Tunnel . . . . 1·00 15

1970

1275 25li Electric train 25 5

1975

1450 70li Steam locomotive driving-wheels 30 5

1979

1588† 170li Electric train (on stamp No. 1275) 50 5

1981

1742†   120li Envelopes forming railway tracks   50   5

1983

1821†   400li Steam train leaving envelope and globe   75   30

1987

1962†   700li Termini Station, Rome   65   30

1988

1990†   650li "ETR 450" electric train in station   55   30

IVORY COAST

West Africa
100 centimes = 1 franc

1906

As Nos. 18/22 of Dahomey

22†	1c General Faidherbe (builder of Dakar–St Louis Railway)	25	40
23†	2c General Faidherbe (builder of Dakar–St Louis Railway)	25	40
24†	4c General Faidherbe (builder of Dakar–St Louis Railway)	60	60
25†	5c General Faidherbe (builder of Dakar–St Louis Railway)	1·50	60
26†	10c General Faidherbe (builder of Dakar–St Louis Railway)	3·00	2·00

1959

184†   200f Houphouet-Boigny Railway Bridge   3·75   1·25

1965

259   30f Abidjan Railway Station   75   30

1966

272   30f Mail train, 1906 ....   1·90   1·25

1975

464   60f Railway Bridge over N'Zi, Dimbokro   ..   50   30

1978

555†   65f Passengers in train   40   20

1979

60f
REPUBLIQUE DE CÔTE D'IVOIRE

594 60f "Flying Scotsman" and Great Britain
£1 stamp, 1878
595 75f Narrow-gauge locomotive and Ivory
Coast 45c stamp, 1936
596 100f Diesel locomotive and Hawaiian 13c
"missionary" stamp, 1852
597 150f Steam locomotive and Japanese 20s
stamp, 1872
598 300f Electric locomotive and French 15c
stamp, 1850
Set of 5   4·50   85
MS599 500f Steam locomotive and Ivory Coast
35c. stamp, 1936 . . . .   2·50   80

1980

635 60f "Le Belier" (Abidjan–Niger Line)
636 65f Abidjan Railway Station, 1904
637 100f Passenger coach, 1908
638 150f Steam locomotive, 1940
Set of 4   2·50   1·75

1983

759 100f Post Office and railway hand trolley,
Grand Bassam, 1903   75   40

1984

RÉPUBLIQUE DE CÔTE-D'IVOIRE

100f

La Gazelle

812 100f Diesel train "La Gazelle"
813 125f "Super Pacific" steam locomotive No.
31251-31290

814 350f "Pacific Type 10" steam locomotive
815 500f "Mallet" Class steam locomotive
Set of 4   4·50   3·25

JAMAICA

West Indies
1938 12 pence = 1 shilling
20 shillings = 1 pound
1969 100 cents = 1 dollar

1938

130† 1s Sugar cane trucks   50   5

1949
As No. 114 of Antigua
145† 1½d Silhouette of steam locomotive   25   15

1970

325 3c The Projector, 1845
326 15c Steam locomotive No. 54, 1946
327 50c Diesel locomotive No. 102, 1967
Set of 3   3·00   2·75

1981
As No. 130, but with World Food Day emblem replacing King's
head
528† $4 Sugar cane trucks . . . .   3·00   2·50

1984

· JAMAICA · 25c ·

612 25c Enterprise, 1845
613 55c Tank locomotive, 1880
614 $1.50 Kitson-Meyer tank locomotive, 1904
615 $3 Super-heated steam locomotive and
bridge, 1916
Set of 4   2·75   2·50

1985

634 25c Baldwin locomotive No. 16
635 55c Rogers locomotive
636 $1.50 Locomotive *Projector*
637 $4 Diesel locomotive No. 102

Set of 4   3·25   2·50

JAPAN

Eastern Asia
100 sen = 1 yen

1942

408 5s Steam locomotive .... 3·00   5·00

1947

MS459 4y Locomotive *Benkei*, 1880 .... 15·00   15·00

1948

507† 500y Locomotive construction .... £325   3·00

1949

547† 8y Globe and passenger coaches ...... 4·00   1·60
549† 24y Globe and passenger coaches .... 14·50   9·25

1956

761 10y Electric train on Tokaido Line .... 7·00   2·10

1962

898 10y Diesel train emerging from Hokuriku
    Tunnel .... 2·00   35

1964

988 10y Electric express train, Tokyo–Osaka
    Line 45   5

1971

1258 15y "Railway Post Office" (S. Onozaki) ..   20   10

1267 50y "Tokyo Horse Tram" (Yoshimura)   60   25

1972

1287 20y High-speed electric train on Sanyo
Line 25 5

1305 20y "Inauguration of Railway Service"
(Hiroshige III)
1306 20y Class "C-62" steam locomotive
Set of 2 70 20

1974

1373 20y Class "D-51" steam locomotive
1374 20y Class "C-57" steam locomotive
Set of 2 70 20

1975

1382 20y Class "C-58" steam locomotive
1383 20y Class "D-52" steam locomotive
Set of 2 70 20

1385 20y Class "8620" steam locomotive
1386 20y Class "C-11" steam locomotive
Set of 2 70 20

1395 20y Class "9600" steam locomotive
1396 20y Class "C-51" steam locomotive
Set of 2 70 20

1398 20y Class "7100" steam locomotive
1399 20y Class "150" steam locomotive
Set of 2 70 20

1977

1484 50y Underground train, Tokyo, 1927
1485 50y Underground train, Tokyo, 1977
Set of 2 1·00 20

1982

1671 60y "SL1290" steam locomotive,
Tohoku–Shinkansen Line
1672 60y Super-express diesel,
Tohoku–Shinkansen Line
Set of 2 1·00 50

1687 60y Joetsu–Shinkansen Express train
1688 60y "ED16" electric locomotive,
Joetsu–Shinkansen Line
Set of 2 1·00 50

1987

1885 60y Early mail sorting carriage
1886 60y Loading mail sacks
        Set of 2   1·10   60

1887 60y Steam tank locomotive No. 137
1888 60y High-speed train No. 002
        Set of 2   1·10   60

1988

1931 60y Class "ED791" locomotive *Sea of Japan* leaving Seikan Railway Tunnel   55   30

1936 60y Seto–Ohashi Road and Rail Bridge from Kagawa side (value at left)
1937 60y Bridge from Kagawa side (value at right)
1938 60y Bridge from Okayama side (value at right)
1939 60y Bridge from Okayama side (value at left)
        Set of 4   2·00   1·10

JERSEY

Western Europe
1969 12 pence = 1 shilling
   20 shillings = 1 pound
1970 100 pence = 1 pound

1969

22† 9d Map showing railways in England and France 55   90
24† 1s6d Map showing railways in England and France .... 1·75   1·75

1970

As Nos. 22 and 24 with face values in decimal currency
49† 4p Map showing railways in England and France 12   12
52† 7½p Map showing railways in England and France 30   40

1973

93 2½p Steam locomotive *North Western*
94 3p Steam locomotive *Calvados*
95 7½p Steam locomotive *Carteret*
96 9p Steam locomotive *Caesarea*
        Set of 4   1·10   90

1985

365 10p Locomotive *Duke of Normandy* at Cheapside
366 13p Saddletank locomotive at First Tower
367 22p Locomotive *La Moye* at Millbrook
368 29p Locomotive *St Heliers* at St Aubin
369 34p Locomotive *St Aubyns* at Corbiere
        Set of 5   3·00   3·00

1989

494†   17p Toy train   35   40

JIND

Indian sub-continent
12 pies = 1 anna
16 annas = 1 rupee

1937

No. 225 of India overprinted **JIND STATE**
117†   4a Mail train ....   1·50   3·50

JOHORE

South-east Asia
100 cents = 1 dollar

1949

As No. 114 of Antigua
148†   10c Silhouette of steam locomotive   20   15

1960

159†   8c Steam train, East Coast Railway ......   1·25   75

JORDAN

Middle East
1949 1000 milliemes = 1 pound
1950 1000 fils = 1 dinar

1949

285†   1m Diesel train   10   25
286†   4m Diesel train   15   40
287†   10m Diesel train   15   30
288†   20m Diesel train   30   50

1970

904†   22f Wrecked railway bridge ....   3·00   3·00
905†   23f Wrecked railway bridge (different
          view) ....   3·00   3·00

1977

1218†   10f Child and toy steam locomotive   10   10

JORDANIAN OCCUPATION OF PALESTINE

Middle East
1000 milliemes = 1 pound

1949

Nos. 285/8 of Jordan overprinted **PALESTINE** *in English and Arabic*
P30†   1m Diesel train   15   30
P31†   4m Diesel train   20   40
P32†   10m Diesel train   25   50
P33†   20m Diesel train   35   70

STANLEY GIBBONS
STAMP COLLECTING SERIES

Introductory booklets on *How to Start, How to Identify Stamps* and *Collecting by Theme.* A series of well illustrated guides at a low price.
Write for details.

KAMPUCHEA

South-east Asia
100 cents = 1 riel

1983

490†	3r Diesel locomotive	1·90	60

1984

542	10c "BB-1002" type diesel locomotive (1966)		
543	40c "BB-1052" type diesel locomotive (1966)		
544	80c Franco-Belgian steam locomotive (1945)		
545	1r "231-505" type steam locomotive (1929)		
546	1r20 "803" type railcar (1968)		
547	2r "BDE-405" type diesel locomotive (1957)		
548	2r50 "DS-01" type diesel railcar (1929)		
	Set of 7	4·00	1·40

1985

MS669†	6r Early steam locomotive at station, Berlin	3·00	90

WHEN YOU BUY AN ALBUM LOOK FOR THE NAME "STANLEY GIBBONS"
It means Quality combined with Value for Money.

KATANGA

Central Africa
100 centimes = 1 franc

1961

73†	3f50 Steam locomotive	3·00	3·00
75†	8f Steam locomotive	3·00	3·00

KEDAH

South-east Asia
100 cents = 1 dollar

1949
As No. 114 *of Antigua*

72†	10c Silhouette of steam locomotive	25	20

1957

96†	8c Steam train, East Coast Railway	2·00	3·50

1959

108†	8c Steam train, East Coast Railway	2·00	1·25

KELANTAN

South-east Asia
100 cents = 1 dollar

1949
As No. 114 *of Antigua*

57†	10c Silhouette of steam locomotive	25	30

1957

87†	8c Steam train, East Coast Railway	80	1·50

1961

100† 8c Steam train, East Coast Railway ...... 1·00 1·75

KENYA

East Africa
100 cents = 1 shilling

1963

13† 10s Railway tracks, Mombasa .... 5·00 1·25

1976

66 50c Diesel train, Tanzania–Zambia Railway
67 1s Diesel train on Nile Bridge, Uganda
68 2s Diesel train at Nakuru Station, Kenya
69 3s Class "A" steam locomotive, 1896
Set of 4 5·00 3·00

1978

136† 5s "Approach Railway Level Crossing
with extreme Caution" .... 1·40 1·50

1983

283† 5s Diesel train on bridge .... 1·00 1·00

286† 3s50 Goods wagons, Mombasa
container terminal 80 50

1986

386† 3s Container depot, Embakasi 50 35

1988

490† 10s New diesel locomotive No. 9401 .... 60 65

KENYA, UGANDA AND TANGANYIKA

East Africa
100 cents = 1 shilling

1935

115† 30c Jinja Railway Bridge, Ripon Falls 80 65
121† 5s Jinja Railway Bridge, Ripon Falls .... 15·00 23·00

1938

As Nos. 115 and 121, but with portrait of King George VI
141b† 30c Jinja Railway Bridge, Ripon Falls .. 30 5
148b† 5s Jinja Railway Bridge, Ripon Falls .... 5·50 25

1949

As No. 114 of Antigua
159† 20c Silhouette of steam locomotive 15 5

1969

256† 30c Railway ferry M.V. *Umoja* 15 5

1971

292 30c Class "11" locomotive
293 70c Class "90" locomotive
294 1s50 Class "59" locomotive
295 2s50 Class "30" locomotive

Set of 4 3·75 3·00

1974

358† 2s50 Diesel train .... 45 1·25

360† 70c Mail-train and post-van 20 5

COLLECT MAMMALS ON STAMPS

A Stanley Gibbons thematic catalogue on this popular subject. Copies available at £7.50 (p. + p. £2) from: Stanley Gibbons Publications Ltd, 5 Parkside, Christchurch Road, Ringwood, Hants BH24 3SH.

KHMER REPUBLIC

South-east Asia
100 cents = 1 riel

Appendix

The following stamps have either been issued in excess of postal needs, or have not been available to the public in reasonable quantities at face value. Miniature sheets, imperforate stamps, etc., are excluded from this section.

1975

Universal Postal Union (2nd issue). Air 500, 2000r, 2000r embossed on gold foil

---

KIRIBATI

Pacific Ocean
100 cents = 1 dollar

1988

MS292† $2 Container ship under Sydney Harbour Bridge .... 1·90 2·00

KOREA

Eastern Asia

South Korea

1949 100 cheun = 1 weun
1953 100 weun = 1 hwan
1962 100 chun = 1 won

1949

129 15w Steam train .... 20·00 15·00

1959

341 40h Diesel train .... 1·40 75

1960

354 40h Diesel train . . . . 1·00 50

1963

483† 4w Miner and coal train, Samch'ok
      region . . . . 1·10 50

1964

507 4w Mine trucks 90 50

1966

634† 7w Diesel train and map . . . . 1·10 50

1967

697† 7w Railway wheel and rail 90 45

1968

743† 5w Silhouette of diesel train 90 45

1969

814 7w Steam locomotive of 1899
815 7w Early steam and modern diesel
     locomotives
                          Set of 2 1·60 75

1970

859† 10w Tramcar, 1899 . . . . 75 40

876† 10w Diesel train . . . . 1·40 45

1971

905† 10w Coal trucks 45 20

916 10w Underground train, Seoul 55 20

1974

1101†   10w Mail-train and communications
        emblem   40   15

1116   10w Underground train, Seoul   30   5

1975

1219   20w Electric train on cross-country line   30   5

North Korea

100 cheun = 1 won

1956

N113   10w Steam train at factory ....   25·00   10·00

1958

N154†   10w Pyongyang Railway Station ......   7·50   1·00

N158   10w Chinese volunteer and troop train   20·00   6·50

1959

N175†   2ch Electric shunting locomotive   ....   1·75   10

N182†   70ch Hoisting rail ....   3·00   1·40

N191†   5ch Loading goods wagon   45   25
N192†   10ch Goods wagons at factory   70   35

N208†   5ch Electric train ....   7·50   1·00

1961

N307   10ch Steam train ....   5·50   1·50

N319　10ch Power station and diesel train on
　　　bridge .... 2·50　60

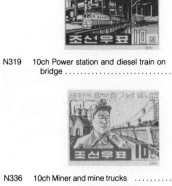

N336　10ch Miner and mine trucks .... 1·75　60

N358　10ch "Red Banner" Class electric
　　　locomotive .... 4·00　1·50

1962

N364†　5ch Coal trucks .... 1·75　30

1963

N440†　5ch Mine train .... 70　20

STANLEY GIBBONS
STAMP COLLECTING SERIES

Introductory booklets on *How to Start, How to Identify Stamps* and *Collecting by Theme*. A series of well illustrated guides at a low price.
Write for details.

N490†　10ch Unloading goods wagon ...... 1·50　20
N491†　10ch Electric train .... 1·50　20

1964

N517　10ch Electric train, Pyongyang–Sinuiju
　　　line .... 2·50　20

N523†　10ch Iron works and trucks .... 1·00　20

N548　10ch Steam train .... 1·25　10

1965

N578†　5ch Railway bridge over Taedong
　　　River .... 1·00　15

N609†　4ch Electric mine train .... 1·25　20

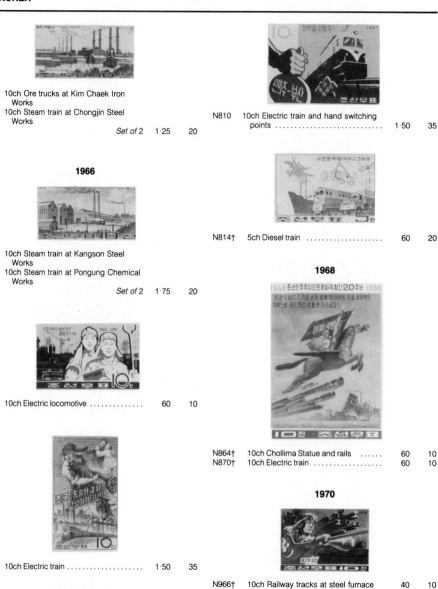

N620 10ch Ore trucks at Kim Chaek Iron
 Works
N621 10ch Steam train at Chongjin Steel
 Works
 Set of 2   1·25   20

1966

N694 10ch Steam train at Kangson Steel
 Works
N695 10ch Steam train at Pongung Chemical
 Works
 Set of 2   1·75   20

N720 10ch Electric locomotive   60   10

N728 10ch Electric train ....   1·50   35

1967

N779† 10ch Blowing-up railway bridge ......   1·10   20

N810 10ch Electric train and hand switching
 points ....   1·50   35

N814† 5ch Diesel train   60   20

1968

N864† 10ch Chollima Statue and rails   60   10
N870† 10ch Electric train   60   10

1970

N966† 10ch Railway tracks at steel furnace   40   10

N970 10ch Electric locomotive and railway
 guard   40   10

N972†   10ch Diesel train   40   10

1971

N1005   5ch Electric train   40   5

N1013†   10ch Electric mine train   80   10
N1015†   10ch Electric train   80   10
N1017†   10ch Electric mine train   80   10
N1020†   10ch Electric locomotive   80   10

N1034   10ch Diesel locomotive   50   10

1972

N1061†   10ch Steam locomotive on construction
         site ....   1·50   20
N1066†   10ch Kim Il Sung with Haeju–Hasong
         Railway survey party ....   1·50   20

COLLECT SHIPS ON STAMPS
The largest Stanley Gibbons thematic catalogue to date
– available at £10.95 (p. + p. £2) from:
Stanley Gibbons Publications Ltd, 5 Parkside,
Christchurch Road, Ringwood, Hants BH24 3SH.

N1083†   5ch Electric train, Pyongyang ....   1·25   35

N1089†   10ch Railway tracks at iron foundry   80   10

N1092†   10ch Coal trucks   80   10

N1099†   10ch Loading freight wagons   50   8

N1110†   10ch Electric train   20   8
N1111†   10ch Laying railway tracks   20   8

N1121†   10ch Diesel locomotive ....   1·25   15

1973

N1224†   10ch Electric train   40   8

1975

N1146†   5ch Electric train and crane lifting
tractor . . . .   1·00   15

N1164†   40ch Diesel train   . . . .   1·00   40

N1392†   10ch Railwayman in "The Blue Signal
Lamp" (painting)   60   5

1976

1974

N1504   5ch "Pulgungi" type electric
locomotive
N1505   10ch "Chaju" type underground train
N1506   15ch "Saebyol" type diesel locomotive
Set of 3   70   20

N1217†   10ch Diesel locomotive and Chollima
Statue   40   8

N1219   10ch Metro train at station, Pyongyang
N1220   10ch Escalator, Pyongyang Metro
N1221   10ch Metro Station Hall, Pyongyang
Set of 3   80   25

MSN1515   40ch Kim Il Sung and electric train   3·00   60

1979

N1570   2ch "Pulgungi" type diesel shunting
locomotive
N1571   5ch "Saebyol" type diesel locomotive
N1572   10ch "Saebyol" type diesel shunting
locomotive
N1573   15ch Electric locomotive
N1574   25ch "Kumsong" type diesel
locomotive
N1575   40ch "Pulgungi" type electric
locomotive
                               Set of 6   3·50   50
MSN1576 50ch "Kumsong" type diesel
locomotive and Pyongyang Station .... 5·00   2·50

N1908†   20ch Boys with toy steam locomotive   2·50   85
N1912†   30ch Boy sitting astride toy electric train 2·50   85
MSN1915† Four sheets 80ch Children with
model train (other sheets show different
subjects) .... 16·00   4·50

1977

N1623†   2ch Electric train on bridge   45   5

1978

N1698†   10ch Electric train and post-van .... 1·00   10

1980

N1941†   10ch Children with toy train .... 1·10   45

N1953†   30ch Rowland Hill and steam goods
train (on No. 645 of Russia) .... 3·25   75

N1961†   10ch Red Cross over map of Korea and
two diesel trains .... 2·50   60

N1968† 10ch "Pulgungi" type electric
locomotive(on stamp No. N1575) .... 1·25   30
MSN1973† 20ch "Pulgungi" type electric
locomotive (on stamp No. N1575) (sheet also
contains other designs) .... 5·50   1·90

N2126† 10ch Electric train and hand switching
points (on stamp No. N810) .... 1·50   30
N2127† 10ch Sir Rowland Hill and steam
locomotive .... 1·50   30
N2129† 30ch Japanese stamp and diesel train 2·50   75

1982

N2174† 20ch Mine locomotive, Komdok Valley   50   20

N2002† 10ch Diesel locomotive 75   20
N2003† 10ch Coach under bridge 75   20

1983

N2031 20ch The Rocket .... 5·00   1·75
MSN2032 1wn Locomotive drawing carriage
and horsebox .... 6·00   2·00

N2320 20ch Locomotion, 1825
N2321 20ch Drache, 1848
N2322 35ch Der Adler, 1835
N2323 35ch Korean steam locomotive
N2324 50ch Austria, 1837
N2325 50ch Bristol and Exeter Railway steam
locomotive, 1853
N2326 80ch Caledonian Railway locomotive,
1859
Set of 7 17·50   5·50
MSN2327 80ch Ilmarinen, 1860 .... 6·00   1·90

N2033 20ch Steam and electric locomotives 5·00   1·75
MSN2034 1wn Siemens electric locomotive .. 9·50   2·00

1981

N2064† 10ch Mine wagons 30   20

N2351† 40ch Electric locomotive .... 3·50   1·10

1984

N2396   20ch Type "202" express locomotive
N2397   30ch Type "E" goods locomotive
                              Set of 2   5·00   1·25
MSN2398   80ch Type "D" locomotive   ....   6·50   1·50

N2423   10ch Inauguration of a French railway
        line, 1860
N2424   20ch Opening of a British railway line,
        "1821"
N2425   30ch Inauguration of Paris–Rouen line,
        1843
                              Set of 3   4·50   1·50
MSN2426   80ch Interior of Wagon-lits car, 1905   5·50   2·25

N2427   10ch Diesel locomotive   ....   2·50   1·00

1985

N2432†   5ch Steam locomotive, 1925   40   5

Appendix
The following stamps have either been issued in excess of postal needs, or have not been available to the public in reasonable quantities at face value. Miniature sheets, imperforate stamps, etc., are excluded from this section.

1981
Nobel Prizes for Medicine. No. N1961 overprinted. 10ch.

1986
40th Anniversary of North Korean Stamps (2nd series). 15ch. ("Kumsong" type diesel locomotive (on stamp No. N1574).

KUWAIT
Arabian Peninsula
1939 12 pies = 1 anna
16 annas = 1 rupee
1961 1000 fils = 1 dinar

1939
No. 255 of India overprinted **KUWAIT**
43†   4a Mail train   ....   11·00   7·50

1974

630   10f Steam train in telephone dial
631   30f Steam train in telephone dial
632   40f Steam train in telephone dial
                              Set of 3   2·00   75

LABUAN
Off north coast of Borneo
100 cents = 1 dollar

1900
No. 107 of North Borneo overprinted **LABUAN**
116a   16c Borneo steam train   ....   19·00   25·00

ALBUM LISTS
Write for our latest list of albums and accessories. This will be sent on request.

LAOS

South-east Asia
100 cents = 1 kip

1962

124†   50c Diesel mail train   60   80

Appendix

The following stamps have either been issued in excess of postal needs, or have not been available to the public in reasonable quantities at face value. Miniature sheets, imperforate stamps, etc., are excluded from this section.

1975

Bicentenary of American Revolution. 100k (Junction of the Trans-Continental Railway), 150k (Tracks, Culebra Cut, Panama Canal).

LATVIA

Eastern Europe
100 santimu = 1 lats

1928

162†   50s Railway bridge, Riga ....   1·75   1·75

169†   1la + 1la10 Railway bridge, Riga ....   1·90   1·90

1933

241†   7-57s Railway bridge, Riga ....   10·00   11·00

1938

MS277   40s Kegums Railway Bridge (sheet also contains 35s stamp) (sold at 2la) ....   8·00   10·00

280†   10s Railway bridge, Riga   20   5

1939

No. **MS277** *overprinted* **1934 1939 15/V**
MS293   40s Kegums Railway Bridge (sheet also contains 35s stamp) (sold at 2la) ....   10·00   20·00

· LEBANON

Middle East
100 centimes = 1 piastre

1967

971†   2p50 Tram, San Francisco   60   20
972†   5p Tram, San Francisco   60   20
973†   7p50 Tram, San Francisco   60   20

1974

1176†   5p Mail van   60   35

WHEN YOU BUY AN ALBUM LOOK FOR THE NAME "STANLEY GIBBONS"

It means Quality combined with Value for Money.

LEEWARD ISLANDS

West Indies
100 cents = 1 dollar

1949

As No. 114 of Antigua
119†   2½d Silhouette of steam locomotive   15   10

1988

844†   20s Sydney Harbour Bridge   10   12

LESOTHO

Southern Africa
1971 100 cents = 1 rand
1979 10 lisente = 1 maloti

1971

215†   4c Mine locomotive   15   5

1984

LESOTHO   6s

605   6s "The Orient Express" (1900)
606   15s German State Railways Class "05"
       No. 05001 (1935)
607   30s Caledonian Railway *Cardean* (1906)
608   60s Santa Fe "Super Chief" (1940)
609   1m L.N.E.R. "Flying Scotsman" (1934)
                Set of 5   2·40   2·00
MS610   2m South African Railways "The Blue
Train" (1972) ....   2·40   2·50

1986

713†   2m Donald Duck operating railway
       mailbag apparatus ....   1·25   1·40

LIBERIA

West Africa
100 cents = 1 dollar

1894

117   5c Steam locomotive ....   3·00   3·00

1953

731†   35c Diesel locomotive (violet)   75   30

1954

As No. 731, but colour changed and inscribed
"COMMEMORATING PRESIDENTIAL VISIT U.S.A.—1954"
752†   35c Diesel locomotive (red) ....   2·75   1·25

1970

1027†   5c Monorail train, Expo '70   15   10

1973

1149	2c G.W.R. steam locomotive	
1150	3c Steam locomotive, Holland	
1151	10c Steam locomotive, France	
1152	15c Steam locomotive, U.S.A.	
1153	20c Steam locomotive, Japan	
1154	25c Steam locomotive, Germany	

Set of 6   5·00   90
MS1155   55c Steam locomotive, Switzerland   ..   2·75   75

1974

1191† 20c British High Speed Train 55 25

1976

1281† 40c Futuristic train .... 1·00 50

1289a† $1 Diesel train carrying iron ore ...... 1·60 25

1979

1383† 27c Stanier Pacific locomotive 60 25

1981
As No. 1289a, *but smaller, size* 33 × 20mm
1510† $1 Diesel train carrying iron ore .... 1·90 1·10

1984

1590† 62c Diesel train carrying iron ore ...... 1·25 90

1988

1690 10c Type "GP10" diesel locomotive,
    Nimba
1691 35c Triple-headed iron ore train
Set of 2   50   35
MS1692 Four sheets (a) $2 *Ince Castle* pulling
"The Bristolian"; (b) $2 Class "57XXm" Steam
tank locomotive No. 3697; (c) $2 Locomotive
King Edward II and passenger train; (d) $2
Steam locomotive No. 1408 on Lostwithiel–
Fowey line
Set of 4 *sheets* 10·00 8·00

OFFICIAL STAMPS
1894
As No. 117 *overprinted* **O S**
O130 5c Steam locomotive .... 1·75 2·00

ALBUM LISTS
Write for our latest list of albums and accessories. This
will be sent on request.

LIBYA

North Africa
100 dirhams = 1 dinar

1984

1450† 100dh Toy steam train 70 40

1491†	100dh Early steam locomotive	70	35
1492†	100dh Steam locomotive (purple and blue)	70	35
1493†	100dh Steam locomotive (cream)	70	35
1494†	100dh Steam locomotive (lavender and brown)	70	35
1495†	100dh Steam locomotive (lavender and black)	70	35
1496†	100dh Steam locomotive (cream and red)	70	35
1497†	100dh Steam locomotive (purple and black)	70	35
1498†	100dh Steam locomotive (green and orange)	70	35

LIECHTENSTEIN

Central Europe
100 rappen = 1 franc

1928

80† 5r + 5r Railway bridge between Buchs and Schaan .... 16·00 13·00

1937

157† 30r Work trucks, Binnen Canal .... 1·50 85

1988

931† 90r Maglev monorail 45 45

LITHUANIA

Eastern Europe
100 centu = 1 litas

1932

320†	5c Kaunas Railway Station	25	25
321†	10c Kaunas Railway Station	25	25

LUXEMBOURG

Western Europe
100 centimes = 1 franc

1921

207†	2f Goods wagons at factory, Esch (blue)	50	50
239†	2f Goods wagons at factory, Esch (brown)	1·10	90
208†	5f Railway bridge over Alzette	15·00	4·50

1931

296a	50c Grand Duke Adolphe Railway Bridge	
297	75c Grand Duke Adolphe Railway Bridge	
298	1f Grand Duke Adolphe Railway Bridge	
299	1½f Grand Duke Adolphe Railway Bridge	
300	1¾f Grand Duke Adolphe Railway Bridge	
300a	3f Grand Duke Adolphe Railway Bridge	
	Set of 6	3·00 5·00

1935

330† 70c Railway bridge over Alzette .... 2·50 3·25

1937

Design as No. 207, but colour changed
MS359 2f × 2 Goods wagons at factory, Esch
(red) (sold at 5f) .... 1·50 5·00

1948

509† 20f Grand Duke Adolphe Railway Bridge 2·00 25

1956

606† 2f Goods wagons and blast furnace .... 21·00 1·00

612 2f Luxembourg Central Station .... 2·75 40

1959

661 2f50 Early locomotive and first bars of
hymn "De Feierwon" .... 1·25 40

1964

751† 1f + 25c Grand Duke Adolphe Railway
Bridge 15 15
754† 6f + 50c Grand Duke Adolphe Railway
Bridge .... 1·00 1·10

1966

785 1f50 Diesel locomotive
786 3f Electric locomotive
Set of 2 45 45

788† 1f50 Grand Duke Adolphe Railway
Bridge 20 20

1967

796† 3f Grand Duke Adolphe Railway Bridge 25 10

807† 3f Goods wagons on quay, Mertert 20 10

1968

828   50f Railway bridges, Luxembourg ....   1·40   40

1977

986†   12f Grand Duke Adolphe Railway Bridge   75   70

1979

1023†   6f Luxembourg Central Station   75   10

1982

1096   8f Deportation Monument, Hollerich
          Railway Station   40   15

1984

1127   10f Lion and locomotive   45   20

1988

1223†   12f Electric locomotive and tanker
          wagon   30   35

OFFICIAL STAMPS

1922

Nos. 207, 239 and 208 overprinted **OFFICIEL**

O267†   2f Goods wagons at factory, Esch
          (blue) ....   1·00   1·25
O279†   2f Goods wagons at factory, Esch
          (brown) ....   1·50   3·00
O269†   5f Railway bridge over Alzette ....   5·00   6·00

MACAO

South-east coast of China
100 avos = 1 pataca

1983

577†   6p Diesel train ....   1·40   75

MADAGASCAR

Indian Ocean off East Africa
100 centimes = 1 franc

1908

53a   1c Steam train leaving tunnel   10   20
54   2c Steam train leaving tunnel   10   20
55   4c Steam train leaving tunnel   10   20
56   5c Steam train leaving tunnel (green and
         olive)   20   10

90	5c Steam train leaving tunnel (red and black)	20	10
57	10c Steam train leaving tunnel (brown and red)	25	5
91	10c Steam train leaving tunnel (olive and green)	15	15
92	10c Steam train leaving tunnel (purple and brown)	30	10
58	15c Steam train leaving tunnel (red and lilac)	30	10
93	15c Steam train leaving tunnel (green and olive)	15	20
94	15c Steam train leaving tunnel (red and blue)	50	90
59	20c Steam train leaving tunnel	25	25
60	25c Steam train leaving tunnel (black and blue)	80	10
95	25c Steam train leaving tunnel (black and violet)	40	10
61	30c Steam train leaving tunnel (black and brown)	1·25	35
96	30c Steam train leaving tunnel (brown and red)	25	40
97	30c Steam train leaving tunnel (purple and green)	20	15
98	30c Steam train leaving tunnel (olive and green)	50	35
62	35c Steam train leaving tunnel	30	30
63	40c Steam train leaving tunnel	30	15
64	45c Steam train leaving tunnel (black and green)	25	25
99	45c Steam train leaving tunnel (red)	15	40
100	45c Steam train leaving tunnel (red and lilac)	40	65
65	50c Steam train leaving tunnel (black and violet)	40	25
101	50c Steam train leaving tunnel (black and blue)	25	5
102	50c Steam train leaving tunnel (yellow and black)	60	25
103	60c Steam train leaving tunnel	50	20
104	65c Steam train leaving tunnel	50	75
66	75c Steam train leaving tunnel (black and red)	30	10
105	85c Steam train leaving tunnel	70	1·25
67	1f Steam train leaving tunnel (olive and brown)	20	10
106	1f Steam train leaving tunnel (blue)	30	20
107	1f Steam train leaving tunnel (green and mauve)	3·50	1·50
108	1f10 Steam train leaving tunnel	80	80
68	2f Steam train leaving tunnel	2·25	5
69	5f Steam train leaving tunnel (brown and violet)	3·00	2·50

1915

*No. 57 surcharged **5c** and Red Cross*

80	10c + 5c Steam train leaving tunnel (brown and red)	20	20

1921

*No. 58 surcharged **1 CENT***

84	1c on 15c Steam train leaving tunnel (red and lilac)	20	50

Stamps of 1908, some with colours changed, surcharged in figures and bars

109	25c on 15c Steam train leaving tunnel (red and lilac)	15	15

85	25c on 35c Steam train leaving tunnel	2·75	2·25
86	25c on 40c Steam train leaving tunnel	2·25	2·00
87	25c on 45c Steam train leaving tunnel (black and green)	1·60	1·40
111	25c on 2f Steam train leaving tunnel	25	30
112	25c on 5f Steam train leaving tunnel	50	60
88	0.30 on 40c Steam train leaving tunnel	65	75
113	50c on 1f Steam train leaving tunnel (olive and brown)	80	20
89	0.60 on 75c Steam train leaving tunnel (black and red)	1·75	1·50
114	60c on 75c Steam train leaving tunnel (violet on red)	30	15
115	65c on 75c Steam train leaving tunnel (black and red)	90	1·50
116	85c on 45c Steam train leaving tunnel (black and green)	90	1·50
117	90c on 75c Steam train leaving tunnel (red)	45	55
118	1f25 on 1f Steam train leaving tunnel (blue)	15	20
119	1f50 on 1f Steam train leaving tunnel (blue)	50	20
120	3f on 5f Steam train leaving tunnel (violet and green)	1·50	1·00
121	10f on 5f Steam train leaving tunnel (mauve and red)	4·50	2·75
122	20f on 5f Steam train leaving tunnel (blue and purple)	4·50	3·50

1942

*Nos. 119 and 121/2 overprinted **FRANCE LIBRE***

229†	1f50 on 1f Steam train leaving tunnel (blue)	75	75
240†	10f on 5f Steam train leaving tunnel (mauve and red)	3·75	3·75
242†	20f on 5f Steam train leaving tunnel (blue and purple)	4·25	4·25

1952

326†	100f Antsirabe Railway Viaduct	4·50	1·00

1956

335†	10f Railway tracks at Pangalanes Canal	20	5

MADEIRA

Atlantic Ocean, north-west of Africa
100 centavos = 1 escudo

1985

219† 40e Mountain railway   50   35

MALACCA

South-east Asia
100 cents = 1 dollar

1949

As No. 114 of Antigua
18† 10c Silhouette of steam locomotive   15   45

1957

43† 8c Steam train, East Coast Railway . . . . . . 1·25 2·25

1960

54† 8c Steam train, East Coast Railway . . . . . . 1·25   70

MALAGASY REPUBLIC

Indian Ocean off East Africa
100 centimes = 1 franc

1960

17† 30f Sugar cane trucks   75   25

1962

35† 20f Diesel train   90   15

1965

108† 30f Early railway postal carriage . . . . 1·25   60

1968

146† 40f Electric train   85   35

1972

210 45f Cable-laying train, Tananarive–
Tamataye . . . . 1·40   80

221† 100f "3600 CV" railway locomotive . . . . . . 2·40   25

1973

252 100f Excursion carriage
253 150f Steam locomotive   *Set of 2* 2·75 1·10

1974

276 50f Micheline railcar
277 85f Track-inspection trolley
278 200f Garratt steam locomotive

Set of 3 4·00 1·40

1976

530 3t Bagnall diesel shunter
531 10t "Shire" class diesel locomotive
532 20t Nippon Sharyo diesel locomotive
533 40t Hunslet diesel locomotive

Set of 4 2·75 2·25

1989

725† 250f Micheline "ZM 517 Tsikirty" railbus,
      Tananarive–Moramanga Line 25 15
727† 350f German Class "1020" electric
      locomotive 35 25
728† 1500f Souleze "710" diesel train,
      Malagasy Republic .... 1·50 1·25
MS730† 2500f Bugatti "Presidentiel" type
      diesel train .... 2·50 2·00

1977

550† 40t Diesel train on bridge, Blantyre–
      Nacala line .... 1·50 1·40

1979

597 5t Diesel train crossing viaduct, Salima–
     Lilongwe line
598 10t Diesel railcar at station, Salima–
     Lilongwe line
599 20t Train rounding bend, Salima–Lilongwe
     line
600 40t Diesel train in cutting, Salima–
     Lilongwe line

Set of 4 1·90 1·50

MALAWI

Central Africa
1968 12 pence = 1 shilling
20 shillings = 1 pound
1970 100 tambalas = 1 kwacha

1968

300 4d Saddleback steam locomotive No. 1
     Thistle
301 9d Class "G" steam locomotive
302 1s6d Diesel locomotive *Zambesi*
303 3s Diesel railcar

Set of 4 2·40 1·75

1980

631† 20t "Shire" Class diesel train (child's
      painting) 20 10

COLLECT MAMMALS ON STAMPS

A Stanley Gibbons thematic catalogue on this popular
subject. Copies available at £7.50 (p. + p. £2) from:
Stanley Gibbons Publications Ltd, 5 Parkside,
Christchurch Road, Ringwood, Hants BH24 3SH.

1985

726† 20t Diesel locomotive 70 35

1987

763 10t Locomotive No. 2 *Shamrock*, 1902
764 25t Class "D" steam locomotive No. 8, 1914
765 30t Locomotive No. 1 *Thistle*, 1902
766 1k Kitson steam locomotive No. 6, 1903
        Set of 4   1·50   1·25

MALAYSIA

South-east Asia
100 cents (sen) = 1 dollar

1966

39† 15c Diesel train on bridge 75 10

1985

315 15c F.M.S.R. steam locomotive No. 1, 1885
316 20c Class "20" diesel locomotive, 1957
317 $1 Class "23" diesel locomotive, 1983
        Set of 3   1·40   1·60
MS318 80c Class "56" steam locomotive, 1938   90   1·50

1987

380† 20c Diesel train at Kuala Lumpur station   8   10

MALDIVE ISLANDS

Indian Ocean
100 larees = 1 rupee

1970

332† 2r Miner and mine trucks . . . . 1·60   1·75

344† 10la Monorail train at "Expo 70"   8   8

1974

507† 1la U.P.U. emblem, steam and diesel
        locomotives   5   5
512† 5r U.P.U. emblem, steam and diesel
        locomotives . . . .   3·50   3·50
MS513† 4r U.P.U. emblem, steam and diesel
        locomotives . . . .   4·00   5·00

1979

MS816†   5r Boy playing with toy diesel train ....   1·60   2·00

1983

1010†   1r Steam locomotive   45   45

1986

1165†   15la John Henry and "Golden Spike
Ceremony, 1869" (on U.S.A. No. 919)   5   5
1168†   14r "Casey" Jones and railway
locomotives (on U.S.A. No. 990)   ....   2·75   3·00

MALI

West Africa
100 centimes = 1 franc

1970

255   20f Gallet 0-3-0T steam locomotive
256   40f Felou 0-3-0T steam locomotive
257   50f Bechevel 2-3-0T steam locomotive
258   80f Type "231" steam locomotive
259   100f Type "141" steam locomotive
Set of 5   10·50   10·00

1972

357†   70f Helsinki Railway Station   ....   1·00   40

367   10f First locomotive to arrive at Bamako,
1906
368   30f Steam locomotive, Thies–Bamako line,
1920
369   60f Type "141" locomotive, Thies–Bamako
line, 1927
370   120f Alsthom "BB" coupled diesel, Dakar–
Bamako line, 1947
Set of 4   10·50   9·50

1973

403   100f Stephenson's *Rocket* and French
Buddicom locomotive
404   150f Union Pacific and Santa Fe
locomotives
405   200f "Mistral" and "Tokaido" electric trains
Set of 3   4·75   2·00

1974

441†   270f Early steam and modern electric
trains ....   2·00   90

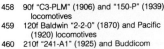

458 90f "C3-PLM" (1906) and "150-P" (1939)
   locomotives
459 120f Baldwin "2-2-0" (1870) and Pacific
   (1920) locomotives
460 210f "241-A1" (1925) and Buddicom
   (1847) locomotives
461 330f Hudson (1938) and *La Gironde*
   (1839) locomotives
                              Set of 4   5·00   2·75

No. 441 *surcharged* **9 OCTOBRE 1974** *and value*
464† 300f on 270f Early steam and modern
   electric trains .... 1·90   80

470 100f Electric train
471 110f Electric train
                              Set of 2   3·50   1·25

1980

738† 220f Globe, Rotary emblem and diesel
   train .... 1·25   50

749 200f Stephenson's *Rocket* and steam
   locomotive, Thies–Bamako line, 1920
   (on stamp No. 368)
750 300f Stephenson's *Rocket* and Bechevel
   2-3-0T steam locomotive (on stamp No.
   257)
                              Set of 2   2·50   1·25

785† 100f Steam locomotive from *Around the
   World in Eighty Days* .... 1·50   75

806 300f Electric train, aircraft and globe .... 1·90   60

808† 120f Diesel train .... 1·40   45

813 120f "Tokaido" train, Japan, and first
   locomotive to arrive at Bamako, 1906
   (on stamp No. 367)
814 130f Amtrack "RTG" train, U.S.A., and
   Gallet 0-3-0T steam locomotive (on
   stamp No. 255)
815 200f "Rembrandt" train, Germany, and
   Type "141" steam locomotive (on stamp
   No. 259)
816 480f "TGV 001" express train, France,
   and Type "231" steam locomotive (on
   stamp No. 258)
                              Set of 4   4·50   1·60

1981

No. 816 *overprinted* **26 Fevrier 1981/Record du monde de
vitesse-380 km/h**
861 480f "TGV 001" express train, France,
   and Type "231" steam locomotive (on
   stamp No. 258) .... 1·75   90

896   700f Diesel locomotive   ....   3·00   1·60

1983

968†   700f Rotary Club emblem and diesel
        railcar   ....   4·00   2·25

1986

1098   110f James Watt   50   45

MALTA

Mediterranean
1949 12 pence = 1 shilling
20 shillings = 1 pound
1972 10 mils = 1 cent
100 cents = 1 pound

1949

As No. 114 of Antigua
251†   2½d Silhouette of steam locomotive   25   5

1974

527†   1c3m Heinrich von Stephan and diesel
        locomotive   25   5

1983

705   3c Locomotive *Manning Wardle*, 1883
706   13c Locomotive *Black Hawthorn*, 1884
707   27c Locomotive *Beyer Peacock*, 1895
                                Set of 3   2·25   1·75

MANCHUKUO

Eastern Asia
100 fen = 1 yen

1936

97†   38f Railway bridge over Sungari River   ....   7·00   7·00
98†   39f Railway bridge over Sungari River   30   90

1939

125   2f Map of railway lines
126   4f "Asia" Express
                                Set of 2   1·25   1·10

MANCHURIA

See under China

MARIENWERDER

Eastern Europe
100 pfennig = 1 mark

1920

Nos. 113/15 of Germany overprinted **Commission Interalliee
Marienwerder**
25†   1m Tram, General Post Office, Berlin   ....   1·90   3·25
26†   1m25 Tram, General Post Office, Berlin   ..   2·25   3·75
27†   1m50 Tram, General Post Office, Berlin   ..   3·00   5·00

MARSHALL ISLANDS

North Pacific
100 cents = 1 dollar

1989

205† 45c Japanese narrow-gauge supply
train, Djarrej Islet, 1940s 55   30

MAURITANIA

West Africa
1906 100 centimes = 1 franc
1973 5 khoum = 1 ouguiya (um)

1906

As Nos. 18/22 of Dahomey
1† 1c General Faidherbe (builder of Dakar–St
Louis Railway) 15   8
2† 2c General Faidherbe (builder of Dakar–St
Louis Railway) 30   20
3† 4c General Faidherbe (builder of Dakar–St
Louis Railway) 40   30
4† 5c General Faidherbe (builder of Dakar–St
Louis Railway) 60   8
5† 10c General Faidherbe (builder of Dakar–St
Louis Railway) .... 3·50 1·25

1962

157 50f Diesel mineral train .... 2·25 85

1963

164† 200f Mine train, Port-Etienne .... 3·00 1·75

COLLECT SHIPS ON STAMPS
The largest Stanley Gibbons thematic catalogue to date
– available at £10.95 (p. + p. £2) from:
Stanley Gibbons Publications Ltd, 5 Parkside,
Christchurch Road, Ringwood, Hants BH24 3SH.

1965

222† 5f Diesel locomotive and Choum Tunnel   90   60
224† 30f Diesel locomotive and Choum Tunnel   1·75 60

1971

390 35f Iron ore train
391 100f Diesel locomotive
                                    Set of 2   3·50   2·00

1980

679 10um Giovi "Mastodont" type steam
locomotive
680 12um SNIM-SEM diesel ore train
681 14um Steam locomotive of Chicago,
Milwaukee and St Paul. Railway
682 20um Bury steam locomotive, 1837
683 67um Steam locomotive of French Reseau
du Nord line
684 100um Steam locomotive of Berlin–
Potsdam line
                                    Set of 6   7·50   2·00

1985

830† 12um German locomotive *Der Adler*,
1835 45   25
831† 18um Class "10" steam locomotive,
Germany, 1956 65   25

838† 50um Dock, iron ore mine and train ...... 1·10   75

MAURITIUS

Indian Ocean
100 cents = 1 rupee

1949
As No. 114 of Antigua
272† 12c Silhouette of steam locomotive 40   40

1974

473† 15c Mail train 30   15

1979

565 20c Whitcomb diesel locomotive "65H.P",
     1949
566 1r Steam locomotive Sir William, 1922
567 1r50 Kitson type steam locomotive, 1930
568 2r Garratt steam locomotive, 1927
                      Set of 4   1·40   1·25

MEMEL

Eastern Europe
100 pfennig = 1 mark

1920
Nos. 114/15 of Germany overprinted **Memelgebiet**
30† 1m25 Tram, General Post Office, Berlin .. 9·00 17·00
31† 1m50 Tram, General Post Office, Berlin .. 3·00 5·50

MEXICO

North America
100 centavos = 1 peso

1895

228† 1p Steam train .... 28·00 10·00
229† 5p Steam train .... £120 75·00
230† 10p Steam train .... £175 85·00

1915

299† 40c Railway map of Mexico (grey) 75   30
433† 40c Railway map of Mexico (mauve) .... 1·25   15

1939

640† 20c Streamlined steam train 50   25

1950

864 15c Rail-laying
865 20c Diesel locomotive and map of Mexico
     City–Yucatan Railway
866 25c Two diesel trains
867 35c Railway bridge
                      Set of 4   2·75   90

869† 25c Steam locomotive 25 10

1957

963 50c Train disaster, Nacozan ....-.. 90 25

1961

995 40c Railway tunnel
996 60c Railway tracks and map of
Chihuahua Railway (air)
997 70c Train on bridge

Set of 3 2·60 80

1963

1041 20c Diesel train
1042 1p20 Steam and diesel locomotives

Set of 2 2·50 1·75

1969

1189 40c Underground train, Mexico City 45 10

WHEN YOU BUY AN ALBUM LOOK FOR THE NAME "STANLEY GIBBONS"
It means Quality combined with Value for Money.

1973

1273 40c "Metlac Viaduct" (painting, J.M.
Velasco) 90 10

1981

1614 1p60 Globe and diesel locomotive 35 10

1984

M E X I C O
14.00

1725† 14p Toy train and Christmas tree 45 12

1987

1866 150p Train on Metlac Railway Viaduct .. 35 5

OFFICIAL STAMPS

1895

Nos. 228/30 optd **OFICIAL**
O241† 1p Steam train .... 35·00 16·00
O242† 5p Steam train .... £150 90·00
O243† 10p Steam train £225 £150

1915

Nos. 299 and 433 overprinted **OFICIAL**
O318† 40c Railway map of Mexico (grey) .... 4·00 2·50
O455† 40c Railway map of Mexico (mauve) 4·50 3·75

1933

No. 433 overprinted **SERVICIO OFICIAL**
O545† 40c Railway map of Mexico (mauve) 5·50 4·00

PARCEL POST STAMPS

1941

P732 10c Steam mail train
P733 20c Steam mail train

Set of 2   3·50   90

1954

P916 10c Diesel mail train
P917 20c Diesel mail train

Set of 2   3·00   40

MIDDLE CONGO

Central Africa
100 centimes = 1 franc

1933

69†	1c Mindouli Railway Viaduct	10	50
70†	2c Mindouli Railway Viaduct	10	50
71†	4c Mindouli Railway Viaduct	10	50
72†	5c Mindouli Railway Viaduct	15	30
73†	10c Mindouli Railway Viaduct	40	50
74†	15c Mindouli Railway Viaduct	75	1·25
75†	20c Mindouli Railway Viaduct	4·50	3·00
76†	25c Mindouli Railway Viaduct	75	75
77†	30c Mindouli Railway Viaduct	1·75	1·25

MONACO

Southern Europe
100 centimes = 1 franc

1922

57†   40c Steam train on St. Devote Viaduct   50   50

1924

97†	1f Steam train on St. Devote Viaduct	20	15
98†	1f05 Steam train on St. Devote Viaduct	20	35
99†	1f10 Steam train on St. Devote Viaduct	8·00	3·50

1926

Nos. 98/9 surcharged

108†	50c on 1f05 Steam train on St. Devote Viaduct	40	35
109†	50c on 1f10 Steam train on St. Devote Viaduct	4·50	2·75

1946

330†	1f Map showing railway lines	30	30
331†	2f + 3f Steam train on St. Devote Viaduct	40	40
332†	3f Map showing railway lines	70	70
334†	10f Map showing railway lines (air)	60	40

1956

Nos. D482/3 and D495 with "Timbre Taxe" obliterated. No. D495 also surcharged

557†	3f Early steam locomotive	35	35
558†	3f Streamlined steam locomotive	35	35
574†	50f on 100f Railway mail van	10·00	10·00

1968

914	20c Type 0-3-0 steam locomotive (1868)	
915	30c Type "C-220" steam locomotive (1898)	
916	60c Type "230-C" steam locomotive (1910)	
917	70c Type "231-F" steam locomotive (1925)	
918	1f Type "241-A" steam locomotive (1932)	
919	2f30 Type "BB" electric locomotive (1968)	

Set of 6   3·00   3·00

1972

1032 30c Toy locomotive in Santa Claus' sack
1033 50c Toy locomotive in Santa Claus' sack
1034 90c Toy locomotive in Santa Claus' sack
Set of 3   65   35

1035 50c Steam locomotive and modern turbo
express   50   30

1978

1373 1f Toy diesel train   55   40

1979

1397† 1f70 Arrival of first train at Monaco   95   70

1984

1661† 5c Tram, Place de la Visitation   5   15
1675† 4f Railway station, 1910 (from painting
by H. Clerissi) . . . .   1·10   80

1702† 5f "Monaco Railway Station" (painting
by H. Clerissi) . . . .   1·10   80

1985

1764† 6f Tram and railway station, 1920 (from
painting "Avenue de la Gare" by H.
Clerissi) . . . .   1·50   1·10

1986

1802† 7f Tram, Avenue du Beau Rivage, 1925   1·40   1·25

1987

1852† 7f Monte Carlo Railway Station, 1925 .. 1·50 1·25

1988

1883† 3f60 High speed mail train 70 60

1901 6f St. Devote Viaduct and Monte Carlo
      harbour, 1910
1902 7f Monte Carlo Station, 1910
                        Set of 2 2·50 2·10

POSTAGE DUE STAMPS

1953

D482† 3f Early steam locomotive 15 15
D483† 3f Streamlined steam locomotive 15 15
D485† 100f Railway mail van .... 11·00 11·00

1960

D700† 5c Arrival of first railway train at
       Monaco 15 25

MONGOLIA

Central Asia
100 mung = 1 tugrik

1956

118† 1t Steam train on bridge .... 22·00 10·00

1961

229† 30m Diesel mail train .... 3·50 80

1966

411 30m Steam train
412 50m Diesel train
                        Set of 2 2·50 50

1969

БНМАУ-ыг
тунхагласны
45
жилийн ой
1969--XI—26

Nos. 411/12 overprinted

544 30m Steam train
545 50m Diesel train
                        Set of 2 4·50 3·50

1971

616†	20m Steam locomotive	40	5
617†	30m Diesel locomotive	40	5

1972

671†	40m Diesel train	60	8

1973

740†	60m Diesel train	1·75	15

755†	30m Early steam locomotive and mail van (on Russia No. 3194)	70	15
763†	30m Steam train and 16th-century postman (on Poland No. 1066)	70	15

1974

821†	50m TEE diesel train	1·50	30

1975

Тээвэр—50
1975—7—15.

Nos 616/17 overprinted

918†	20m Steam locomotive	2·25	2·25
919†	30m Diesel locomotive	2·25	2·25

1976

1003	60m Diesel train	75	20

1977

1062	60m Diesel locomotive and ore trucks, Erdenet	75	20

1063	60m Diesel goods train	40	15

1979

1213† 1t Travelling post office, London–
Birmingham Railway . . . . 1·50 1·00

1360 30m Diesel train on bridge 50 10

1982

1215 10m Stephenson's *Rocket*
1216 20m German *Der Adler* locomotive, 1835
1217 30m American locomotive, 1860
1218 40m Mongolian locomotive, 1931
1219 50m Mongolian locomotive, 1936
1220 60m Mongolian locomotive, 1970
1221 70m Japanese high-speed electric train,
1963
1222 80m French "Orleans" aerotrain
1223 1t20 Russian experimental jet train
Rapidity
Set of 9 4·50 1·50

1448 60m Diesel train 50 30

1983

MS1233 1t50 Postal tramcar (on Brazil No.
1735) (there are two other 1t50 values in the
sheet) . . . . 7·00 6·00

1546† 80m Diesel mail train 90 50

1984

1584† 1t20 Diesel train . . . . 2·50 1·00

1981

1353† 1t Diesel mail train (on stamp No. 229) 1·75 50
1356† 1t Electric express train, Tokyo–Osaka
line (on Japan No. 988) . . . . 1·75 50

MONTSERRAT

West Indies
12 pence = 1 shilling
20 shillings = 1 pound

1949

As No. 114 of Antigua
117† 2½d Silhouette of steam locomotive 15 25

MOROCCO

North-west Africa
100 francs = 1 dirham

1966

190† 25f Diesel train 75 35

1982

620 1d40 Diesel train and route map of Unity
Railway 65 50

1983

655 2d Diesel train 75 45

MOSUL

Western Asia
12 pies = 1 anna
16 annas = 1 rupee

1919

Turkey Fiscal stamp surcharged POSTAGE I.E.F. "D" ½ Anna
1† ½a on 1pi Steam locomotive .... 1·40 1·40

MOZAMBIQUE

South-east Africa
1944 100 centavos = 1 escudo
1980 100 centavos = 1 metical

1944

385† 1e75 Lourenco Marques Central Railway
Station .... 3·50 60

1948

409† 10c River Zambesi railway bridge 15 8
417† 1e20 River Zambesi railway bridge 50 20

1952

468 1e50 Railway tracks 50 20

1953

492 1e Railway tracks (on stamp No. 468)
493 3e Railway tracks (on stamp No. 468)
Set of 2 2·50 60

1954

496 10c Railway lines on map of Mozambique
497 20c Railway lines on map of Mozambique
498 50c Railway lines on map of Mozambique
499 1e Railway lines on map of Mozambique
500 2e30 Railway lines on map of
Mozambique
501 4e Railway lines on map of Mozambique
502 10e Railway lines on map of Mozambique
503 20e Railway lines on map of Mozambique
Set of 8 3·50 1·00

1966

579 1e Beira Railway Station 30 30

1975

Nos. 496 and 503 overprinted **INDEPENDENCIA 25 JUN 75**
631† 10c Railway lines on map of
Mozambique 25 25
645† 20e Railway lines on map of
Mozambique .... 1·75 1·75

1979

759† 12e50 Child's drawing of steam train 90 35

779 50c 0-6-0T steam locomotive
780 1e50 0-4-0T steam locomotive
781 3e 4-4-0 steam locomotive
782 7e50 2-4-0T steam locomotive
783 12e50 0-8-2T steam locomotive
784 15e 4-8-4 steam locomotive
Set of 6 2·50 85

1981

846† 3m50 Railway tracks 75 25

ALBUM LISTS
Write for our latest list of albums and accessories. This
will be sent on request.

1982

934† 15m Envelope forming railway wagon .. 75 75

1983

998 1m Mallet type steam locomotive
999 2m Baldwin Series "200" steam
locomotive
1000 4m Henschel Series "600" steam
locomotive
1001 8m Baldwin Series "05" steam
locomotive
1002 16m Henschel Garratt type steam
locomotive
1003 32m Henschel Series "50" steam
locomotive
Set of 6 4·00 1·75

1016 8m Diesel locomotive 85 40

1028† 20m Mail train .... 1·75 1·00

1985

1080† 16m Tanker wagons 55   50

1105 1m Railway tracks, sisal plantation (on
      Mozambique Company No. 210)   5   5

MOZAMBIQUE COMPANY
South-east Asia
100 centavos = 1 escudo

1918

206†	5c Goods wagons on dock, Beira	15	10
228†	7c Steam train	45	25
210†	10c Railway tracks, sisal plantation	40	15
211†	15c Steam train	30	20
252†	25c Steam goods train, Beira	40	25
231†	80c Railway tracks, sisal plantation (brown and blue)	1·10	40
248†	80c Railway tracks, sisal plantation (black and red)	60	30
254†	1e40 Steam goods train, Beira	1·00	30
232†	2e Goods wagons on dock, Beira (violet and red)	1·25	75
250†	2e Goods wagons on dock, Beira (black and lilac)	1·00	40

1920
No. 206 surcharged
220† 1½c on 5c Goods wagons on dock, Beira   1·10   70

1935

260   1e Steam train on Zambesi Railway
      Bridge and goods wagons .... 2·00   50

1937
Design as No. 260, but with redesigned border
302† 5e Steam train on Zambesi Railway
      Bridge and goods wagons   60   20

NABHA
Indian subcontinent
12 pies = 1 anna
16 annas = 1 rupee

1938
No. 255 of India overprinted **NABHA STATE**
85†   4a Mail train .... 1·60 2·25

NAURU
Pacific Ocean
100 cents = 1 dollar

1975

130† 7c Phosphate mine wagon   25   25
131† 15c Electric phosphate train   65   65

1980

224   8c Steam phosphate train
225   32c Electric locomotive
226   60c Diesel locomotive
                               Set of 3   80   80

1982

268† 10c Steam locomotive *Nellie* 40 15
269† 30c Class "Clyde" diesel locomotive and
phosphate ore trucks 60 35

1985

NAURU 25c

323† 25c Diesel locomotive hauling crushed
ore 50 50
325† 50c Early steam locomotive 85 85

1986

334† 30c German 2ft gauge steam
locomotive, 1910 .... 45 45

NEGRI SEMBILAN

South-east Asia
100 cents = 1 dollar

1949

As No. 114 of Antigua
63† 10c Silhouette of steam locomotive 20 10

1957

72† 8c Steam train, East Coast Railway 85 60

COLLECT BIRDS ON STAMPS

New second edition available at £8.50 (p. + p. £2) from:
Stanley Gibbons Publications Ltd, 5 Parkside,
Christchurch Road, Ringwood, Hants BH24 3SH.

NETHERLANDS

North-west Europe
100 cents = 1 gulden

1932

402† 7½c + 3½c Railway bridge, Schipluiden 30·00 23·00

1939

499 5c Early steam locomotive *Der Arend*
500 12½c Modern electric locomotive
Set of 2 8·25 3·25

1952

754† 2c Telegraph poles and steam train
(violet) 70 10

As No. 754, but colour changed
757a 2c Telegraph poles and steam train
(brown) .... 20·00 15·00

1955

811† 5c + 3c Post Office Annexe, Hague
Railway Station and railway viaduct .. 55 35
812† 7c + 5c Tram tracks, Amsterdam ...... 1·25 1·25

1964

976 15c Station signal
977 40c Electric train at speed

Set of 2 1·10 80

1969

1052† 20c + 10c Railway bridge, Culemborg 1·50 25

1975

1206† 30c Underground railway lines on map,
Amsterdam 40 15

1980

1343† 60c UCES-type hopper truck 40 10

1981

1365† 45c Map of railway marshalling yard 30 10

1985

1464† 70c Women prisoners and construction
of Burma railway 55 10

1989

1557 55c Wheel on rail
1558 65c Early to modern steam, electric and
diesel locomotives
1559 75c Modern diesel train

Set of 3 1·10 12

NETHERLANDS INDIES

South-east Asia
100 cents = 1 gulden

1946

484† 1c Railway viaduct near Soekaboemi 30 60

1947

No. 484 surcharged
504† 4c on 1c Railway viaduct near
Soekamboemi .... 45 1·50

NEVIS

West Indies
100 cents = 1 dollar

1983

132/133 55c Locomotive County of Oxford, Great
Britain (1945)

134/135 $1 Locomotive *Evening Star*, Great
Britain (1960)
136/137 $1 Locomotive Stanier Class "5", Great
Britain (1934)
138/139 $1 Locomotive *Pendennis Castle*, Great
Britain (1924)
140/141 $1 Locomotive *Winston Churchill*, Great
Britain (1946)
142/143 $1 Locomotive *Mallard*, Great Britain
(1935)
144/145 $1 Locomotive *Britannia*, Great Britain
(1951)
146/147 $1 Locomotive *King George V*, Great
Britain (1927)

                               Set of 16   6·25   6·75
The first stamp in each pair shows technical drawings and the
second the locomotive at work.

1984

219/220 5c Class "EF81" locomotive, Japan
(1968)
221/222 10c Class "5500" electric locomotive,
France (1927)
223/224 60c Class "240P" locomotive, France
(1940)
225/226 $2.50 Shinkansen electric train, Japan
(1964)

                               Set of 8   4·00   4·00
The first stamp in each pair shows technical drawings and the
second the locomotive at work.

1985

277/278 1c Class "Wee Bogie" locomotive, Great
Britain (1882)
279/280 60c Locomotive *Comet*, Great Britain
(1851)
281/282 90c Class "8H" locomotive, Great Britain
(1908)
283/284 $2 Class "A" locomotive No. 23, Great
Britain (1866)

                               Set of 8   4·00   4·00
The first stamp in each pair shows technical drawings and the
second the locomotive at work.

297/298 5c Locomotive *Snowdon Ranger*, Great
Britain (1878)

299/300 30c Large Belpaire passenger
locomotive, Great Britain (1904)
301/302 60c Great Western Railway Class
"County" locomotive, Great Britain
(1904)
303/304 75c Locomotive *Nord L'Outrance*,
France (1877)
305/306 $1 Q.R. Class "PB-15" locomotive,
Australia (1899)
307/308 $2.50 D.R.G. Class "64" locomotive,
Germany (1928)

                               Set of 12   5·00   5·50
The first stamp in each pair shows technical drawings and the
second the locomotive at work.

318   25c Isambard Kingdom Brunel
319   25c Royal Albert Bridge, 1859
320   50c William Dean
321   50c Locomotive *Lord of the Isles*, 1895
322   $1 Locomotive *Lode Star*, 1907
323   $1 G. J. Churchward
324   $2.50 Locomotive *Pendennis Castle*, 1924
325   $2.50 C. B. Collett

                               Set of 8   5·25   5·25
The two designs for each value were printed together,
se-tenant, forming composite designs of Great Western Railway
engineers and their achievements.

1986

352/353 30c Locomotive *Stourbridge Lion*,
U.S.A. (1829)
354/355 75c "EP-2 Bi-Polar" locomotive, U.S.A.
(1919)
356/357 $1.50 U.P. "BO x 4" gas turbine
locomotive, U.S.A (1953)
358/359 $2 N.Y., N.H. and H.R. "FL9"
locomotive, U.S.A. (1955)

                               Set of 8   6·25   6·25
The first stamp in each pair shows technical drawings and the
second the locomotive at work.

COLLECT MAMMALS ON STAMPS

A Stanley Gibbons thematic catalogue on this popular
subject. Copies available at £7.50 (p. + p. £2) from:
Stanley Gibbons Publications Ltd, 5 Parkside,
Christchurch Road, Ringwood, Hants BH24 3SH.

427/428 15c Conner "Single Class" locomotive, Great Britain (1859)
429/430 45c Class "P2" locomotive *Cock o'the North*, Great Britain (1934)
431/432 60c Class "7000" locomotive, Japan (1926)
433/434 75c Palatinate Railway Class "P3" locomotive, Germany (1897)
435/436 $1 Locomotive *Dorchester*, Canada (1836)
437/438 $1.50 Class "Centennial" diesel locomotive, U.S.A. (1969)
439/440 $2 Locomotive *Lafayette*, U.S.A (1837)
441/442 $3 Class "C-16" locomotive, U.S.A. (1882)

Set of 16   7·75   8·50

The first stamp in each pair shows technical drawings and the second the locomotive at work.

NEW BRUNSWICK

North America
100 cents = 1 dollar

1860

9† 1c Steam locomotive .... 17·00 18·00

NEW CALEDONIA

South Pacific
100 centimes = 1 franc

1955

339† 14f Nickel train .... 2·50   55

1970

481† 20f Mount Fuji and Japanese electric express train .... 1·50   75

1971

484 10f Steam mail train, Dumbea .... 2·40 1·25

NEWFOUNDLAND

North Atlantic
100 cents = 1 dollar

1908

94 2c Map showing railway lines .... 14·00   30

1910

103† 10c Steam goods train, Grand Island .... 38·00 48·00

1928

183†	5c Steam train	2·75	1·00
173†	12c Tram tracks, St. Johns	1·50	7·50
177†	28c Tram tracks, St. Johns	14·00	27·00

1959

774†	8d Loading hopper trucks, Lake Grassmere	60	80

NEW ZEALAND

Australasia
1936 12 pence = 1 shilling
20 shillings = 1 pound
1967 100 cents = 1 dollar

1936

597† 6d Tracks.on dock, Wellington .... 90 3·25

1938

610 1d + 1d Children playing with toy train .... 1·25 1·40

1940

619† 4d Steam train .... 6·50 70

1963

818 3d Steam locomotive *Pilgrim* and "DG" diesel locomotive
819 1s9d Diesel express and Mount Ruapehu
Set of 2 2·25 1·25

1973

998† 4c Coal trucks at mine, Westport 15 8

1003 3c Class "W" steam locomotive
1004 4c Class "X" steam locomotive
1005 5c Class "Ab" steam locomotive
1006 10c Class "Ja" steam locomotive
Set of 4 3·50 2·10

1982

1264† 30c Dunedin Railway Station 30 30

1985

1360 24c Nelson horse-drawn tram, 1862
1361 30c Graham's Town steam tram, 1871
1362 35c Dunedin cable car, 1881
1363 40c Auckland electric tram, 1902
1364 45c Wellington electric tram, 1904
1365 58c Christchurch electric tram, 1905
Set of 6   2·00   2·25

1368† 45c South Rangitikei Railway Bridge   50   40

1987

1422† 40c Diesel mail train   40   40

OFFICIAL STAMPS

1940
No. 619 overprinted **Official**
O147† 4d Steam train ....   27·00   2·00

NICARAGUA
Central America
1890 100 centavos = 1 peso
1912 100 centavos de cordoba = 1 peso de cordoba
1925 100 centavos = 1 cordoba

1890

27 1c Steam locomotive and telegraph key
28 2c Steam locomotive and telegraph key

29 5c Steam locomotive and telegraph key
30 10c Steam locomotive and telegraph key
31 20c Steam locomotive and telegraph key
32 50c Steam locomotive and telegraph key
33 1p Steam locomotive and telegraph key
34 2p Steam locomotive and telegraph key
35 5p Steam locomotive and telegraph key
36 10p Steam locomotive and telegraph key
Set of 10   1·60   55·00

1900

137 1c Steam locomotive on dock, Mount
Momotombo   30   10
138 2c Steam locomotive on dock, Mount
Momotombo   60   15
139 3c Steam locomotive on dock, Mount
Momotombo   70   20
140 4c Steam locomotive on dock, Mount
Momotombo   90   25
184 5c Steam locomotive on dock, Mount
Momotombo   75   25
185 5c Steam locomotive on dock, Mount
Momotombo   55   15
142 6c Steam locomotive on dock, Mount
Momotombo ....   18·00   5·50
186 10c Steam locomotive on dock, Mount
Momotombo   55   10
144 15c Steam locomotive on dock, Mount
Momotombo ....   9·50   35
145 20c Steam locomotive on dock, Mount
Momotombo ....   8·50   30
146 50c Steam locomotive on dock, Mount
Momotombo ....   8·50   1·50
147 1p Steam locomotive on dock, Mount
Momotombo ....   18·00   6·50
148 2p Steam locomotive on dock, Mount
Momotombo ....   7·50   75
149 5p Steam locomotive on dock, Mount
Momotombo ....   13·00   2·50
Stamps of this issue exist overprinted **B Dpto Zelaya**, **Cabo** or
CABO for local use in those areas where silver currency
circulated.

1901
Nos. 142 and 147/9 surcharged **1901** and value
151 2c on 1p Steam locomotive on dock,
Mount Momotombo ....   7·00   6·00
169 3c on 6c Steam locomotive on dock,
Mount Momotombo ....   6·50   3·75
163 4c on 6c Steam locomotive on dock,
Mount Momotombo ....   5·50   3·50
173 5c on 1p Steam locomotive on dock,
Mount Momotombo ....   9·00   4·25
168 10c on 2p Steam locomotive on dock,
Mount Momotombo ....   7·00   1·75
152 10c on 5p Steam locomotive on dock,
Mount Momotombo ....   12·50   10·00
153 20c on 2p Steam locomotive on dock,
Mount Momotombo ....   12·50   12·50
176 20c on 5p Steam locomotive on dock,
Mount Momotombo ....   4·75   3·75
No. 176 exists overprinted **B Dpto Zelaya** or **CABO** for local
use in those areas where silver currency circulated

1902

Nos. 137/8 surcharged **1902** *and value*
187 15c on 2c Steam locomotive on dock,
Mount Momotombo
188 30c on 1c Steam locomotive on dock,
Mount Momotombo
Set of 2 3·50 4·50

1904

No. 186 surcharged
205 5c on 10c Steam locomotive on dock,
Mount Momotombo
200 15c on 10c Steam locomotive on dock,
Mount Momotombo
Set of 2 6·50 3·50

No. 186 surcharged **Vale,** *value and wavy lines*
203 5c on 10c Steam locomotive on dock,
Mount Momotombo
204 15c on 10c Steam locomotive on dock,
Mount Momotombo
Set of 2 1·90 65
Nos. 200 and 203/5 exist overprinted **B Dpto Zelaya Cabo** or **CABO** for local use in those areas where silver currency circulated.

1911

Railway tickets, sucharged **TIMBRE FISCAL** *or* **Timbre Fiscal** *and new value on the front, further surcharged on back* **vale cts**
CORREO DE 1911
319 2c on 5c on 2nd class ticket
320 05c on 5c on 2nd class ticket
321 10c on 5c on 2nd class ticket
322 15c on 10c on 1st class ticket
Set of 4 1·40 1·75

Railway tickets, with fiscal surcharge on front, as Nos. 319/22, further surcharged on front **CORREO** *and value*
323 02c on 10c on 1st class ticket
324 20c on 10c on 1st class ticket
325 50c on 10c on 1st class ticket
Set of 3 11·00 11·00

Railway tickets, with fiscal surcharge on front, as Nos. 319/22, further surcharged on front **Correo Vale 1911** *and value*
326 2c on 10c on 1st class ticket
327 5c on 10c on 1st class ticket
328 5c on 5c on 2nd class ticket
329 10c on 10c on 1st class ticket
Set of 4 1·75 1·40
No. 328 exists overprinted **B Dpto Zelaya** for local use in those areas where silver currency circulated

Railway tickets, with fiscal surcharge on front, as Nos. 319/22, surcharged on back **Vale CORREO DE 1911** *and value*
331 5c on 10c on 1st class ticket
332 10c on 10c on 1st class ticket
Set of 2 25·00 —

1913

Silver Currency Nos. Z1/4, Z6, Z9/15 surcharged
367 ½c on 2c Steam locomotive
368 1c on 3c Steam locomotive
369 1c on 4c Steam locomotive
370 1c on 6c Steam locomotive
371 1c on 20c Steam locomotive
372 1c on 25c Steam locomotive
384 2c on 1c Steam locomotive
373 2c on 25c Steam locomotive
274 5c on 35c Steam locomotive
375 5c on 50c Steam locomotive
376 6c on 1p Steam locomotive
377 10c on 2p Steam locomotive
378 1p on 5p Steam locomotive
Set of 13 24·00 22·00

1932

726 1c Tracks on wharf, Port San Jorge
727 2c Steam work train, El Nacascolo Halt
728 5c Rivas Railway Station
729 10c Steam train at San Juan del Sur
730 15c Steam train at Rivas Station
731 15c Tracks at La Chocolata Cutting (air)
732 20c Steam locomotive at El Nacascolo
733 25c Tracks at La Cuesta Cutting
734 50c Tracks on quay, San Juan del Sur
735 1cor View of El Estero
Set of 10 £175

739 1c Railway construction, El Sauce
740 2c Railway bridge, Santa Lucia
741 5c View of Santa Lucia
742 10c Railway construction
743 15c Tracks, Santa Lucia Cutting
744 15c Railway Bridge, Santa Lucia (air)
745 20c Santa Lucia River Halt
746 25c Malpaicillo Railway Station
747 50c Railway panorama
748 1cor Steam locomotive, San Andres
Set of 10 £175

1937

991† 55c Tracks, San Juan del Sur 80 60

999† 7½c Steam mail train .... 2·50 75

1974

1935† 2c Steam mail train (on stamp No. 999) 5 15

1976

2071† 4cor "Amtrak" turboliner train .... 1·90 1·25

2097† 5cor Ulau Railway Bridge (on Honduras
No. 236c) .... 1·50 90

1978

2155 1c Passenger and freight locomotive
2156 2c Lightweight cargo locomotive
2157 3c American steam locomotive
2158 4c Baldwin heavy freight locomotive
2159 5c Baldwin light freight and passenger
locomotive
2160 15c Presidential Pullman coach
2161 35c Lightweight American locomotive
(air)
2162 4cor Baldwin locomotive
2163 10cor Juniata locomotive
Set of 9 6·75 2·50
MS2164 20cor Map of Nicaraguan railway
system .... 6·00 6·00

2170† 10cor Indian steam locomotive (scene
from *Around the World in Eighty
Days*) .... 4·00 3·00

1980

2211† 2cor20 Children playing with toy steam
train .... 2·00 2·00
MS2213† 5cor Children playing with toy train
(sheet also contains a 15cor value) .... 20·00 20·00

No. 2211 overprinted **1980 ANO DE LA ALFABETIZACION**
2246† 2cor20 Children playing with toy steam
train .... 2·00 2·00

1981

2318 50c Locomotive "EL93" at Lago Grenada
2319 1cor Vulcan Iron Works 0-6-0 locomotive, 1946
2320 1cor20 Philadelphia Iron Works 0-6-0 locomotive, 1911
2321 1cor80 Steam hoist, 1909
2322 2cor "U-10B" diesel locomotive, 1956
2323 2cor50 German diesel railbus
2324 6cor Japanese diesel railbus (air)

Set of 7   3·75   80

1982

2357† 3cor50 Steam train .... 1·50   15

1983

2474 15c Passenger coach
2475 65c Goods wagon
2476 1cor Tanker
2477 1cor50 Ore hopper

2478 4cor Passenger railcar (air)
2479 5cor Tipper truck
2480 7cor Railbus

Set of 7   4·75   2·00

1984

2607† 15cor Steam locomotive .... 4·00   2·10

2619† 1cor Pacific–Atlantic Railway diesel locomotive 50   20

1985

2659 1cor Early German steam locomotive
2660 1cor German electric locomotive

2661 9cor Steam locomotive No. 88 (air)
2662 9cor Double deck tram
2663 15cor German steam passenger locomotive
2664 21cor German mountain steam locomotive

Set of 6   2.75   75

MS2665 42cor Early German locomotive *Der Adler* .... 2·40   60

SILVER CURRENCY

1912

Z1   1c Steam locomotive
Z2   2c Steam locomotive
Z3   3c Steam locomotive
Z4   4c Steam locomotive
Z5   5c Steam locomotive
Z6   6c Steam locomotive
Z7   10c Steam locomotive
Z8   15c Steam locomotive
Z9   20c Steam locomotive
Z10 25c Steam locomotive
Z11 35c Steam locomotive
Z12 50c Steam locomotive
Z13 1p Steam locomotive
Z14 2p Steam locomotive
Z15 5p Steam locomotive

Set of 15   42·00   25·00

OFFICIAL STAMPS

1890

Nos. 27/36 overprinted **FRANQUEO OFICIAL**

O37	1c Steam locomotive and telegraph key	
O38	2c Steam locomotive and telegraph key	
O39	5c Steam locomotive and telegraph key	
O40	10c Steam locomotive and telegraph key	
O41	20c Steam locomotive and telegraph key	
O42	50c Steam locomotive and telegraph key	
O43	1p Steam locomotive and telegraph key	
O44	2p Steam locomotive and telegraph key	
O45	5p Steam locomotive and telegraph key	
O46	10p Steam locomotive and telegraph key	

Set of 10   1·50   14·00

1903

Nos. 139 and 186 surcharged **OFICIAL** and value

O197   1c on 10c Steam locomotive on dock,
　　　 Mount Momotombo
O198   2c on 3c Steam locomotive on dock,
　　　 Mount Momotombo
O199   4c on 3c Steam locomotive on dock,
　　　 Mount Momotombo
O200   4c on 10c Steam locomotive on dock,
　　　 Mount Momotombo
O201   5c on 3c Steam locomotive on dock,
　　　 Mount Momotombo

Set of 5   8·75   9·25

1911

Railway tickets surcharged **Timbre Fiscal Vale 10 ctvs.** further
surcharged **Correo oficial Vale** and new value

O334	10c on 10c on 1st class ticket	
O335	15c on 10c on 1st class ticket	
O336	20c on 10c on 1st class ticket	
O337	50c on 10c on 1st class ticket	
O338	$1 on 10c on 1st class ticket	
O339	$2 on 10c on 1st class ticket	

Set of 6   22·00   27·00

Railway tickets surcharged **Timbre Fiscal Vale 10 ctvs.** further
surcharged **CORREO OFICIAL** and new value

O340	10c on 10c on 1st class ticket	
O341	15c on 10c on 1st class ticket	
O342	20c on 10c on 1st class ticket	
O343	50c on 10c on 1st class ticket	

Set of 4   75·00   60·00

As No 322, but with the surcharge on the back obliterated with a
heavy bar, surcharged on front **Correo oficial Vale 1911** and new
value

O344	5c on 10c on 1st class ticket	
O345	10c on 10c on 1st class ticket	
O346	15c on 10c on 1st class ticket	
O347	20c on 10c on 1st class ticket	
O348	50c on 10c on 1st class ticket	

Set of 5   22·00   28·00

1912

As No. 322, but with the surcharge on the back obliterated with a
heavy bar, surcharged on front **Correo Oficial 1912** and new
value

O349	5c on 10c on 1st class ticket	
O350	10c on 10c on 1st class ticket	
O351	15c on 10c on 1st class ticket	
O352	20c on 10c on 1st class ticket	
O353	35c on 10c on 1st class ticket	
O354	50c on 10c on 1st class ticket	
O355	$1 on 10c on 1st class ticket	

Set of 7   35·00   30·00

NIGER

West Africa
100 centimes = 1 franc

1967

258   100f Monorail, Expo '67, Montreal .... 1·75   50

1969

327   100f Child and toy train .... 1·75   50

1973

496	25f Rudolf Diesel and engine	
497	50f Type "BB-610ch" diesel locomotive	
498	75f Type "060-DB1" diesel locomotive	
499	125f Type "CC72004" diesel locomotive	

Set of 4   4·75   2·25

1974

527	50f Locomotive No. 230K (1948) and U.S.A locomotive No. 2222 (1938)	
528	75f P.L.M. locomotive No. C21 (1893)	
529	100f U.S.A. "220" (1866) and British "231" (1939) class locomotives	
530	150f Seguin locomotive (1829) and Stephenson's *Rocket* (1829)	

Set of 4   5·75   2·25

809   45f Shimbashi–Yokohama steam
         locomotive
810   60f American steam locomotive
811   90f German State Railway Series "61"
         steam locomotive

544†   100f Japanese woman and electric
         locomotive .... 1·50   60

812   100f Prussian State Railway "P-2" type
         steam locomotive
813   130f French steam locomotive L'Aigle
                                    Set of 5   4·50   1·00
MS814   425f Locomotive The Rocket, 1830 ....   4·00   75

1975

562   50f Locomotive City of Truro (G.W.R.
         England, 1903)
563   75f No. 5003 steam locomotive (Germany,
         1937)
564   100f Locomotive The General (U.S.A.,
         1863)
565   125f Type "BB-15000" electric locomotive
         (France, 1971)
                                    Set of 4   4·75   2·25

1985
No. **MS**814 overprinted **TSUKUBA EXPO '85**
MS1025   Five sheets (b) 425f Locomotive The
Rocket, 1830 (Different designs on other
sheets)
                    Set of 5 miniature sheets   12·50   12·50

1976

1037   110f Diesel train   85   30

628†   300f Zeppelin "LZ-130" over trams in
         front of Essen Railway Station .... 3·25   60

NIGERIA
West Africa
1936 12 pence = 1 shilling
20 shillings = 1 pound
1973 100 kobo = 1 naira

1979

1936

767†   200f British Advanced Passenger Train   1·90   50
MS768†   400f French electric train ....   3·00   75

34†   ½d Tracks on Apapa Wharf   35   40
44†   10s Niger River railway bridge, Jebba ....   38·00   48·00

1938

As No. 44, but with portrait of King George VI
59c† 5s Niger River railway bridge, Jebba .... 2·25 90

1949

As No. 114 of Antigua
64† 1d Silhouette of steam locomotive 15 10

1953

72† 2d Mine trucks at tin mine (black and
ochre).......................... 40 10
72cc† 2d Mine trucks at tin mine (slate) 70 10
73† 3d Steam train and Niger River railway
bridge, Jebba 35 5

1956

No. 72 overprinted ROYAL VISIT 1956
81 2d Mine trucks at tin mine 5 5

1961

101† £1 Lagos Railway Station and diesel
locomotive .... 5·00 3·25

102† 1d Diesel locomotive 5 5

1965

166† 3d I.C.Y. emblem and diesel locomotive 60 5

1966

191† 2s6d Niger River railway bridge, Jebba 1·50 2·25

1974

324† 30k Diesel locomotive on map of Nigeria 1·90 2·75

326† 18k Diesel train and world transport map 1·00 1·00

1980

412 10k Steam locomotive
413 20k Loading goods train
414 30k Diesel goods train
Set of 3 1·50 1·25

1986

517† 15k Loading railway wagons on dock 5 5

STAMP MONTHLY
— finest and most informative magazine for all
collectors. Obtainable from your newsagent or by
postal subscription — details on request.

NIUAFO'OU

South Pacific
100 seniti = 1 pa'anga

1988

MS107   42s Early Australian Trans Continental locomotive; 42s Train carriages; 42s Sydney Harbour Bridge (sheet also contains nine other designs) .... 4·75 5·00

NIUE

South Pacific
100 cents = 1 dollar

1979

290†   50c French 1849 20c stamp, and part of French post office railway van, 1849 .... 50 35
291†   50c Sir Rowland Hill and part of French post office railway van, 1849 .... 50 35

1980

Nos. 290/1 surcharged **HURRICANE RELIEF Plus 2c**
316†   50c + 2c French 1849 20c stamp, and part of French post office railway van, 1849 .... 50 55
317†   50c + 2c Sir Rowland Hill and part of French post office railway van, 1849 .... 50 55

No. 290 overprinted **ZEAPEX '80 AUCKLAND** *and No. 291 overprinted* **NEW ZEALAND STAMP EXHIBITION** *and emblem*
359†   50c French 1849 20c stamp, and part of French post office railway van, 1849 .... 45 30
360†   50c Sir Rowland Hill and part of French post office railway van, 1849 .... 45 30

WHEN YOU BUY AN ALBUM LOOK FOR THE NAME "STANLEY GIBBONS"
It means Quality combined with Value for Money.

NORFOLK ISLAND

Australasia
100 cents = 1 dollar

1988

444†   37c Sydney Harbour Bridge 35 40

NORTH BORNEO

South-east Asia
100 cents = 1 dollar

1897

107†   16c Borneo steam train .... 50·00 55·00

1901

No. 107 overprinted **BRITISH PROTECTORATE**
136†   16c Borneo steam train .... 28·00 18·00

1909

161†   3c Jesselton Railway Station (black and red) .... 1·75 90
279†   3c Jesselton Railway Station (black and green) .... 2·00 1·25

1916

No. 161 surcharged
186†   2c on 3c Jesselton Railway Station (black and red) .... 8·00 7·00

No. 161 overprinted with Maltese Cross
204†   3c Jesselton Railway Station (black and red) .... 22·00 50·00

1918

No. 161 surcharged **RED CROSS TWO CENTS**
216†   3c + 2c Jesselton Railway Station (black and red) .... 3·50 8·50

No. 161 surcharged **FOUR CENTS** *and cross*
237†   3c + 4c Jesselton Railway Station (black and red) .... 75 3·25

1922

No. 161 overprinted **MALAYA—BORNEO EXHIBITION 1922**
256† 3c Jesselton Railway Station (black and
red) .... 3·25 22·00

1949

As No. 114 of Antigua
352† 8c Silhouette of steam locomotive 30 20

1956

387† 10c Borneo steam train, 1902 .... 60 15

POSTAGE DUE STAMPS

1902

No. 107 overprinted **POSTAGE DUE**
D44† 16c Borneo steam train .... 12·50 14·00

1920

No. 279 overprinted **POSTAGE DUE**
D58† 3c Jesselton Railway Station (black and
green)........................... 1·50 6·00

NORTH KOREA

See under Korea

NORTH VIETNAM

See under Vietnam

NORTHERN RHODESIA

Central Africa
12 pence = 1 shilling
20 shillings = 1 pound

1949

As No. 114 of Antigua
50† 2d Silhouette of steam locomotive 20 30

1953

54 ½d Cecil Rhodes and Victoria Falls Railway
Bridge
55 1d Cecil Rhodes and Victoria Falls Railway
Bridge

56 2d Cecil Rhodes and Victoria Falls Railway
Bridge
57 4½d Cecil Rhodes and Victoria Falls Railway
Bridge
58 1s Cecil Rhodes and Victoria Falls Railway
Bridge
Set of 5 1·10 5·00

NORWAY

Northern Europe
100 ore = 1 krone

1947

390† 45 ore First Norwegian steam locomotive
Caroline .... 3·25 50

1954

446 20 ore First railway steam locomotive
Caroline and flat car
447 30 ore Diesel express train
448 55 ore Engine driver
Set of 3 2·75 1·50

1969

625 50 ore Diesel railcar 40 30

1979

848† 1k25 Steam train on Kylling Bridge,
Verma, Romsdal 40 10

1980

MS862 2k Steam locomotive and passenger
carriage (sheet contains 3 other designs and
was sold at 15k) .... 7·00 7·00

1981

883† 2k30 Train Ferry *Storegut* 40 30

1984

946† 2k50 Tram in Kardemomme Town 80 25

NYASALAND PROTECTORATE

Central Africa
12 pence = 1 shilling
20 shillings = 1 pound

1949

As No. 114 of Antigua
163† 1d Silhouette of steam locomotive 30 20

PAHANG

South-east Asia
100 cents = 1 dollar

1949

As No. 114 of Antigua
49† 10c Silhouette of steam locomotive 20 20

1957

79† 8c Steam train, East Coast Railway 80 80

PAKISTAN

Indian subcontinent
100 paisa = 1 rupee

1961

153 13p Locomotive *Eagle*, 1861
154 50p Diesel locomotive
Set of 2 1·25 15

1969

276 15p Dacca Railway Station 30 10

1970

288 50p Monorail tracks, World Fair, Osaka .. 15 25

1971

313 20p Early locomotive and boy with toy
train 50 25

COLLECT BIRDS ON STAMPS

New second edition available at £8.50 (p. + p. £2) from:
Stanley Gibbons Publications Ltd, 5 Parkside,
Christchurch Road, Ringwood, Hants BH24 3SH.

1981

570 40p Coal wagons at steel works
571 2r Coal wagons at steel works

Set of 2   20   25

1988

755† 50r Locomotive *Eagle* of 1861 .... 2·75   3·00

PALAU

North Pacific
100 cents = 1 dollar

1987

209† 22c Train at phosphate mine and steam
locomotive (on Japan No. 408) 25   15

PANAMA

Central America
100 centesimos = 1 balboa

1915

166† 5c Electric towing engine, Gatun Locks   1·25   50

1918

180†	24c Electric towing engine, Gatun Locks	24·00	7·50
181†	50c Goods wagon, Balboa docks	22·00	16·00
182†	1b Electric towing engine, Pedro Miguel Locks	30·00	18·00

1929

No. 182 overprinted **CORREO AEREO** *and plane*

239† 1b Electric towing engine, Pedro Miguel
Locks .... 18·00 14·00

1936

287† 50c Electric towing engine, Pedro Miguel
Locks .... 22·00 15·00

1937

No. 287 overprinted **UPU**

303† 50c Electric towing engine, Pedro Miguel
Locks .... 18·00 18·00

No. 182 surcharged **CORREO AEREO 5c**

322† 5c on 1b Electric towing engine, Pedro
Miguel Locks .... 2·50 1·25

1939

357† ½c Tracks and overhead wires, Gatun
Locks .... 1·25 1·25
358† 1c Electric towing engine, Pedro Miguel
Locks .... 1·50 1·00
361† 10c Panama Railways ferryboat .... 2·00 50

1948

470† 50c C. C. Arosemena (engineer) .... 1·75 70

1953

548†   20c C. C. Arosemena (engineer) in
Revolutionary Council   90   25

1955

571†   25c Steam work train, Panama Canal ....   2·25   1·25

1979

1144†   3c Electric towing engine, Panama
Canal   10   5

1980

1150   1c Colon Railway Station, Trans-
Panamanian Railway   10   25

PARAGUAY
South America
100 centimos = 1 guarani

1944

589†   5c First Paraguayan railway locomotive   2·00   50
600†   20c First Paraguayan railway locomotive
(air)   ....   3·50   1·25

1946
No. 600 surcharged **1946 5 Centimos 5**
636†   5c on 20c First Paraguayan railway
locomotive   ....   4·25   4·50

1950

691   20c Streamlined steam locomotive
692   30c Streamlined steam locomotive
693   50c Streamlined steam locomotive
694   1g Streamlined steam locomotive
695   5g Streamlined steam locomotive
Set of 5   2·25   2·50

OFFICIAL STAMPS

1886

O37†   15c Steam train (blue) (imperf)   ....   4·00   5·00
O44†   15c Steam train (brown) (perf)   ....   3·00   1·75

Appendix
The following stamps have either been issued in excess of
postal needs, or have not been made available to the public in
reasonable quantities at face value. Miniature sheets, imperforate
stamps, etc. are excluded from this section.

1972
Early Railway Locomotives (1st series). Postage 10, 15, 20, 25,
30, 50, 75c; Air 12g45, 18g15, 50g.
Visit of President of Paraguay to Japan. Postage 15c (early steam
train), 75c (high speed train).
Early Railway Locomotives (2nd series). Postage 10, 15, 20, 25,
30, 50, 75c; Air 12g45, 18g15.

1974
U.P.U. Centenary. Air 10g (American mail train).

1976
Early Railway Locomotives (3rd series). Postage 1, 2, 3, 4, 5g; Air
10, 15, 20g
American Revolution and U.S. Postal Service Bicentenaries. 3g
(U.S.A. Western steam locomotive).

1979
Electric Locomotives. Centenary. Postage 3, 4, 5, 6, 7, 8, 20g; Air
10, 25g

1983
*Third International Railways Congress, Malaga (1982). Steam
Locomotives.* 25, 50c, 1, 2, 3, 4, 5g.
"Philatelia 83" International Stamp Exhibition, Dusseldorf. 1983
International Railway Congress issue overprinted. 25, 50c, 1, 2,
3, 4g.

PATIALA

Indian subcontinent
12 pies = 1 anna
16 annas = 1 rupee

1937
No. 255 of India overprinted **PATIALA**
88†   4a Mail train .... 4·00   4·00

PENANG

South-east Asia
100 cents = 1 dollar

1949
As No. 114 of Antigua
23†   10c Silhouette of steam locomotive 15   5

1957

48†   8c Steam train, East Coast Railway 80   40

1960

59†   8c Steam train, East Coast Railway 80   65

PERAK

South-east Asia
100 cents = 1 dollar

1949
As No. 114 of Antigua
124†   10c Silhouette of steam locomotive 15   5

1957

154†   8c Steam train, East Coast Railway ...... 1·40   30

PERLIS

South-east Asia
100 cents = 1 dollar

1949
As No. 114 of Antigua
3†   10c Silhouette of steam locomotive 25   60

1957

33†   8c Steam train, East Coast Railway ...... 1·10   80

PERU

South America
1871 100 centavos = 1 peso
1874 100 centavos = 1 sol

1871

21a   5c Steam locomotive, Callao–Lima–
      Chorillos Railway .... £110   24·00

1925

451†   2c Steam train at Morro Arica 70   30
452†   5c Steam train at Morro Arica (blue) .... 1·50   50
453†   5c Steam train at Morro Arica (red) ...... 1·25   40
454†   5c Steam train at Morro Arica (green) .... 1·25   40

1927
As Nos. 451/4, but figures of value not encircled
457   2c Steam train at Morro Arica (orange)
458   2c Steam train at Morro Arica (brown)
459   2c Steam train at Morro Arica (blue)
460   2c Steam train at Morro Arica (violet)
461   2c Steam train at Morro Arica (green)
462   20c Steam train at Morro Arica
               Set of 6   16·00   7·50

1928

465   2c Steam train at Morro Arica   40   10

1930
No. 465 overprinted **Habilitada Franqueo**
469   2c Steam train at Morro Arica   60   60

1936

578†   35c Early locomotive *La Callao* . . . .   6·00   3·00

589†   15c Tram, Paseo de la Republica, Lima
        (blue) . . . .   1·00   25
601†   50c Goods wagons at mine (yellow) (air)   75   35
603†   80c Tracks in Infiernillo Canyon, Andes
        (black) . . . .   11·00   8·00
604†   1s Steam train at La Cima (blue) . . . .   9·50   1·50

1937
No. 603 surcharged **Habilit 25 Cts**
614†   25c on 80c Tracks in Infiernillo Canyon,
        Andes . . . .   7·50   10·00

As Nos. 601, 603, 604 but colours changed
629†   50c Goods wagons at mine (red) . . . .   1·50   20
631†   80c Tracks in Infiernillo Canyon, Andes
        (green) . . . .   3·75   1·25
632†   1s Steam train at La Cima (brown) . . . . . .   4·25   40

COLLECT SHIPS ON STAMPS
The largest Stanley Gibbons thematic catalogue to date
– available at £10.95 (p. + p. £2) from:
Stanley Gibbons Publications Ltd, 5 Parkside,
Christchurch Road, Ringwood, Hants BH24 3SH.

1938

656†   70c Tracks in Infiernillo Canyon, Andes
        (grey) . . . .   1·50   15

1948
No. 656 surcharged **Habilitada S/o** *and value*
718†   10c on 70c Tracks in Infiernillo Canyon,
        Andes   40   15
719†   15c on 70c Tracks in Infiernillo Canyon,
        Andes   80   15
720†   20c on 70c Tracks in Infiernillo Canyon,
        Andes   40   15
721†   55c on 70c Tracks in Infiernillo Canyon,
        Andes   60   15

1949
As No. 656, but colour changed
736†   70c Tracks in Infiernillo Canyon, Andes
        (blue)   65   10

1952

776†   10c Tracks at Matarani Docks   25   8
777†   15c Steam train (grey)   10   10
777a† 15c Steam train (brown)   90   20

1957

811†   10s Locomotive *La Callao* (on stamp No.
        578) . . . .   2·25   1·50

1962
Design as No. 777, but new value with De La Rue imprint
875†   1s80 Steam train   45   15

PHILIPPINES

South-east Asia
1955 100 centavos = 1 peso
1962 100 sentimos = 1 piso

1955

777 5c Steam locomotive .... 1·50   60

1959

820 6c Goods wagon on Seal of Bacolod
     Province
821 10c Goods wagon on Seal of Bacolod
     Province
                              Set of 2   60   40

1966

MS1028 70s Diesel locomotive .... 2·00   2·00

1969

1117 10s Diesel locomotive
1118 40s Diesel locomotive
1119 75s Diesel locomotive
                              Set of 3   1·60   75

1970

1140 10s Diesel locomotive at Iligan steel mill
1141 20s Diesel locomotive at Iligan steel mill
1142 30s Diesel locomotive at Iligan steel mill
                              Set of 3   1·10   40

1971

1199† 70s Diesel train and Mayon Volcano ....   1·75   50

1974

1331† 15s Diesel train   10   10

1978

MS1462 7p50 Early steam locomotive (sheet
        also contains three other 7p50 designs) ...... 14·00 14·00

1466 2p30 Miner and mine train ....   1·25   50

1983

| 1772† | 40s Ore truck | 35 | 15 |

1984

| 1842 | 1p20 Electric train on viaduct | 20 | 8 |

1861	60s Manila–Dagupan steam locomotive, 1892		
1862	1p20 Light Railway Transit train, 1984		
1863	6p Bicol express, 1955		
1864	7p20 Electric tram, 1905		
1865	8p40 Commuter train, 1972		
1866	20p Horse-drawn tram, 1898		
	Set of 6	5·25	2·50

1985

Nos. 1863/4 surcharged **PHILATELIC WEEK 1985** and new value. No. 1937 also overprinted **AIRMAIL**

1936	60s on 6p Bicol express, 1955		
1937	3p on 7p20 Electric tram, 1905 (air)		
	Set of 2	40	25

PITCAIRN ISLANDS

South Pacific
12 pence = 1 shilling
20 shillings = 1 pound

1949

As No. 114 of Antigua

| 13† | 2½d Silhouette of steam locomotive | 2·00 | 3·00 |

POLAND

Eastern Europe
100 groszy = 1 zloty

1935

| 318† | 10g Tracks on dock, Gdynia | 60 | 10 |

1943

| 492† | 1z Saboteurs damaging railway lines | 3·00 | 3·00 |

1948

| 629 | 18z Steam locomotive, clock and winged wheel emblem of European Railway Conference | 6·50 | 8·50 |

1952

| 741† | 5z Steam goods train at steel mill | 1·25 | 40 |

783	5g Tracks, Gdansk Shipyards		
784	15g Tracks, Gdansk Shipyards		
	Set of 2	30	10

1953

| 815† | 1z35 Goods wagons on dock | 1·25 | 3·00 |

| 841† | 10g Children playing with toy steam locomotive | 50 | 10 |

1954

844 60g Electric train from front
845 80g Electric train from back

Set of 2   7·00   4·25

847† 40g Front of tram 50   10

873† 10g Hopper trucks at coal mine 60   10
876† 25g Steam goods train at steel mill 90   10

885 40g Steam train and signal
886 60g Steam night express

Set of 2   4·50   70

1957

1035† 90g Goods wagons at steel works 15   10

1958

1066† 2z10 Silhouette of steam train 50   15

1964

1503† 60g Goods wagons at Chelm Cement
Works 8   5

1966

1631 60g Electric locomotive 15   10

1636† 60g Electric train 20   10

**STANLEY GIBBONS
STAMP COLLECTING SERIES**

Introductory booklets on *How to Start, How to Identify Stamps* and *Collecting by Theme.* A series of well illustrated guides at a low price.
Write for details.

1976

2414 50g Trevithick's steam locomotive, 1803
2415 1z Murray and Blenkinsop's steam
 locomotive, 1810
2416 1z50 George Stephenson's locomotive
 Rocket, 1829
2417 1z50 Polish "Universal" Type ET-22
 electric locomotive, 1969
2418 2z70 Robert Stephenson's locomotive
 North Star, 1837
2419 3z Joseph Harrison's steam locomotive,
 1840
2420 4z50 Thomas Roger's steam locomotive,
 1855
2421 4z90 Polish Chrzanow Works steam
 locomotive, 1922
                              Set of 8   3·75   90

2465† 1z50 Goods wagons, Gdynia docks   25   10
2467† 2z Goods wagons, Szczecin docks   30   5
2468† 4z20 Coal wagons, Swinoujscie docks   60   15

1978

2530 50g Electric locomotive and Katowice
 Railway Station
2531 1z Steam locomotive No. Py 27,
 Znin–Gasawa narrow gauge railway
2532 1z Steam locomotive No. Pm 36 and
 Cegielski's factory, Poznan
2533 1z50 Electric locomotive and Otwock
 Station
2534 1z50 Steam locomotive and Warsaw
 Stalowa Station
2535 4z50 Steam locomotive No. Ty51 and
 Gdynia Station
2536 5z Steam locomotive No. Tr21 and
 locomotive works. Chrzanow
2437 6z Cockerill steam locomotive and
 Vienna Station
                              Set of 8   2·75   65

MS2547 8z40 + 4z Kazimierz Stanislaw
 Gzowski (engineer) ....   1·10   65

1979

2591† 50g Child's painting of steam
 locomotive   15   5

2640† 4z50 Loading mail onto train   45   10

1980

2716† 6z Horse-drawn tram   50   20

1985

3006 5z Type "20K" goods wagon
3007 10z Type "201E" electric locomotive
3008 17z Type "OMMK" two-axle coal truck
3009 20z Type "111A" passenger coach
                              Set of 4   1·90   45

1988

3190†	15z Tracks on coal wharf, Gdynia	5	5
3191†	20z Hipolit Cegielski (industrialist) and early steam locomotive	5	5

PORT ARTHUR & DAIREN

See under China

PORTUGAL

South-west Europe
100 centavos = 1 escudo

1956

1136	1e Early steam locomotive		
1137	1e50 Electric locomotive		
1138	2e Electric locomotive		
1139	2e50 Early steam locomotive		
		Set of 4 13·00	2·50

1966

1294	1e Salazar Bridge, Lisbon		
1295	2e50 Salazar Bridge, Lisbon		
1296	2e80 Salazar Bridge, Lisbon		
1297	4e30 Salazar Bridge, Lisbon		
		Set of 4 3·25	1·75

1973

1509†	1e Diesel train	35	10

1516†	1e Horse-drawn tram-car, Oporto	25	10
1518†	7e50 Early tram-car, Oporto	1·40	40

1974

1541†	20e Steam and electric locomotives	2·50	1·50

1977

1671	4e Early steam locomotive		
1672	10e Steam train on Maria Pia Bridge		
		Set of 2 1·60	95

1978

1700†	30e Goods wagon at factory	90	15

1979

1742†	5e Emigrant at railway station	30	10
1744†	17e Man greeting child at railway station	60	30

1981

1851 8e50 Steam locomotive *Dom Luiz*, 1862
1852 19e Pacific type steam locomotive, 1925
1853 27e "Alco 1500" diesel locomotive, 1948
1854 33e50 Alsthom "BB2600" electric
    locomotive, 1974

                              Set of 4 3·00 1·00

1983

1925 30e Passenger in train 65   25

1989

2138† 29e Cable railway, Lisbon 25   15
2139† 65e Electric tram-car, Lisbon 55   45

QATAR

Arabian Peninsula
100 dirhams = 1 riyal

1970

336† 2r Japanese "Hikari Express" on viaduct 2·50 2·00

1974

502† 3d Early mail wagon and electric
    express train 10   20

RAS AL KHAIMA

Arabian Peninsula
100 dirhams = 1 riyal

Appendix
The following stamps have either been issued in excess of postal needs, or have not been made available to the public in reasonable quantities at face value. Miniature sheets, imperforate stamps, etc. are excluded from this section.

1970
"EXPO '70" World Fair, Osaka, Japan, Air 80d.

1971
Japanese Locomotives. Postage 30, 35, 75d; Air 90d, 1r, 1r75.

REUNION

Indian Ocean
100 centimes = 1 franc

1949
No. 1056 *of France surcharged* **100F CFA**
330† 100f on 200f Railway bridge, Bordeaux 60·00 28·00

RHODESIA

Central Africa
1969 12 pence = 1 shilling
20 shillings = 1 pound
1970 100 cents = 1 dollar

1969

431 3d 2ft gauge steam locomotive, Beira–
    Salisbury line, 1899
432 9d Steam locomotive. 1904
433 1s6d Articulated steam locomotive, 1950
434 2s6d Diesel locomotive, 1955

                              Set of 4 16·00 9·50

1974

488 14c George Pauling (railway engineer) .. 1·00 1·50

RHODESIA AND NYASALAND

Central Africa
12 pence = 1 shilling
20 shillings = 1 pound

1959

24a† 9d Rhodesian Railways trains .... 2·50 1·75

RUANDA-URUNDI

Central Africa
100 centimes = 1 franc

1916

No. 75 of Belgian Congo overprinted **RUANDA**
6† 50c Railway bridge over the M'pozo ...... 18·00

No. 75 of Belgian Congo overprinted **URUNDI**
13† 50 Railway bridge over the M'pozo ...... 18·00

No. 75 of Belgian Congo overprinted **EST AFRICAIN**
ALLEMAND OCCUPATION BELGE DUITSCH OOST AFRIKA
BELGISCHE BEZETTING
20† 50c Railway bridge over the M'pozo ...... 5·50 4·00

1918

No. 83 of Belgian Congo overprinted **A.O.**
28† 50c + 50c Railway bridge over the
M'pozo .... 50 1·50

1922

No. 20 surcharged **5c**
32† 5c on 50c Railway bridge over the
M'pozo .... 35 1·50

STAMP MONTHLY
— finest and most informative magazine for all
collectors. Obtainable from your newsagent or by
postal subscription — details on request.

RUMANIA

South-east Europe
100 bani = 1 leu

1928

1107† 10le Cernavoda Bridge over the
Danube .... 3·75 75
1108† 20le Cernavoda Bridge over the
Danube .... 4·50 75

1939

1422 1le Railway locomotives of 1869 and
1939
1423 4le Steam train crossing railway bridge
1424 5le Steam train leaving station
1425 7le Steam train leaving station
1426 12le Diesel train crossing railway bridge
1427 15le Railway Headquarters and trams,
Bucharest
Set of 6 8·50 5·50

1945

1713† 36le + 164le Filimon Sarbu (saboteur)
and German train 70 80

1760† 80le Steam train on Cernavoda Bridge 60 60

1761† 80le Cernavoda Bridge 35 25

1762†   10le + 490le German electric train
      (perf) .... 1·40   1·50
1767†   10le + 490le German electric train
      (imperf) .... 1·40   1·50

1954†   2le + 2le Steam train 40   40

1947

1883†   1000le + 1000le Tracks and mine
      tunnel 25   30
1887†   3000le + 3000le Steam train 25   30

2006†   100le Steam train .... 4·00   3·25

1898†   12le Cernavoda Bridge 60   20
1899†   15le Tracks on dock, Constantza ...... 1·00   20
1901†   32le Tracks on dock, Constantza ...... 4·75   2·25
1902†   36le Cernavoda Bridge .... 4·00   1·25

2007†   1le + 1le Goods wagon on dock (black
      and green) 60   60
2010†   15le + 15le Steam train (black and red) 5·50   3·75
MS2011   As Nos. 2007 and 2010 (both in
      brown and red). Imperf (sheet contains two
      other designs) .... 24·00   25·00

1949

2033†   30le Steam locomotive .... 1·75   1·75

1906†   3le + 3le Steam train at petroleum
      refinery 20   20

1948

Nos. 1898/9 and 1901/2 overprinted **R.P.R.**

1939†   12le Cernavoda Bridge .... 2·00   30
1940†   15le Tracks on dock, Constantza ...... 2·00   40
1942†   32le Tracks on dock, Constantza ...... 8·50   3·75
1943†   36le Cernavoda Bridge .... 6·50   2·50

COLLECT BIRDS ON STAMPS

New second edition available at £8.50 (p. + p. £2) from:
Stanley Gibbons Publications Ltd, 5 Parkside,
Christchurch Road, Ringwood, Hants BH24 3SH.

2036†   11le Steam locomotive (perf or imperf)
2037†   20le Steam locomotive (perf or imperf)
                        Set of 2   2·00   2·25

1951

2125†	2le Mine trucks	30	15
2135†	50le Steam locomotive on dock (air)	5·00	3·50

1952
Nos. 2006, 2125 and 2135 surcharged

2159†	3b on 100le Steam train	4·00	3·00
2207†	35b on 2le Mine trucks	3·00	3·00
2217†	1le on 50le Steam locomotive on dock	8·50	4·50

No. 2033 surcharged **AERIANA 5 LEI** *and aeroplane*

2163	5le on 30le Steam locomotive	25·00	20·00

2229	55b Railwayman	3·00	30

1955

2385†	10b Model railway	60	8

1956

2439†	55b Lumber train	4·00	30

1957

2561†	55b Steam goods train on viaduct	75	25

1958

2601†	75b Goods wagons at factory	40	15

1959

2665†	40b Trams, Bucharest	1·75	25

1960

2732†	5b Diesel locomotive leaving tunnel	25	5
2741†	75b Cattle wagons	50	10
2744†	1le50 Goods wagons at iron works	75	10

1961

2835†	20b A. Saligny (engineer) and Saligny Bridge	25	8

2901† 40b Constantza Railway Station 60 15

1963

2992 1le75 Railway strikers, Grivitsa . . . . 1·75 30

3002† 1le55 Goods wagons, Hunedoara Metal
Works 75 15

3031† 40b Steam locomotive 60 15
3032† 55b Diesel freight locomotive 60 15

1966

3395† 1le55 "The Third Class Compartment"
(painting by Daumier) . . . . 5·00 60

**WHEN YOU BUY AN ALBUM LOOK
FOR THE NAME "STANLEY GIBBONS"**
It means Quality combined with Value for Money.

1967

3511† 20b Railway T.P.O. coach 40 5
3516† 60b Electric parcel trucks 40 8
3517† 1le Diesel train (23 × 29mm) 40 10
3528† 4le Electric train (29 × 23mm) . . . . 2·50 15

3531† 55b Canadian monorail train and globe 30 8

1969

3679 55b Trains of 1869 and 1969 . . . . 60 15

1971
As Nos. 3517 and 3528, but in smaller format
3842† 1le Diesel train (17 × 23mm) 45 5
3854† 4le Electric train (23 × 17mm) . . . . 1·50 5

1972

3902 55b Modern trains and symbol of
International Railway Union 70 15

3910† 1le35 Train on Saligny Bridge,
Cernavoda 55 10
3912† 2le75 Train on Prieteniei Bridge,
Giurgiu–Ruse . . . . 2·00 40

3913　55b North Railway Station, Bucharest,
　　　　1872 .... 70　15

1974

4076†　40b Loading mail train .... 40　5

1979

4515†　1le20 Friendship Bridge in coat of arms
　　　　of Giurgiu .... 20　5

4535　55b Locomotive No. 43 *Calugareni*
4536　1le Locomotive No. 458 *Orleans*
4537　1le50 Locomotive No. 1059
4538　2le15 Locomotive No.15021
4539　3le40 Locomotive No. 231085 "Pacific"
　　　　type
4540　4le80 Electric locomotive "060-EA"
　　　　　　　　　　　　　　 Set of 6　3·75　60
MS4541　10le Diesel locomotive .... 4·50　4·00

1982

4686　60b Entrance to Union Square
　　　　Underground Station, Bucharest
4687　2le40 Platform and train at Heroes'
　　　　Square Underground Station,
　　　　Bucharest
　　　　　　　　　　　　　　 Set of 2　90　30

1983

MS4830　10le "Orient Express" at Bucharest,
　　　　1883 .... 3·50　2·75

1985

4932†　2le Canal and railway bridge,
　　　　Cernavoda .... 60　25

4954†　3le Bucharest Underground train ...... 80　25

1987

5135　50b Class "L 45H" diesel shunter
5136　1le Class "LDE 125" diesel goods
　　　　locomotive
5137　2le Class "LDH 70" diesel goods
　　　　locomotive
5138　3le Class "LDE 2100" diesel locomotive
　　　　leaving tunnel
5139　4le Class "LDE 3000" diesel locomotive
5140　5le Class "LE 5100" electric locomotive
　　　　　　　　　　　　　　 Set of 6　3·00　50

1988

MS5179 Two sheets. 3le Bucharest Underground train in station; 3le "ICE" express electric train (sheets contain six other designs)

Set of 2 sheets   8·00   1·75

5206   2le + 1le Electric mail train   40   10

1989

5229†   50b Railway tracks, Tasca Bicaz
      Cement Factory   8   5
5230†   1le50 Railway bridge, Cernavoda   20   8
5232†   3le Underground train in station,
      Bucharest   40   10

RUSSIA

Eastern Europe and Northern Asia
100 kopeks = 1 rouble

1922

287†   20r + 5r Steam train leaving tunnel   30   1·50

1932

597†   20k Steam goods train, Magnitogorsk   ..   5·50   1·75

1933

608†   1k Steam goods train   ....   1·50   30

1934

643†   5k Steam goods train at steel furnace,
      Kuznetzk   ....   5·00   1·75
645†   20k Steam goods train   ....   8·50   2·75

670†   10k Steam train at factory (dated
      "1924–1934")   ....   2·25   2·00

1935

688   5k Excavating Moscow Underground
      Railway tunnel
689   10k Section of roadbed, escalator and
      station
690   15k Underground station and train
691   20k Underground train in station
                    Set of 4   30·00   25·00

1938

796†	50k Model train	4·50	60
797†	80k Model train	5·50	70

819	10k Mayakovsky Square Underground Station, Moscow
820	15k Sokol Terminus Underground Station, Moscow
821	20k Kiev Underground Station, Moscow
822	30k Dynamo Stadium Underground Station, Moscow
823	40k Underground train, Moscow
824	50k Revolution Square Underground Station, Moscow

Set of 6   15·00   5·00

1939

843†	80k Khimki River Station, Moscow	4·00	1·50
844†	1r Dynamo Underground Station, Moscow	8·50	1·75

878†	15k Incline railway, Kislovodsk	45	30

1941

945a†	20k Steam train on railway bridge over Moscow–Volga canal	1·75	70
946†	30k Steam locomotives	1·75	70
949†	1r Petroleum trucks at refinery	1·00	80

1942

996†	30k Guerillas attacking German train	85	80
997†	30k Goods wagon at munition factory	85	80

1002†	30k Steam goods train	1·50	45

1943

1006†	10k Steam train	80	15

1944

As No. 670, *but dated* "1924–1944"

1063†	60k Steam train at factory	1·25	20

1946

1215†	5k Steam goods train	25	5
1216†	10k Petroleum trucks at refinery	30	5
1217†	15k Coal trucks at coal mine	35	8
1219†	30k Ladle truck	60	25

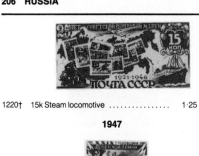

1220†   15k Steam locomotive ....   1·25   20

1947

1258†   20k Steam goods train (perf or imperf)   45   10

1280   30k Izmailovsky Underground Station, Moscow
1281   30k Power plant, Moscow Underground
1282   45k Falcon Underground Station, Moscow
1283   45k Stalinsky Underground Station, Moscow
1284   60k Kiev Underground Station, Moscow
1285   60k Mayakovsky Underground Station, Moscow

     Set of 6   5·25   1·50

1286†   5k Tram on Crimea Bridge, Moscow   50   10
1288†   30k Kiev Station, Moscow ....   1·25   25
1289†   30k Kazan Station, Moscow ....   1·25   25

1312†   50k Steam goods train on bridge (perf or imperf) ....   1·25   20
1315†   1r Steam goods train on bridge (perf or imperf) ....   2·25   35

1317†   15k Steam ladle train at foundry, Konstantinovka (perf or imperf)   40   12
1319†   30k Steam ladle train at foundry, Konstantinovka (perf or imperf) ......   1·00   20
1321†   30k Tractors on flat trucks (perf or imperf) ....   1·00   20
1326†   1r Tractors on flat trucks (perf or imperf) ....   2·75   75

1948

1340†   1r Coal trucks at metallurgical works and colliery ....   3·50   1·25

1361†   60k Steam train ....   20·00   10·00

1374†   15k Steam goods train ....   2·50   1·00
1376†   60k Steam goods train ....   6·50   1·75

1403†   30k Steam and electric locomotives ....   2·00   60
1404†   50k Steam and electric locomotives ....   3·50   1·00
1405†   60k Tram ....   3·00   1·50

1416   30k Coal mine locomotive
1417   60k Coal mine locomotive
1418   60k Oil wells and tanker train
1419   1r Oil wells and tanker train

     Set of 4   24·00   9·00

1951

1447† 40k Tram, Lenin St., Sverdlovsk 80 20

1949

1523 40k Steam train (perf or imperf)
1524 50k Steam train (perf or imperf)
Set of 2 2·50 35

1554 25k Electric tram
1555 40k Diesel train
1556 50k Steam train
1557 1r Diesel train
Set of 4 14·00 1·90

1950

1571† 40k Trams, Tashkent 65 20

1620 40k Kaluzhskaya Underground Station, Moscow
1621 40k Culture Park Underground Station, Moscow
1622 40k Taganskaya Underground Station, Moscow
1623 1r Kurskaya Underground Station, Moscow
1624 1r Paveletskaya Underground Station, Moscow
1625 1r Culture Park Underground Station, Moscow
1626 1r Taganskaya Underground Station, Moscow
Set of 7 12·00 2·40

1678† 40k Trams, Lenin Square, Sofia, Bulgaria .... 4·00 2·50

1952

1759† 40k Steam train .... 2·50 2·00

1791 40k Byelorussia Koltsevaya Underground Station, Moscow
1792 40k Botanical Gardens Underground Station, Moscow
1793 40k Novoslobodskaya Underground Station, Moscow
1794 40k Komsomolskaya Koltsevaya Underground Station, Moscow
Set of 4 6·25 70

1953

1814† 40k Leningrad Station (black on yellow) 1·25 80
1815† 40k Leningrad Station (brown on pink) 1·25 80

1955

1883   40k "Construction of Railway" (painting
        by Savitsky) .... 1·50   15

1957

2081†   40k Leningrad Station 50   15

2126†   40k Railway worker (perf or imperf) 50   10

2133†   40k Diesel and electric locomotives at
        factory 75   20

1958

2242†   60k Steam parcels train .... 1·50   25
2245†   1r Diesel locomotive and globe .... 1·40   40

COLLECT MAMMALS ON STAMPS

A Stanley Gibbons thematic catalogue on this popular
subject. Copies available at £7.50 (p. + p. £2) from:
Stanley Gibbons Publications Ltd, 5 Parkside,
Christchurch Road, Ringwood, Hants BH24 3SH.

2276†   40k Steam locomotive and tractors on
        flat trucks, Chelyabinsk 80   12
2278†   40k Ladle trucks at Zaporozhe foundry   80   12

2299†   60k Type "TE3" diesel locomotive ...... 3·00   50

1959

2380   40k Loading mail train
2381   60k Loading mail train
                              Set of 2   65   20

2406†   1r Steam train in Hibinsky Mountains .. 2·25   60

1960

2447†   40k Trams, Ordzhonikidze, North
        Ossetian Republic 90   20

1961

2624   4k Diesel train under Angara River
        Bridge, Irkutsk 30   10

2625   4k Diesel locomotive   45   10

2629†   4k Goods wagons at factory   40   5

2649†   3k Power workers and railway signal   35   15

1962

2737   4k Trams, Vinnitsa   20   5

2738   4k Electric locomotive   25   5

2773†   4k Electric train and diesel train on
bridge   55   12

1963

2898   4k Electric locomotive and mail van   30   5

1964

2963†   4k K. S. Zaslonov and sabotaged train   35   5

3008   6k Petroleum trucks   30   5

3040   6k Electric goods train   40   10

1965

3110†   6k Diesel railcar   40   5

3150†   4k V. Ivanov and armoured train   40   10

3167†	2k Ladle truck at steel works	10	5
3171†	10k Steam train	45	10
3172†	12k Electric train	50	10

| 3338† | 4k Electric train | 15 | 5 |
| 3340† | 4k Ladle truck | 15 | 5 |

3194†	2k Early steam locomotive and mail van	20	5
3196†	6k Diesel locomotive and mail van	55	5
3198†	16k Monorail at airport	1·25	15

| 3357† | 50k Mail van (ultramarine, blue and grey) | 2·75 | 50 |
| 3568† | 50k Mail van (blue) | 3·00 | 65 |

3213	6k Oktyabrskaya Underground Station, Moscow		
3214	6k Leninsky Prospekt Underground Station, Moscow		
3215	6k Moskovian Gate Underground Station, Leningrad		
3216	6k Bolshevik Factory Underground Station, Kiev		
	Set of 4	1·40	30

1966

Учредительная конференция
Всесоюзного общества
филателистов. 1966

No. 3198 overprinted

| 3265 | 16k Monorail at airport | 1·75 | 50 |

| 3269† | 4k Electric train | 45 | 5 |

STAMP MONTHLY
— finest and most informative magazine for all collectors. Obtainable from your newsagent or by postal subscription — details on request.

1967

| 3479† | 4k Steam train at factory (in painting "Dawn of the Five-Year Plan" by Romas) | 35 | 10 |

| 3495† | 6k Electric locomotive | 25 | 5 |

| 3503† | 4k Goods wagon | 15 | 5 |
| 3506† | 4k Electric train on bridge | 15 | 5 |

3516† 16k Train (in painting "Moscow Suburb in February" by Nissky) .... 1·50 40

1968

3572† 6k Electric locomotive and mail van 15 8

3590† 3k Steam construction train 10 5

3634 4k Electric train, map and emblem
3635 10k Track-laying train
Set of 2 60 15

1969

3665 4k Petroleum truck at refinery 10 5

3711 4k Electric locomotive, Donetsk 10 5

1970

3796† 10k Boy and toy electric train 25 10

3803† 4k Electric goods train 10 5

1971

3939† 6k Early steam locomotive 25 5
3940† 6k Diesel train 25 5

3960† 4k Diesel railcar 10 5

3979† 4k Ladle trucks 15 5

1972

4052† 4k Mine train, Yakut Republic 20 5

1973

4175† 4k Diesel locomotive, Buriat
Autonomous Republic 15 5

1974

4291 4k Modern passenger coach from
Egorov Wagon Works, Leningrad 25 5

4333† 4k Diesel locomotive 15 5

COLLECT SHIPS ON STAMPS
The largest Stanley Gibbons thematic catalogue to date
– available at £10.95 (p. + p. £2) from:
Stanley Gibbons Publications Ltd, 5 Parkside,
Christchurch Road, Ringwood, Hants BH24 3SH.

1975

4425† 10k "Excavating the Metro Tunnel"
(painting by I. I. Lansere) 60 10

4452† 4k Track-laying machine and
Baikal–Amur Railway 25 5

1976

4509 4k Electric goods train on bridge,
Dnepropetrovsk 8 5

4523 4k Electric train and bridge 25 5

4559† 4k Diesel train and railway signalman 12 5

4716† 4k Electric locomotive 12 5

1978

4936† 3k Girl in compartment (from painting
"Into Service" by K. K. Kostandi) 15 5
4937† 4k Lenin on footplate (from painting "To
Petrograd" by A. M. Lopukhov) 30 10

4757 1k First Russian locomotive and its
designers
4758 2k "D series" steam freight train, 1845
4759 3k First passenger locomotive, 1845
4760 16k "GV series" locomotive, 1863–67
4761 20k "BV series" passenger locomotive,
1863–67

Set of 5 2·25 45

1980

4991† 1r + 50k Underground Railway bridge
over Dnieper, Kiev .... 2·50 1·75

4781† 4k Diesel locomotive 20 5

1979

5061† 5k Mail van 10 5

4861 2k "A" series passenger locomotive
4862 3k "Shch" series locomotive
4863 4k "L-Putilov" series locomotive
4864 6k "Su" series locomotive
4865 15k "L" series locomotive

Set of 5 1·25 35

4901 4k Lenin Square Underground Station,
Tashkent 20 5

5079 6k Luzhniki Underground Railway
bridge, Moscow 25 5

1981

5093†	4k Baikal–Amur Railway train and map	20	5
5098†	4k Diesel coal train	20	5

5151†	4k Diesel train	15	5

5163	4k Diesel goods train	25	5

5188†	6k 19th-century horse-drawn tram	20	8
5192†	32k Electric tram, 1912	90	40

1982

5194	10k Diesel railcar on bridge, Kiev	25	12

5229	4k "VL-80T" electric locomotive	
5230	6k "TEP-75" diesel locomotive	
5231	10k "TEM-7" diesel locomotive	
5232	15k "VL-82M" electric locomotive	
5233	32k "EP-200" electric locomotive	
	Set of 5	2·75	85

1983

5325	4k Diesel locomotive	10	5

1984

5456	5k Diesel locomotive	12	5

5500	5k Medal, workers, diesel train and map of Baikal–Amur Railway	12	5

MS5509	50k Diesel train	1·60	50

1985

5564	10k "VL80R" electric locomotive	
5565	10k Coal wagon	
5566	10k Oil tanker wagon	
5567	10k Goods wagon	
5568	10k Refrigerated wagon	
5569	10k "TEM 2" diesel locomotive	
5570	10k "Sv" passenger coach	
5571	10k Mail van	
	Set of 8	2·50	70

1986

5690   15k Murkan–Klaipeda railway ferry   30   15

5697   4k Class "3u" steam locomotive No.
        EU684-37 (1929), Slavyansk
5698   5k Class "FD" steam locomotive No.
        21-3000 (1941), Novosibirsk
5699   10k Class "Ov" steam locomotive No.
        5109 (1907), Volgograd
5700   20k Class "SO" steam locomotive No.
        17-1613 (1944), Dnepropetrovsk
5701   30k Class "FDp" steam locomotive No.
        20-578 (1941), Kiev
                                    Set of 5   1·60   60

1987

5789†   30k 19th-century steam locomotive and
         mail vans   60   30

EXPRESS STAMPS

1932

E590†   80k Steam express locomotive . . . .   30·00   12·00

RWANDA

Central Africa
100 centimes = 1 franc

1976

756†   8f Steam train   60   12

1984

1186†   20c Diesel train   5   5

SAAR

Western Europe
1920 100 pfennig = 1 mark
1921 100 centimes = 1 franc

1920

Nos. 114/15 of Germany overprinted **SAARGEBIET**
46†   1m25 Tram, General Post Office, Berlin . .   2·50   1·25
47†   1m50 Tram, General Post Office, Berlin . .   2·50   1·25

1921

55†   20pf Steam coal train at Reden Mine,
       Landsweiler   50   15
59†   50pf Signal gantry, Saarbrucken . . . .   1·40   1·50

Nos. 55 and 59 surcharged in centimes
70†   3c on 20pf Steam coal train at Reden
       Mine, Landsweiler   40   15
74†   20c on 50pf Signal gantry, Saarbrucken   70   15

1926

118†	1f50 Goods wagons at Burbach steelworks	6·00	15
119†	2f Goods wagons at Burbach steelworks	6·00	25
120†	3f Goods wagons at Burbach steelworks	14·00	60
121†	5f Goods wagons at Burbach steelworks	16·00	5·50

1934

Nos. 118/21 overprinted **VOLKSABSTIMMUNG 1935**

187†	1f50 Goods wagons at Burbach steelworks	3·00	2·50
188†	2f Goods wagons at Burbach steelworks	4·50	4·25
189†	3f Goods wagons at Burbach steelworks	7·50	5·50
190†	5f Goods wagons at Burbach steelworks	32·00	25·00

1949

268†	5f Steam train at slag heap	2·00	10
269†	6f Mine trucks at colliery	13·00	60
273†	15f Mine trucks at colliery	8·50	15
277†	30f Steam train, St. Arnual	16·00	45
279†	60f Train at Reden Mine, Landsweiler	5·50	1·50

1957

As No. 1192 of Germany (West Germany), but inscribed "SAARLAND"

404†	30f + 10f Mine truck	45	70

1958

As No. 1203 of Germany (West Germany), but inscribed "SAARLAND"

429	12f Rudolf Diesel (engineer) and first oil engine	15	25

OFFICIAL STAMPS

1922

No. 119 overprinted **DIENSTMARKE**

O127†	2f Goods wagons at Burbach steelworks	3·25	55

ST. HELENA

South Atlantic
12 pence = 1 shilling
20 shillings = 1 pound

1949

As No. 114 of Antigua

145†	3d Silhouette of steam locomotive	60	30

ST. KITTS

West Indies
100 cents = 1 dollar

1987

232†	75c Front of sugar cane locomotive	35	40
233†	75c Locomotive cab and tender	35	40
234†	75c Sugar cane wagons and boy on bicycle	35	40
235†	75c Sugar cane wagons and tractor	35	40
236†	75c Loading sugar cane wagon	35	40

ST. KITTS-NEVIS

West Indies
12 pence = 1 shilling
20 shillings = 1 pound

1949

As No. 114 of Antigua

82†	2½d Silhouette of steam locomotive	15	10

ST. LUCIA

West Indies
100 cents = 1 dollar

1949

As No. 114 of Antigua

160†	5c Silhouette of steam locomotive	15	15

1983

651/652	35c Locomotive *Duke of Sutherland*, Great Britain (1930)	
653/654	35c Locomotive *City of Glasgow*, Great Britain (1940)	
655/656	50c Locomotive *Lord Nelson*, Great Britain (1926)	
657/658	50c Locomotive *Leeds United*, Great Britain (1928)	
659/660	$1 Locomotive *Bodmin*, Great Britain (1945)	

661/662 $1 Locomotive *Eton*, Great Britain
(1930)
663/664 Locomotive *Flying Scotsman*, Great
Britain (1923)
665/666 $2 Locomotive *Rocket*, Great Britain
(1829)
Set of 16   7·75   7·00
The first stamp in each pair shows technical drawings and the
second the locomotive at work.

1984

SAINT LUCIA

715/716 1c Locomotive *Taw*, Great Britain (1897)
717/718 15c "Crocodile 1.C.C.1." type
locomotive, Switzerland (1920)
719/720 50c Locomotive *The Countess*, Great
Britain (1903)
721/722 75c Class "GE 6/6 C.C." electric
locomotive, Switzerland (1921)
723/724 $1 Class "P8", Germany (1906)
725/726 $2 Locomotive *Der Adler*, Germany
(1835)
Set of 12   6·50   6·00
The first stamp in each pair shows technical drawings and the
second the locomotive at work.

1985

SAINT LUCIA

761/762 5c Class "C53" locomotive, Japan
(1928)
763/764 15c Class "Heavy L" locomotive, India
(1885)
765/766 35c Class "B18¼" locomotive, Australia
(1926)
767/768 60c Locomotive *Owain Glyndwr*, Great
Britain (1923)
769/770 75c Locomotive *Lion*, Great Britain
(1838)
771/772 $1 Coal type locomotive, Great Britain
(1873)
773/774 $2 Class "Q6" locomotive No. 2238,
Great Britain (1921)
775/776 $2.50 Class "H" locomotive, Great
Britain (1920)
Set of 16   10·00   8·50
The first stamp in each pair shows technical drawings and the
second the locomotive at work.

ALBUM LISTS

Write for our latest list of albums and accessories. This
will be sent on request.

SAINT LUCIA

824/825 10c Tank locomotive No. 28, Great
Britain (1897)
826/827 30c Class "M" locomotive No. 1621,
Great Britain (1893)
828/829 75c Class "Dunalastair" locomotive,
Great Britain (1896)
830/831 $2.50 "Big Bertha" type locomotive No.
2290, Great Britain (1919)
Set of 8   3·75   3·75
The first stamp in each pair shows technical drawings and the
second the locomotive at work.

1986

SAINT LUCIA

858/859 5c Rack locomotive *Tip Top*, U.S.A.
(1983)
860/861 15c Electric locomotive *Stephenson*,
Great Britain (1975)
862/863 30c Class "D" locomotive No. 737,
Great Britain (1901)
864/865 60c Class "2-CO-2" locomotive No. 13,
Great Britain (1922)
866/867 75c Electric locomotive *Electra*, Great
Britain (1954)
868/869 $1 Locomotive *City of Newcastle*, Great
Britain (1922)
870/871 $2.25 Von Kruckenburg propeller-driven
railcar, Germany (1930)
872/873 $3 Locomotive No. 860, Japan (1893)
Set of 16   9·50   9·50
The first stamp in each pair shows technical drawings and the
second the locomotive at work.

ST. THOMAS AND PRINCE ISLANDS

In Atlantic off West Africa
100 cents = 1 dobra

Appendix

The following stamps have either been isssued in excess of
postal needs, or have not been made available to the public in
reasonable quantities at face value. Miniature sheets, imperforate
stamps, etc. are excluded from this section.

1978

Universal Postal Union Centenary. 15d × 2 (monorail and steam
train)

ST. VINCENT

West Indies
100 cents = 1 dollar

1949

As No. 114 of Antigua
178† 5c Silhouette of steam locomotive 15 15

1983

744/745 10c Locomotive *King Henry VIII*, Great
Britain (1927)
746/747 10c Diesel locomotive *Royal Scots
Greys*, Great Britain (1961)
748/749 25c Locomotive *Hagley Hall*, Great
Britain (1928)
750/751 50c Locomotive *Sir Lancelot*, Great
Britain (1926)
752/753 60c Class "B12" locomotive, Great
Britain (1912)
754/755 75c Deeley "Compound type"
locomotive, Great Britain (1902)
756/757 $2.50 Locomotive *Cheshire*, Great
Britain (1927)
758/759 $3 Bulleid "Austerity Class Q1"
locomotive, Great Britain (1942)
Set of 16 4·75 4·75
The first stamp in each pair shows technical drawings and the
second the locomotive at work.

1984

792/793 1c Class "Liberation" locomotive,
France (1945)
794/795 2c Diesel locomotive *Dreadnought*,
Great Britain (1967)
796/797 3c Locomotive No. 242A1, France
(1946)
798/799 50c Class "Dean Goods" locomotive,
Great Britain (1883)
800/801 75c Hetton Colliery locomotive No. 1,
Great Britain (1822)
802/803 $1 Locomotive *Penydarren*, Great
Britain (1804)
804/805 $2 Locomotive *Novelty*, Great Britain
(1829)
806/807 $3 Class "44" locomotive, Germany
(1925)
Set of 16 5·00 5·00
The first stamp in each pair shows technical drawings and the
second the locomotive at work.

WHEN YOU BUY AN ALBUM LOOK FOR THE NAME "STANLEY GIBBONS"
It means Quality combined with Value for Money.

834/835 5c Class "20" locomotive, Rhodesia
(1954)
836/837 40c Locomotive *Southern Maid*, Great
Britain (1928)
838/839 75c Locomotive *Prince of Wales*, Great
Britain (1911)
840/841 $2.50 Class "05" locomotive, Germany
(1935)
Set of 8 4·50 5·25
The first stamp in each pair shows technical drawings and the
second the locomotive at work.

1985

872/873 1c Locomotive *Glen Douglas*, Great
Britain (1913)
874/875 10c Locomotive *Fenchurch*, Great
Britain (1872)
876/877 40c Class "Stirling Single" locomotive
No. 1, Great Britain (1870)
878/879 60c Locomotive No. 158A, Great Britain
(1866)
880/881 $1 Class "Jones Goods" locomotive No.
103, Great Britain (1893)
882/883 $2.50 Locomotive *The Great Bear*,
Great Britain (1908)
Set of 12 4·50 5·00
The first stamp in each pair shows technical drawings and the
second the locomotive at work.

893/894 5c Tank locomotive *Loch*, Great Britain
(1874)
895/896 30c Class "47XX" locomotive, Great
Britain (1919)
897/898 60c Class "121" locomotive, France
(1876)
899/900 75c Class "24" locomotive, Germany
(1927)
901/902 $1 Tank locomotive No. 1008, Great
Britain (1889)
903/904 $2.50 Class "PS-4" locomotive, U.S.A.
(1926)
Set of 12 5·00 5·50
The first stamp in each pair shows technical drawings and the
second the locomotive at work.

1986

1001/1002 30c Class "ED41 BZZB" rack and
adhesion locomotive, Japan
(1926)
1003/1004 50c Locomotive *The Judge*,
Chicago Railroad Exposition,
U.S.A. (1883)
1005/1006 $1 Class "E60C" electric
locomotive, U.S.A. (1973)
1007/1008 $3 Class "SD40-2" diesel
locomotive, U.S.A. (1972)
Set of 8   4·75   4·75
The first stamp in each pair shows technical drawings and the
second the locomotive at work.

1988

1159 1c Mickey Mouse in parcels van
1160 2c Mordie and Ferdie on low-loader
wagon
1161 3c Wagon full of Christmas trees
1162 4c Donald Duck and nephews in
reindeer truck
1163 5c Donald and Daisy Duck in restaurant
car
1164 10c Disney characters in railway
carriage
1165 $5 Mickey Mouse driving steam
locomotive
1166 $6 Father Christmas in guard's van
Set of 8   4·50   4·75
MS1167 Two sheets (b) $5 American steam
locomotive painted on carousel (other stamp
shows Disney characters)
Set of 2 sheets   4·25   4·50

1989

1171† 5c Mickey Mouse with diamond mine
truck 5   5

SAMOA

West Pacific
100 sene = 1 tala

1985

MS704† $2 Queen Elizabeth II and Queen
Mother arriving at Tattenham Corner Station   1·25   1·50

1988

780† 70s Monorail train, "Expo 88" World Fair,
Brisbane 35   40

SAN MARINO

Southern Europe
100 centesimi = 1 lira

1932

179 20c Electric train at San Marino Railway
Station
180 50c Electric train at San Marino Railway
Station
181 1li25 Electric train at San Marino Railway
Station
182 5li Electric train at San Marino Railway
Station
Set of 4   32·00   32·00

COLLECT BIRDS ON STAMPS
New second edition available at £8.50 (p. + p. £2) from:
Stanley Gibbons Publications Ltd, 5 Parkside,
Christchurch Road, Ringwood, Hants BH24 3SH.

1951

420† 75li Train under Archway of Murata
Nuova .... 9·00 6·00

1955

491† 5li Train under Archway of Murata Nuova 5 15
494† 25li Train under Archway of Murata
Nuova 10 10
797† 40li Train under Archway of Murata
Nuova 10 10

1956

Design as No. 491, but larger, 36½ × 27mm and inscribed
"CONGRESSO INTERNAZ PERITI FILATELICI SAN MARINO
SALSO-MAGGIORE 6-8 OTTOBRE 1956"
520† 80li Train under Archway of Murata
Nuova .... 4·00 2·50

1964

755 1li Murray Blenkinsop locomotive (1812)
756 2li Locomotive *Puffing Billy* (1813)
757 3li Locomotive *Locomotion No. 1* (1825)
758 4li Locomotive *Rocket* (1829)
759 5li Locomotive *Lion* (1838)
760 15li Locomotive *Bayard* (1839)
761 20li Crampton type locomotive (1849)
762 50li Locomotive *Little England* (1851)
763 90li Locomotive *Spitfire* (c1860)
764 110li Locomotive *Rogers* (c1865)
Set of 10 1·40 1·40

1973

961† 300li Brooklyn Bridge, New York 40 40

1981

1161† 300li St. Charles Square Underground
Station, Vienna 60 60

1984

1231† 2000li Flinders Street Station and
railway bridge, Melbourne .... 2·75 2·75

1988

1316† 600li Maglev Monorail "Bullet" train 60 50

SARAWAK

South-east Asia
100 cents = 1 dollar

1949

As No. 114 of Antigua
167† 8c Silhouette of steam locomotive 50 50

SAUDI ARABIA

Arabia
1916 40 paras = 1 piastre
1929 110 guerche = 1 riyal
1960 100 halalah = 1 riyal

Hejaz

1916

11† 1pa Stucco work over entrance to Cairo
Railway Station .... 2·00   50

1921

No. 11 overprinted in Arabic without frame
21† 1pa Stucco work over entrance to Cairo
Railway Station .... 20·00 10·00

No. 21 further surcharged with new values in Arabic
29 ½pi on 1pa Stucco work over entrance to
Cairo Railway Station .... £180 60·00
30 1pi on 1pa Stucco work over entrance to
Cairo Railway Station .... £180 60·00

1922

No. 11 overprinted in Arabic with frame
31† 1pa Stucco work over entrance to Cairo
Railway Station .... 3·00   1·00

No. 31 further surcharged with new values as Nos. 29/30
37 ½pi on 1pa Stucco work over entrance to
Cairo Railway Station .... 15·00 15·00
38 1pi on 1pa stucco work over entrance to
Cairo Railway Station .... 4·00   25

1924

Nos. 11 and 31 overprinted in Arabic
66† 1pa Stucco work over entrance to Cairo
Railway Station (No. 11) .... 15·00   6·00
77† 1pa Stucco work over entrance to Cairo
Railway Station (No. 31) .... £100 50·00

No. 77 further surcharged with new values in Arabic as Nos. 29/30
84 ½pi on 1pa Stucco work over entrance to
Cairo Railway Station .... £120 50·00
85 1pi on 1pa Stucco work over entrance to
Cairo Railway Station .... £100 45·00

Nejd

1925
Turkish Railway Tax stamps overprinted in Arabic
195 1pi Steam locomotive
196 2pi Steam locomotive
197 3pi Steam locomotive

Set of 3 42·00 42·00

Turkish Railway Tax stamp overprinted twice in Arabic
214 3pi Steam locomotive .... £175 60·00

Turkish Railway Tax stamps overprinted in Arabic
218b 1pi Steam locomotive
219 2pi Steam locomotive
220 3pi Steam locomotive
221 5pi Steam locomotive

Set of 4 60·00 26·00

Turkish Railway Tax stamps surcharged in Arabic
244 1pi on 10pi Steam locomotive
245 2pi on 50pi Steam locomotive
246 3pi on 100pi Steam locomotive
247 4pi on 500pi Steam locomotive
248 5pi on 1000pi Steam locomotive

Set of 5 £250 £160

Turkish Railway Tax stamps surcharged in Arabic
249 1pi on 10pi Steam locomotive
250 2pi on 50pi Steam locomotive
251 3pi on 100pi Steam locomotive
252 4pi on 500pi Steam locomotive
253 5pi on 1000pi Steam locomotive

Set of 5 £250 £160

POSTAGE DUE STAMPS

1925

Nos. 218b/19 and 221 further overprinted in Arabic
D232† 1pi Steam locomotive . . . . 15·00
D233† 2pi Steam locomotive . . . . 15·00
D236† 5pi Steam locomotive . . . . 25·00

Saudi Arabia

1952

372 ½g Diesel goods train on Dammam–
       Riyadh Railway
373 1g Diesel goods train on
       Dammam–Riyadh Railway
374 3g Diesel goods train on
       Dammam–Riyadh Railway
375 10g Diesel goods train on
       Dammam–Riyadh Railway
376 20g Diesel goods train on
       Dammam–Riyadh Railway

Set of 5 £110 32·00

1977

1201 20h Diesel train and route map of
        Dammam–Riyadh Railway . . . . 10·00 1·50

SELANGOR
South-east Asia
100 cents = 1 dollar

1949
As No. 114 *of Antigua*
111† 10c Silhouette of steam locomotive 15 5

1957

120† 8c Steam train, East Coast Railway . . . . . . 1·10 25

1961

133† 8c Steam train, East Coast Railway 60 70

SENEGAL
West Africa
100 centimes = 1 franc

1906
As Nos. 18/22 *of Dahomey*
33† 1c General Faidherbe (builder of
       Dakar–St Louis Railway) 70 30
34† 2c General Faidherbe (builder of
       Dakar–St Louis Railway)(name in red) 40 40
34a† 2c General Faidherbe (builder of
       Dakar–St Louis Railway) (name in
       blue) 80 80
35† 4c General Faidherbe (builder of
       Dakar–St Louis Railway) 60 60
36† 5c General Faidherbe (builder of
       Dakar–St Louis Railway) . . . . 1·50 30
37† 10c General Faidherbe (builder of
       Dakar–St Louis Railway) . . . . 4·50 30
38† 15c General Faidherbe (builder of
       Dakar–St Louis Railway) . . . . 3·00 1·75

1964

281† 85f Mine trucks on mineral wharf, Dakar 1·10 90

1974

559 100f Diesel locomotive .... 1·00 40

SERBIA

South-east Europe
100 paras = 1 dinar

1943

G84† 9d Railway van .... 75 1·00

SEYCHELLES

Indian Ocean
100 cents = 1 rupee

1949

As No. 114 of Antigua
154† 18c Silhouette of steam locomotive 15 15

1976

388† 1r50 Steam train, Transcontinental
Railroad, U.S.A. (1869) 60 35

1989

754† 10r "The White Train" (Red Cross
hospital train), South Africa,
1899–1902 .... 2·00 2·10

SHANGHAI

East Asia
100 cents = 1 dollar

1893

176 2c Winged railway wheel 35 45

SHARJAH

Arabia
1965 100 naye paise = 1 rupee
1966 100 dirhams = 1 riyal

1965

125† 1r Steam train .... 1·75 80
126† 1r Diesel train .... 1·75 80

Appendix
The following stamps have either been issued in excess of
postal needs, or have not been made available to the public in
reasonable quantities at face value. Miniature sheets, imperforate
stamps, etc. are excluded from this section.

1971

Post Day. Trains. Postage 1, 2, 3, 4, 5d: Air 25, 50, 60d, 1, 2r.

SIERRA LEONE

West Africa
1949 12 pence = 1 shilling
20 shillings = 1 pound
1964 100 cents = 1 leone

1949

As No. 114 of Antigua
205† 1½d Silhouette of steam locomotive 15 10

1956

215† 4d Ore truck, Marampa .... 1·00 25
219† 2s6d Steam train on Orugu Bridge ...... 4·00 70

1963

No. 219 *overprinted* **2nd Year Independence Progress Development 1963 AIRMAIL**

265† 2s6d Steam train on Orugu Bridge 40 15

1986

927† 40c Tram, Times Square, New York, 1905 .... 5 8

941 50c Chicago–Milwaukee "Hiawatha Express"
942 2le Rock Island Line "The Rocket"
943 4le Rio Grande "Prospector"
944 7l Southern Pacific "Daylight Express"
                    Set of 4 2·50 2·50
MS945 12le Pennsylvania "Broadway Limited" 1·75 1·90

1987

MS1067† 100le "Rhinegold Express" (first electric express) .... 3·00 3·25

1094† 50le Sydney Harbour Bridge .... 1·50 1·60

COLLECT MAMMALS ON STAMPS

A Stanley Gibbons thematic catalogue on this popular subject. Copies available at £7.50 (p. + p. £2) from: Stanley Gibbons Publications Ltd, 5 Parkside, Christchurch Road, Ringwood, Hants BH24 3SH.

1105† 2le Mickey Mouse, Goofy and Chip n'Dale on Western River Railroad train, Tokyo Disneyland 5 5
1107† 10le Mickey Mouse, Goofy and children aboard Big Thunder Mountain train, Tokyo Disneyland 30 35

SINGAPORE

South-east Asia
100 cents = 1 dollar

1949

As No. 114 *of Antigua*
33† 10c Silhouette of steam locomotive 75 5

1988

572 10c Mass Rapid Transit System route map
573 50c Train on elevated section
574 $1 Train in tunnel
                    Set of 3 80 95

SINKIANG

See under China

SLOVAKIA

Central Europe
100 haleru = 1 koruna

1943

109 70h Route map of Strazke–Presov Railway and Presov Church
110 80h Steam locomotive and route map
111 1k30 Railway tunnel and route map
112 2k Railway viaduct and route map
                    Set of 4 3·50 5·00

SLOVENIA

South-east Europe
100 centesimi = 1 lira

1945

120† 20c Railway viaduct, Borovnice 50 75

SOLOMON ISLANDS

Pacific Ocean
12 pence = 1 shilling
20 shillings = 1 pound

1949

As No. 114 of Antigua
77† 2d Silhouette of steam locomotive 75 30

SOMALILAND PROTECTORATE

East Africa
12 pies = 1 anna
16 annas = 1 rupee

1949

As No. 114 of Antigua
121† 1a on 10c Silhouette of steam locomotive ·12 12

SOUTH AFRICA

South Africa
1960 12 pence = 1 shilling
20 shillings = 1 pound
1961 100 cents = 1 rand

1960

183 1s3d Locomotives of 1860 and 1960 .... 1·50 30

1973

326† 4c Electric train 20 5

1978

441 15c Steel rail 20 20

442 15c Railway lines, Richards Bay
443 15c Railway lines, Saldanhabaai
                                    Set of 2 70 1·40

1983

541 10c Class "S2" light shunting locomotive
542 20c Class "16E" express locomotive
543 25c Class "6H" locomotive
544 40c Class "15F" main-line locomotive
                                    Set of 4 1·75 1·90

1984

564† 30c Electric ore train on Mfolozi Railway
      Bridge 65 55

SOUTH KOREA

See under Korea

SOUTH VIETNAM

See under Vietnam

SOUTH WEST AFRICA

Southern Africa
1937 12 pence = 1 shilling
20 shillings = 1 pound
1961 100 cents = 1 rand

1937

96   1½d Steam mail train .... 4·50   1·40
No. 96 exists inscribed in either English or Afrikaans. The prices quoted are for one of each in a horizontal pair.

1984

424†   20c Swakopmund Railway Station 30   25

1985

446†   50c Windhoek Railway Station 50   55

447   12c Zwilling narrow-gauge steam
        locomotive
448   25c Feldspur narrow-gauge side-tank
        locomotive
449   30c Jung and Henschel narrow-gauge
        side-tank locomotive
450   50c Henschel Hd narrow-gauge
        locomotive
                            Set of 4   1·40   95

OFFICIAL STAMPS

1938

No. 96 overprinted alternately **OFFICIAL** or **OFFISIEEL**
O20†   1½d Steam mail train .... 10·00 15·00
Prices quoted are for one of each in horizontal pair.

SOUTHERN CAMEROONS

West Africa
12 pence =1 shilling
20 shillings = 1 pound

1960

Nos. 72a and 73 of Nigeria overprinted **CAMEROONS U.K.T.T.**
4†   2d Mine trucks at tin mine 5   15
5†   3d Steam train and Niger River railway
        Bridge, Jebba 15   5

SOUTHERN RHODESIA

Central Africa
12 pence = 1 shilling
20 shillings = 1 pound

1937

36   1d Steam train on Victoria Falls Bridge
37   2d Steam train on Victoria Falls Bridge
38   3d Steam train on Victoria Falls Bridge
39   6d Steam train on Victoria Falls Bridge
                            Set of 4   5·50   7·00

1940

58†   4d Victoria Falls Bridge 70   70

1953

75†   1s Steam train on bridge .... 2·50   60

83†   4½d Victoria Falls Bridge 70   1·00

SPAIN

South-west Europe
100 centimos = 1 peseta

1930

534 1c Steam locomotive
535 2c Steam locomotive
536 5c Steam locomotive
537 10c Steam locomotive
538 15c Steam locomotive
539 20c Steam locomotive
540 25c Steam locomotive
541 30c Steam locomotive
542 40c Steam locomotive
543 50c Steam locomotive
544 1p Steam locomotive
545 4p Steam locomotive
546 10p Steam locomotive

547 5c Steam locomotive emblem of Int.
   Railway Congress, Madrid (air)
548 10c Steam locomotive emblem of Int.
   Railway Congress, Madrid
549 25c Steam locomotive emblem of Int.
   Railway Congress, Madrid
550 50c Steam locomotive emblem of Int.
   Railway Congress, Madrid
551 1p Steam locomotive emblem of Int.
   Railway Congress, Madrid
552 4p Steam locomotive emblem of Int.
   Railway Congress, Madrid
                    Set of 19   £425   £425

1936

802† 2c Tram outside Press Association
   Building, Madrid   15   15
804† 10c Tram outside Press Association
   Building, Madrid   15   15
807† 25c Tram outside Press Association
   Building, Madrid   15   15
811† 60c Tram outside Press Association
   Building, Madrid   50   30

1948

1106 50c Marquis of Salamanca (builder of
   first Spanish railway)
1107 5p Steam train on Garganta de
   Pancorbo Viaduct
1108 2p Diesel train and signal (air)
                    Set of 3   4·50   1·50

1953

1230† 50p Torres Quevedo (engineer and
   inventor) . . . .   9·50   1·25

1958

1295 15c Talgo Express and Escorial
1296 60c Diesel train on viaduct,
   Despenaperros
1297 80c Steam locomotive and Castillo de la
   Mota
1298 1p Talgo Express and Escorial
1299 2p Diesel train on viaduct,
   Despenaperros
1300 3p Steam locomotive and Castillo de la
   Mota
                    Set of 6   4·50   1·60

1964

1645† 2p Steam locomotive   15   5

1970

2032 2p Spanish 12c stamp of 1860 and
railway cachet 15 10

1974

2231 2p M. Biada (construction engineer) and
early locomotive of Barcelona–Mataro
Railway 20 10

1976

2375† 3p Railway mail-sorting van 55 5

1978

2528 5p Steam train and U.P.U. emblem 25 10

1980

2606† 3p Electric train 5 5
2608† 5p Underground train 5 5

1982

2690 9p Modern locomotive and storks
2691 14p Steam locomotive *Antigua*
2962 33p Steam locomotive *Montana* (wrongly
inscribed "Santa Fe")
Set of 3 1·10 20

1985

2839 17p Steam train, Asturias 40 12

1988

2961† 20p *La Junta* (first Cuban locomotive),
1837 .... 20 5

EXPRESS LETTER STAMPS

1930

E553 20c Electric locomotive .... 75·00 85·00

COLLECT SHIPS ON STAMPS

The largest Stanley Gibbons thematic catalogue to date
– available at £10.95 (p. + p. £2) from:
Stanley Gibbons Publications Ltd, 5 Parkside,
Christchurch Road, Ringwood, Hants BH24 3SH.

SPANISH MOROCCO

North Africa
100 centimos = 1 peseta

1948

307†	2c Steam goods train	5	5
316†	2p50 Steam goods train	7·50	7·50

1950

350†	10p Steam mail train	11·50	9·25

SRI LANKA

Indian Ocean
100 cents = 1 rupee

1983

821†	2r Steam train	20	25

1986

924	1r "Viceroy Special" Train, Colombo–Kandy line	30	30

1988

1041	75c Diesel locomotive		
1042	5r75 Diesel locomotive		
	Set of 2	25	30

SUDAN

North-east Africa
1000 milliemes = 100 piastres = 1 pound

1950

115†	2p Blue Nile Railway Bridge, Khartoum	1·75	10

OFFICIAL STAMPS

1950

No. 115 *overprinted* **S.G.**

O59†	2p Blue Nile Railway Bridge, Khartoum	3·50	90

SURINAM

South America
100 cents = 1 gulden

1945

No. 321 *surcharged* **5 CENT VOOR HET NATIONAL STEUNFONDS**

307†	7½c + 5c Sugar-cane train	7·00	8·00

313†	1c Goods wagon at bauxite mine, Moengo	50	50
319†	5c Mine truck at gold mine	1·25	45
321†	7½c Sugar-cane train	2·75	75

1950

No. 321 surcharged **1 Cent**

383 1c on 7½c Sugar-cane train . . . . 1·00 1·60

1965

563† 10c Diesel locomotive and side-dump
     trucks, Moengo bauxite mine 25 25

1973

764† 30c Diesel mail train 60 60

1978

MS929 60c Diesel locomotive (sheet also
     contains 20c and 95c values) . . . . 2·75 2·75

1982

1091† 100c Diesel locomotive and sugar-cane
     trucks . . . . 1·10 1·10

1985

1236 5c Sugar-cane train (on No. 321)
1237 5c Steamlined steam locomotive (on
     Monaco No. D483)
1238 10c Steam locomotive *Dam*

1239 10c Modern electric locomotive and
     carriage unit
1240 20c Steam locomotive "3737"
1241 20c Electric locomotive "NS–IC III"
1242 30c Stephenson's locomotive *Rocket*
1243 30c French "TGV" high speed
     locomotive
1244 50c Stephenson's locomotive *Der Adler*
1245 50c French double-decker "UB2N" train
1246 75c American locomotive *The General*
1247 75c Japanese "Shinkansen" train
     Set of 12 6·00 3·50

1986

Nos. 1244/5 surcharged

1282 15c on 50c Stephenson's *Der Adler*
1283 15c on 50c French double-decker
     "UB2N" train
     Set of 2 90 35

1988

Nos. 1246/7 surcharged

1368† 60c on 75c American locomotive *The
     General* . . . . 1·40 1·00
1369† 60c on 75c Japanese "Shinkansen"
     train . . . . 1·40 1·00

SWAZILAND

Southern Africa
1949 12 pence = 1 shilling
20 shillings = 1 pound
1961 100 cents = 1 rand
1975 100 cents = 1 lilangeni (plural emalangeni)

1949

As No. 114 of Antigua

48† 1½d Silhouette of steam locomotive 10 5

1964

109 2½c Steam goods train and route map of
     Swaziland Railway
110 3½c Steam goods train and route map of
     Swaziland Railway
111 15c Steam goods train and route map of
     Swaziland Railway
112 25c Steam goods train and route map of
     Swaziland Railway
     Set of 4 75 25

ALBUM LISTS

Write for our latest list of albums and accessories. This
will be sent on request.

1968

140†   25c Iron-ore mine and railway route map   45   30

1979

325   25c Iron-ore mine and railway route map
      (on No. 140) and Sir Rowland Hill   25   30

1981

371†   1e Steam goods train leaving tunnel ....   2·00   2·00

1982

411†   1e Steam sugar-cane train ....   1·00   1·40

1984

466   10c King Sobhuza opening Swaziland
      Railway, 1964
467   25c Type "15A" locomotive at Siweni Yard
468   30c Container loading, Matsapha Station
469   1e Locomotive No. 268 leaving Alto
      Tunnel
                       Set of 4   2·50   1·50

SWEDEN

Northern Europe
100 ore = 1 krona

1924

173†   1k Steam train on globe ....   60·00   75·00
174†   2k Steam train on globe ....   £175   65·00
175†   5k Steam train on globe £250   £175

1936

195†   40 ore Steam mail train (green) ....   7·50   1·50

1956

378   10 ore Railway construction
379   25 ore First Swedish steam locomotive
      Fryckstad
380   40 ore Diesel train on Arsta Bridge,
      Stockholm
                       Set of 3   3·50   2·75

1970

624†   70 ore Electric locomotive and dam ....   5·50   3·75
625†   70 ore Electric ore train and mine ......   5·50   3·75

1972

As No. 195, but colour changed
702†   40 ore Steam mail train (blue)   60   60

1974

826† 1k Train ferry *Skanes* 60 60

1975

861 5 ore Steam locomotive *Fryckstad*
862 5 ore Steam locomotive *Gotland*
863 90 ore Steam locomotive *Prince August*
Set of 3   75   30

1977

937† 1k10 Horse-drawn tram 50   40
938† 1k10 Electric tram 50   40
941† 1k10 Underground train, Stockholm 50   40

1981

1086 1k50 Par Lagerkvist riding railway trolley
with father (illustration from
autobiography *Guest of Reality*) 30   10

1087† 2k40 Electric locomotive 50   40

1985

1252† 2k Tram (in painting "View of Slussen"
by Sigrid Hjerten) 40   40

1986

1310† 2k10 Interior of 19th-century sorting
carriage .... 2·50   3·00

1988

1408 2k20 "X2" High-speed train
1409 3k10 "X2" High-speed train
1410 3k10 Narrow-gauge steam locomotive
Set of 3   1·25   70

SWITZERLAND

Central Europe
100 centimes = 1 franc

1931

J56† 5c (+ 5c) Tracks at Silvaplana Lakes 40   45

1932

352 10c Louis Favre (engineer of St. Gotthard
Railway)
353 20c Alfred Escher (President of St.
Gotthard Railway)
354 30c Emil Welti (founder of St. Gotthard
Railway)
Set of 3   70   1·40

1934

357† 10c Tracks at Chillon Castle 20 10
359† 20c Tracks and Landwasser Viaduct,
Filisur 40 5
361† 30c Railway viaduct, Schaffhausen ...... 30·00 40

1936

As Nos. 357, 359 and 361, but redrawn with figures of value lower
373b† 10c Tracks at Chillon Castle (purple) .. 25 5
373c† 10c Tracks at Chillon Castle (brown) 20 5
490† 10c Tracks at Chillon Castle (green) 30 5
375b† 20c Tracks and Landwasser Viaduct,
Filisur .... 7·00 5
377† 30c Railway viaduct, Schaffhausen
(blue) 75 5
493† 30c Railway viaduct, Schaffhausen
(turquoise) .... 16·00 1·00

1939

J89† 10c + 5c Railway viaduct, Freiburg 20 20

1942

J100† 5c + 5c Niklaus Riggenbach (rack
railway pioneer) 20 25

1945

J112† 5c + 5c Ludwig Forrer (railway
director) 30 25

1947

473 5c + 5c Platelayers
474 10c + 10c Rorschach Station
475 20c + 20c Luen-Castiel Railway Station
476 30c + 30c Fluelen Railway Station
Set of 4   6·00   9·25

477 5c First Swiss steam locomotive *Limmat*
478 10c Steam freight locomotive
479 20c Electric train crossing Melide
Causeway
480 30c Trains on railway bridge
Set of 4   2·00   2·00

STANLEY GIBBONS
STAMP COLLECTING SERIES

Introductory booklets on *How to Start, How to Identify
Stamps* and *Collecting by Theme*. A series of well
illustrated guides at a low price.
Write for details.

1949

511†	5c Sitter Viaducts near St. Gall	30	5
512†	10c Mountain cog railway, Rochers de Naye	25	5
513†	15c Rotary snow-plough	30	5
515†	25c Melide Railway Causeway, Lake Lugano	50	5
518†	40c Goods wagons on dock, Rhine harbour, Basel	3·00	5
520†	60c Railway viaduct, Landwasser	6·00	5

1955

563†	10c + 10c Grandfey Railway Viaduct, River Saane	60	30

1956

568†	10c Electric train emerging from Simplon Tunnel and Stockalper Palace	40	10

1957

577†	10c Electric train emerging from St. Gotthard Tunnel	1·75	8

1959

597†	5c Electric railcar	25	10

1962

659†	5c Electric TEE train	40	10
661†	20c Jungfraujoch Railway Station	65	8

1963

672†	20c Electric train on Luegelkinn Viaduct and Tunnel, Lotschberg Railway	1·50	10

1967

754†	50c Railway wheel emblem of Central Office for International Railway Transport	40	35

1972

825†	20c Signal-box switch table	25	8

1974

885†	30c Berne Railway Station	30	25

1976

921† 40c St. Gotthard Railway 30 10

J286† 80c + 40c Toy steam locomotive, 1900 70 75

1985

1981

1017† 20c Voltage regulator from Jungfrau
Railway's power station 15 10

1076† 35c Railway conductor's equipment 40 15

1986

1982

1021 40c Class "C4/5" steam locomotive
1022 40c Class "Re6/6" electric locomotive
Set of 2 60 40

1112† 90c Interior of railway sorting carriage 55 65

1987

1046† 20c Articulated tram, Zurich 15 15

1122† 90c Electric train, Geneva Airport rail
link 80 65

1983

1989

1055† 80c Niklaus Riggenbach's rack and
pinion railway 45 40

1159† 80c Rhaetian Railway diesel train
crossing viaduct 60 45

OFFICIAL STAMPS

1938

Nos. 373b and 377 overprinted with Geneva Cross
O383† 10c Tracks at Chillon Castle . . . . 1·00 40
O387† 30c Railway viaduct, Schaffhausen . . 75 75

1942

Nos. 373c and 377 overprinted **Officiel**

O430†	10c Tracks at Chillon Castle	15	20
O434†	30c Railway viaduct, Schaffhausen . .	1·75	60

1950

Nos. 511/13, 515, 518 and 520 overprinted **Officiel**

O522†	5c Sitter Viaduct near St. Gall	70	60
O523†	10c Mountain cog railway, Rochers de		
	Naye	1·25	60
O524†	15c Rotary snow-plough	5·50	9·50
O526†	25c Melide Railway Causeway, Lake		
	Lugano	3·75	5·50
O529†	40c Goods wagons on dock, Rhine		
	harbour, Basel	5·00	2·50
O531†	60c Railway viaduct, Landwasser	8·50	4·00

International Organizations in Switzerland

I. LEAGUE OF NATIONS

1934

No. 361 overprinted **SOCIETE DES NATIONS**

LN46†	30c Railway viaduct, Schaffhausen	—	1·10

1937

Nos. 373b/c, 375b and 377 overprinted **SOCIETE DES NATIONS**

LN49aa†	10c Tracks at Chillon Castle		
	(purple)	—	80
LN49b†	10c Tracks at Chillon Castle		
	(brown)	35	60
LN51†	20c Tracks and Landwasser		
	Viaduct, Filisur	—	1·40
LN53†	30c Railway viaduct, Schaffhausen		
	(blue)	60	70

1944

Nos. 373c and 377 overprinted **COURRIER DE LA SOCIETE DES NATIONS**

LN69†	10c Tracks at Chillon Castle (brown)	30	40
LN73†	30c Railway viaduct, Schaffhausen		
	(blue)	60	65

II. INTERNATIONAL LABOUR OFFICE

1937

Nos. 373b/c, 375b and 377 overprinted **S.d.N. BUREAU INTERNATIONAL du TRAVAIL**

LB41†	10c Tracks at Chillon Castle (purple)	—	90
LB41b†	10c Tracks at Chillon Castle (brown)	45	60
LB43†	20c Tracks and Landwasser Viaduct,		
	Filisur	—	70
LB45†	30c Railway viaduct, Schaffhausen		
	(blue)	40	70

1944

Nos. 373c and 377 overprinted **COURRIER DU BUREAU INTERNATIONAL DU TRAVAIL**

LB61†	10c Tracks at Chillon Castle (brown)	30	30
LB65†	30c Railway viaduct, Schaffhausen		
	(blue)	70	1·00

1950

Nos. 511/13, 515, 518 and 520 overprinted **BUREAU INTERNATIONAL DU TRAVAIL**

LB80†	5c Sitter Viaducts near St. Gall	4·50	3·25
LB81†	10c Mountain cog railway, Rochers de		
	Naye	4·50	3·00
LB82†	15c Rotary snow-plough	6·00	4·50
LB84†	25c Melide Railway Causeway, Lake		
	Lugano	6·50	4·75
LB87†	40c Goods wagon on dock, Rhine		
	harbour, Basel	7·00	5·50
LB89†	60c Railway viaduct, Landwasser	9·50	7·50

III. INTERNATIONAL EDUCATION OFFICE

1944

Nos. 373c and 377 overprinted **COURRIER DU BUREAU INTERNATIONAL D'EDUCATION**

LE3†	10c Tracks at Chillon Castle (brown)	55	1·25
LE7†	30c Railway viaduct, Schaffhausen		
	(blue)	1·75	2·50

1948

Nos. 490 and 493 overprinted **BUREAU INTERNATIONAL D'EDUCATION**

LE24†	10c Tracks at Chillon Castle (green)	2·50	2·50
LE27†	30c Railway viaduct, Schaffhausen		
	(turquoise)	2·50	2·50

1950

Nos. 511/13, 515, 518 and 520 overprinted **BUREAU INTERNATIONAL D'EDUCATION**

LE29†	5c Sitter Viaducts near St. Gall	55	55
LE30†	10c Mountain cog railway, Rochers de		
	Naye	65	65
LE31†	15c Rotary snow-plough	75	75
LE33†	25c Melide Railway Causeway, Lake		
	Lugano	8·00	7·50
LE36†	40c Goods wagon on dock, Rhine		
	harbour, Basel	4·50	5·00
LE38†	60c Railway viaduct, Landwasser	6·50	7·50

IV. WORLD HEALTH ORGANIZATION

1948

No. 490 overprinted **ORGANISATION MONDIALE DE LA SANTE**

LH2†	10c Tracks at Chillon Castle (green)	3·00	3·00

Nos. 511/13, 515, 518 and 520 overprinted **ORGANISATION MONDIALE DE LA SANTE**

LH6†	5c Sitter Viaducts near St. Gall	40	30
LH7†	10c Mountain cog railway, Rochers de		
	Naye	75	60
LH8†	15c Rotary snow-plough	85	1·00
LH10†	25c Melide Railway Causeway, Lake		
	Lugano	3·50	2·75
LH13†	40c Goods wagon on dock, Rhine		
	harbour, Basel	1·90	1·50
LH15†	60c Railway Viaduct, Landwasser	2·75	2·25

V. INTERNATIONAL REFUGEES ORGANIZATION

1950

Nos. 511/12, 515 *and* 518 *overprinted* **ORGANISATION INTERNATIONALE POUR LES REFUGIES**

LR1†	5c Sitter Viaducts near St. Gall	15·00	8·50
LR2†	10c Mountain cog railway, Rochers de Naye	15·00	8·50
LR4†	25c Melide Railway Causeway, Lake Lugano	15·00	8·50
LR5†	40c Goods wagon on dock, Rhine harbour, Basel	15·00	8·50

VI. UNITED NATIONS

1950

Nos. 511/13, 515, 518 *and* 520 *overprinted* **NATIONS UNIES OFFICE EUROPEEN**

LU1†	5c Sitter Viaducts near St. Gall	45	80
LU2†	10c Mountain cog railway, Rochers de Naye	45	80
LU3†	15c Rotary snow-plough	75	1·10
LU5†	25c Melide Railway Causeway, Lake Lugano	2·50	3·00
LU8†	40c Goods wagon on dock, Rhine harbour, Basel	3·00	3·75
LU10†	60c Railway viaduct, Landwasser	4·25	5·50

VIII. UNIVERSAL POSTAL UNION

1976

LP11†	80c Railway mail van	55	60

SYRIA

Middle East
100 centimes = 1 piastre

1960

714	12½p Diesel train, Latakia–Aleppo Railway	1·50	65

COLLECT BIRDS ON STAMPS

New second edition available at £8.50 (p. + p. £2) from:
Stanley Gibbons Publications Ltd, 5 Parkside,
Christchurch Road, Ringwood, Hants BH24 3SH.

1963

814†	17½p Hejaz Railway Station, Damascus	1·00	10

1968

985	12½p Railway tracks	
986	27½p Railway tracks	
	Set of 2	2·50	2·00

1981

1509	60p Diesel train	1·50	35

1985

1607	60p Steam and diesel locomotives	1·25	45

1986

1633	110p Diesel train	1·50	80

SZECHWAN

See under China

TAIWAN

See under China

TANZANIA

East Africa
100 cents = 1 shilling

1976

187 50c Diesel train, Tanzania–Zambia
 Railway
188 1s Diesel train on Nile Bridge, Uganda
189 2s Diesel train at Nakuru Station, Kenya
190 3s Class "A" steam locomotive, 1896
 Set of 4 1·90 1·00

1985

417† 5s Diesel train 60   85

430 5s Steam locomotive No. 3022
431 10s Steam locomotive No. 3107
432 20s Steam locomotive No. 6004
433 30s Steam locomotive No. 3129
 Set of 4 6·00 6·50

445 1s50 Class "64" diesel locomotive
446 2s Class "36" diesel locomotive
447 5s "DFH1013" diesel shunter

448 10s "DE1001" diesel-electric locomotive
449 30s Steam locomotive, Zanzibar, 1906
 Set of 5 3·75 3·75
MS450 15s Class "30" steam locomotive; 20s
 Class "11" steam locomotive .... 3·00 3·25

1987

533† 2s Diesel locomotive on emblem of
 Tanzanian Railway Corporation 5   5
MS535† 20s Diesel express train 30 35

Nos. 445/9 overprinted **10th Anniversary of TANZANIA ZAMBIA RAILWAY AUTHORITY 1976–1986.**
541 1s50 Class "64" diesel locomotive
542 2s Class "36" diesel locomotive
543 5s "DFH1013" diesel shunter
544 10s "DE1001" diesel-electric locomotive
545 30s Steam locomotive, Zanzibar, 1906
 Set of 5 70 80

1988

MS566 40s Diesel express train 55 60

THAILAND

South-east Asia
100 satangs = 1 baht

1977

918 1b Alsthom electric locomotive
919 2b Davenport electric locomotive
920 4b Pacific steam locomotive
921 5b George Egestoff's steam locomotive
 Set of 4 4·00 1·90

1981

ประเทศไทย THAILAND

1057 75s Diesel locomotive 15 10

1982

1094† 5b Nineteenth-century steam train 45 25

1985

1193 1b50 Diesel mail train 25 10

1987

1278 2b Diesel passenger train 15 5

ALBUM LISTS

Write for our latest list of albums and accessories. This will be sent on request.

TOGO

West Africa
100 centimes = 1 franc

1961

288† 25f Electric train and gantry 70 15

1963

321† 1f Steam mail train 25 10

1964

373† 5f Goods wagon at phosphate mine,
      Kpeme 20 10
375† 60f Diesel phosphate train 90 50

1967

531† 105f Monorail train, "Expo '67", Montreal 1·40 55

No. 531 overprinted **JOURNEE NATIONALE DU TOGO 29 SEPTEMBRE 1967**

576† 105f Monorail train, "Expo '67", Montreal 1·75 60

1969

666† 45f Hand holding diesel locomotive on
bridge .... 1·50   40

1970

REPUBLIQUE TOGOLAISE **20**^F

745† 20f Monorail car and British Pavilion,
"Expo '70", Osaka   20   15
746† 30f Monorail and French Pavilion, "Expo
'70", Osaka   30   15
747† 50f Monorail and station, Russian
Pavilion, "Expo '70", Osaka   55   30
748† 60f Monorail train and Japanese Pavilion,
"Expo '70", Osaka   60   35

1973

961† 25f Steam and diesel locomotives   40   20

1977

1181† 50f Tracks, phosphate complex, Kpeme   80   25

COLLECT MAMMALS ON STAMPS

A Stanley Gibbons thematic catalogue on this popular
subject. Copies available at £7.50 (p. + p. £2) from:
Stanley Gibbons Publications Ltd, 5 Parkside,
Christchurch Road, Ringwood, Hants BH24 3SH.

1978

1326† 200f Steam locomotive, 1870 ....   1·60   55

1979

1372† 200f French post office carriage, 1848   1·25   40

1374 35f Stephenson's locomotive *Rocket*,
1829
1375 50f William Norris' locomotive *Austria*,
1843
1376 60f U.S.A. locomotive *The General*, 1862
1377 85f Stephenson locomotive, 1843
1378 100f Locomotive *De Witt Clinton*, 1831
1379 200f D. Joy's locomotive *Jenny Lind*,
1847
                                    Set of 6   4·25   1·50

1980

1477† 100f Spaceship resembling steam train
(*From the Earth to the Moon* by Jules
Verne) ....   1·40   60

REPUBLIQUETOGOLAISE

1515† 100f Cologne Railway Station in
background 85 45

1984

1682† 45f Constructing Lome–Atakpame
Railway 30 25
1685† 70f Railway tracks, Lome wharf, 1903 45 35
1702† 270f Steam train, Ancho Railway, 1905 1·10 95
1703† 270f "Mallet" train, Kpalime Railway,
1907 .... 1·10 95

1749 1f Rack railway steam train, Madeira
1750 2f British-made steam locomotive, Egypt
1751 3f "Garratt" steam locomotive, Algeria
1752 4f Diesel train, Congo-Ocean Railway
1753 50f Italian-made steam locomotive, Libya
1754 90f Northern Railway steam locomotive
No. 49 (air)
1755 105f "Mallet" steam locomotive, Togo
1756 500f Steam locomotive, Rhodesia
1757 1000f Beyer-Garratt steam locomotive,
East African Railway
Set of 9 9·50 6·50
MS1758 Two sheets (a) 1000f First horse-
drawn train to Dakar, Senegal; (b) 1000f
American-made locomotive, Ghana
Set of 2 sheets 8·50 7·00

1985

Nos. 1752, 1755 *and* 1757/8 *overprinted* **80e ANNIVERSAIRE du
ROTARY INTERNATIONAL**
1853 4f Diesel train, Congo-Ocean Railway
1854 10f "Mallet" steam locomotive, Togo (air)
1855 1000f Beyer-Garratt steam locomotive,
East African Railway
Set of 3 4·50 4·25

MS1856 Two sheets (a) 1000f First horse-
drawn train to Dakar, Senegal; (b) 1000f
American-made locomotive, Ghana
Set of 2 sheets 9·00 8·50

Nos. 1753/4, 1756 *and* **MS**1758 *overprinted* **150e
ANNIVERSAIRE DE CHEMIN FER "LUDWIG"**
1857 50f Italian-made steam locomotive, Libya
1858 90f Northern Railway steam locomotive
No. 49 (air)
1859 500f Steam locomotive, Rhodesia
Set of 3 2·75 2·25
MS1860 Two sheets (a) 1000f First horse-
drawn train to Dakar, Senegal; (b) 1000f
American-made locomotive, Ghana
Set of 2 sheets 9·00 8·50

1988

No. **MS**1758 *overprinted* **Praga 88** (c) *or* **FINLANDIA 88** (d)
MS1977 Four sheets (c) 1000f First horse-
drawn train to Dakar, Senegal; (d) 1000f
American-made locomotive, Ghana (other two
sheets show different subjects)
Set of 4 sheets 15·00 14·00

TOKELAU

South Pacific
100 cents = 1 dollar

1988

157† 50c Sydney Harbour Bridge 35 40

TONGA

South Pacific
1949 12 pence = 1 shilling
20 shillings = 1 pound
1967 100 seniti = 1 pa'anga

1949

As No. 114 *of Antigua*
88† 2½d Silhouette of steam locomotive 20 10

1984

889† 2p Sir Sanford Fleming (Canadian
railway engineer) .... 2·00 2·25

1988

MS989   42s Cover from first overland mail by
Australian Trans-Continental Railway; 42s
Sydney Harbour Bridge (sheet also contains
ten other 42s designs) .... 4·75   5·00

TRANSKEI
Southern Africa
100 cents = 1 rand

1985

169†   25c White Kei Railway Bridge 15   20

1989

229   16c Two Class "14 CRB" steam
locomotives pulling passenger train
230   30c Class "14 CRB" locomotive and
passenger train at Toleni Halt
231   40c Double-headed steam train on Great
Kei River Bridge
232   50c Double-headed steam train in Kei
Valley
                              Set of 4   60   75

TRANSVAAL
Southern Africa
12 pence = 1 shilling
20 shillings = 1 pound

1895

215b   1d Rack steam train emerging from
tunnel 35   15

TRAVANCORE
Indian subcontinent
16 cash = 1 chuckram
26 chuckrams = 1 rupee

1941

72†   ½ch Marthanda Varma Bridge, Alwaye ....   1·00   8

1943
No. 72 *surcharged* **4 CASH**
74†   4 cash on ½ch Marthanda Varma Bridge,
Alwaye   80   10

OFFICIAL STAMPS

1942
No. 72 *overprinted* **SERVICE**
O104†   ½ch Marthanda Varma Bridge, Alwaye   40   8

No. 74 *overprinted* **SERVICE**
O107†   4 cash on ½ch Marthanda Varma
Bridge, Alwaye   60   10

TRENGGANU
South-east Asia
100 cents = 1 dollar

1949
As No. 114 *of Antigua*
63†   10c Silhouette of steam locomotive   20   35

1957

93†   8c Steam train, East Coast Railway ......   2·75   60

TRIESTE
Southern Europe

Zone A
Allied Military Government
100 centesimi = 1 lira

1949
No. 725 *of Italy overprinted* **A.M.G.–F.T.T.**
91   50li Globes and diesel railcar ....   2·25   2·50

1954
No. 871 *of Italy overprinted* **AMG–FTT**
297   25li Train on bridge   50   55

Zone B
Yugoslav Military Government
100 paras = 1 dinar

1949

Nos. 612/13 of Yugoslavia overprinted **VUJA–STT**
B24 5d Steam mail train
B25 12d Steam mail train
Set of 2 10·00 6·00

1950

Nos. 631/3b of Yugoslavia overprinted **VUJA–STT**
B33 2d Steam locomotive of 1849
B34 3d Modern steam locomotive
B35 5d Diesel train
B36 10d Electric train on bridge (orange)
Set of 4 13·50 9·00
MSB36a 10d Electric train on bridge (purple) .... 70·00 45·00

1953

No. 714 of Yugoslavia overprinted **STT–VUJNA**
B85† 50d Steam locomotive .... 2·50 2·50

1954

No. 683c of Yugoslavia overprinted **STT–VUJNA**
B118† 500d Tracks on bank of River Save,
Belgrade .... 8·50 12·50

TRINIDAD AND TOBAGO
West Indies
100 cents = 1 dollar

1949

As No. 114 of Antigua
261† 5c Silhouette of steam locomotive 15 10

1969

293† 35c Side-dump truck, Pitch Lake 60 5

1974

451 40c Diesel train
452 50c Diesel train
Set of 2 40 50

1980

557† 50c Steam locomotive used for Royal
Train, 1880 .... 35 60

1986

705 65c Steam tank locomotive *Arima*
706 95c Canadian-built steam locomotive No.
22
707 $1.10 Steam tender locomotive
708 $1.50 Steam saddle-tank locomotive
Set of 4 1·40 1·75

1987

730† 95c Railway tracks at oil field 35 40
731† $1.10 Belmont Tramway Company early
tramcar 40 50

1988

747† $1.10 Governor's train at Arima Station,
1888 .... 30 35

COLLECT SHIPS ON STAMPS
The largest Stanley Gibbons thematic catalogue to date
– available at £10.95 (p. + p. £2) from:
Stanley Gibbons Publications Ltd, 5 Parkside,
Christchurch Road, Ringwood, Hants BH24 3SH.

TUNISIA

North Africa
1951 100 centimes = 1 franc
1959 1000 milliemes = 1 dinar

1951

No. 1107 of France overprinted **TUNISIE**
349   12f + 3f Travelling Post Office sorting van   2·25   2·50

1978

897†   20m Electric train and Underground train   60   40

TURKEY

South-east Europe and Asia Minor
1926 40 paras = 1 piastre or grush
1929 40 paras = 1 kurus
100 kurus = 1 lira

1926

1024†	2gr Tracks in Sakarya Gorge	50	10
1025†	2½gr Tracks in Sakarya Gorge	50	10
1026†	3gr Tracks in Sakarya Gorge	60	10

1927

١١٢٧

لملبا.

Nos. 1024/6 overprinted in Turkish

1036†	2gr Tracks in Sakarya Gorge	1·60	40
1037†	2½gr Tracks in Sakarya Gorge	1·60	40
1038†	3gr Tracks in Sakarya Gorge	2·25	75

STAMP MONTHLY

— finest and most informative magazine for all collectors. Obtainable from your newsagent or by postal subscription — details on request.

1928

Nos. 1024/6 overprinted in Turkish

1056†	2gr Tracks in Sakarya Gorge	1·10	30
1057†	2½gr Tracks in Sakarya Gorge	1·10	40
1058†	3gr Tracks in Sakarya Gorge	1·10	75

1929

1077†	20p Steam goods train on bridge over Kizil-Irmak	25	10
1078†	1k Steam goods train on bridge over Kizil-Irmak	50	10
1070†	2k Steam goods train on bridge over Kizil-Irmak (black)	1·00	10
1080†	2k Steam goods train on bridge over Kizil-Irmak (violet)	2·00	10
1071†	2½k Steam goods train on bridge over Kizil-Irmak	1·40	10
1072†	3k Steam goods train on bridge over Kizil-Irmak (purple)	1·60	10
1082†	3k Steam goods train on bridge over Kizil-Irmak (red)	2·75	10
1086†	7½k Tracks in Sakarya Gorge	65	10
1090†	17½k Tracks in Sakarya Gorge	65	50
1092†	25k Tracks in Sakarya Gorge	1·75	15
1094†	40k Tracks in Sakarya Gorge	2·00	15

1930

Nos. 1076/98 surcharged **SIVAS D.Y. 30 ag. 930** *and value for opening of Ankara–Sivas Railway*

1099	10pa on 10pa Legendary blacksmith
1100	10pa on 20pa Steam goods train on bridge over Kizil-Irmak
1101	20pa on 1k Steam goods train on bridge over Kizil-Irmak
1102	1k on 1½k Legendary blacksmith
1103	1½k on 2k Steam goods train on bridge over Kizil-Irmak (violet)
1104	2k on 2½k Steam goods train on bridge over Kizil-Irmak
1105	2½k on 3k Steam goods train on bridge over Kizil-Irmak (red)
1106	3k on 4k Legendary blacksmith
1107	4k on 5k Fortress of Ankara
1108	5k on 6k Legendary blacksmith
1109	6k on 7½k Tracks in Sakarya Gorge
1110	7½k on 12½k Fortress of Ankara
1111	12½k on 15k Fortress of Ankara
1112	15k on 17½k Tracks in Sakarya Gorge

1113	17½k on 20k Fortress of Ankara
1114	20k on 25k Tracks in Sakarya Gorge
1115	25k on 30k Fortress of Ankara
1116	30k on 40k Tracks in Sakarya Gorge
1117	40k on 50k Kemal Ataturk
1118	50k on 100k Kemal Ataturk
1119	100k on 200k Kemal Ataturk
1120	250k on 500k Kemal Ataturk

Set of 22   £110   48·00

1934

Nos. 1086, 1092 and 1094 overprinted **1934** and aeroplane or surcharged also

1157†	7½k Tracks in Sakarya Gorge	40	25
1159†	20k on 25k Tracks in Sakarya Gorge	70	35
1160†	25k Tracks in Sakarya Gorge	90	55
1161†	40k Tracks in Sakarya Gorge	1·25	70

Nos. 1086, 1090 and 1092 surcharged **IZMIR 9 Eylul 934 Sergisi** and value

1164†	2k on 25k Tracks in Sakarya Gorge	2·50	80
1165†	5k on 7½k Tracks in Sakarya Gorge	3·50	80
1166†	6k on 17½k Tracks in Sakarya Gorge	2·00	50
1169†	20k on 25k Tracks in Sakarya Gorge	32·00	32·00

1936

Nos. 1090 and 1092 surcharged **BOGAZLAR MUKAVELESININ IMZASI 20/7/1936** and value in figures

| 1186† | 4k on 17½k Tracks in Sakarya Gorge | 1·25 | 65 |
| 1187† | 5k on 25k Tracks in Sakarya Gorge | 1·25 | 65 |

1938

Nos. 1086 and 1094 surcharged **1937** with aeroplane above and value

| 1198† | 4½k on 7½k Tracks in Sakarya Gorge | 2·00 | 1·25 |
| 1200† | 35k on 40k Tracks in Sakarya Gorge | 3·25 | 9·75 |

| 1214† | 7½k Steam train on bridge | 1·00 | 30 |

1939

No. 1092 surcharged **Hatayin Anavatana Kavusmasi 23/7/1939** and value

| 1235† | 3k on 25k Tracks in Sakarya Gorge | 70 | 20 |
| 1237† | 7½k on 25k Tracks in Sakarya Gorge | 1·00 | 30 |

1241	3k Railway bridge, Ankara–Erzurum Railway
1242	6k Steam locomotive, Ankara–Erzurum Railway
1243	7½k Railway track in gorge, Ankara–Erzurum Railway
1244	12½k Tunnel entrance at Atma-Bogazi

Set of 4   22·00   30·00

1941

No. 1092 surcharged with aeroplane, new value and squares

| 1286† | 4½k on 25k Tracks in Sakarya Gorge | 75 | 1·40 |

1943

| 1316† | 4½k Steam train entering tunnel | 2·25 | 30 |

| 1338† | 6¾k Railway bridge | 60 | 60 |

1947

1373	15k Steam express train
1374	20k Steam express train
1375	60k Steam express train

Set of 3   3·50   2·75

1949

| 1399† | 5k Tram at Izmir | 25 | 5 |
| 1402† | 40k Tram at Izmir | 85 | 15 |

1950

| 1437† | 60k Railway bridge, Istanbul | 1·75 | 75 |

1951

No. 1399 overprinted **SANAYI KONGRESI 9-NISAN-1951**

1454† 5k Tram at Izmir 50 80

1953

1527† 30k Diesel train .... 3·50 1·75

1955

1591† 55k Railway bridge .... 1·00 40

1959

1856† 15k Goods wagon at steel works 20 5
1864† 75k Electric train .... 2·75 10
1865† 90k Tracks on dock .... 2·75 10
1867† 120k Tracks beside highway .... 2·00 10

1961

1934† 30k Diesel train on bridge 30 15
1935† 40k Tracks beside highway 60 25

1968

2254† 60k Kemal Ataturk at railway carriage
window 50 20

1971

2387 100k Diesel train on bridge,
Turkey–Bulgaria line
2388 110k Train ferry, Lake Van, Turkey–Iran
line
2389 250k Diesel train and map, Turkey–Iran
line
Set of 3 1·90 65

1972

2439 100k International Railway Union (U.I.C.)
emblem 60 15

1979

2652 2½li Diesel mail train 35 10

2669 5li Railway tunnel in figure "8" 60 25

1988

2989† 200li Steam locomotive 30 8

2995 50li American Standard steam
      locomotive, 1850s
2996 100li Steam locomotive, 1913
2997 200li Henschel Krupp steam locomotive,
      1926
2998 300li Toshiba "E 43001" electric
      locomotive, 1987
2999 600li MTE-Tulomsas diesel locomotive,
      1984

Set of 5 1·40 80

3003† 300li Seto–Ohashi Road and Rail
       Bridge, Japan 35 12

COLLECT MAMMALS ON STAMPS

A Stanley Gibbons thematic catalogue on this popular
subject. Copies available at £7.50 (p. + p. £2) from:
Stanley Gibbons Publications Ltd, 5 Parkside,
Christchurch Road, Ringwood, Hants BH24 3SH.

POSTAGE DUE STAMPS

1926

D1035 20pa Steam goods train on bridge
       over Kizil-Irmak
D1036 1gr Steam goods train on bridge over
       Kizil-Irmak
D1037 2gr Steam goods train on bridge over
       Kizil-Irmak
D1038 3gr Steam goods train on bridge over
       Kizil-Irmak
D1039 5gr Steam goods train on bridge over
       Kizil-Irmak

Set of 5 7·00 25·00

TURKS AND CAICOS ISLANDS

West Indies
1949 12 pence = 1 shilling
20 shillings = 1 pound
1969 100 cents = 1 dollar

1949

As No. 114 of Antigua
217† 2½d Silhouette of steam locomotive 10 15

1950

221† ½d Side-dump trucks on salt dock 15 40

1979

559† 25c Early steam locomotive (self-
      adhesive) 60 45

1980

628† $1 Steam locomotive and Harriet
      Tubman .... 1·10 80

1982

706† 15c Interior of railway dining car (from painting "The Proper Gratuity" by Norman Rockwell) 50   50

1983

731 15c West Caicos trolley tram
732 55c West Caicos steam locomotive
733 90c East Caicos sisal steam train
734 $1.60 East Caicos steam locomotive
                                    Set of 4   3·25   3·50
MS735 $2.50 Sisal steam train .... 2·75   2·75

1984

824† 35c Donald Duck and Chip n'Dale
     playing with train set 75   65

STANLEY GIBBONS
STAMP COLLECTING SERIES

Introductory booklets on *How to Start, How to Identify Stamps* and *Collecting by Theme.* A series of well illustrated guides at a low price.
Write for details.

TUVA

Central Asia
100 kopecks = 1 aksha

1936

90† 30k Steam goods train and camel .... 6·00   1·00

TUVALU

Pacific Ocean
100 cents = 1 dollar

1984

241/242 1c Class "GS-4" locomotive, U.S.A. (1941)
243/244 15c Class "AD60" locomotive, Australia (1952)
245/246 40c Class "C38" locomotive, Australia (1943)
247/248 60c Locomotive *Lord of the Isles*, Great Britain (1892)
                                    Set of 8   1·90   2·40
The first stamp in each pair shows technical drawings and the second the locomotive at work.

253/254 10c "Casey Jones" type locomotive, U.S.A. (1896)
255/256 15c "Triplex" type locomotive, U.S.A. (1914)
257/258 20c Class "370" Advanced Passenger Train, Great Britain (1981)
259/260 25c Class "4F" locomotive, Great Britain (1924)

261/262 40c Class "Tornado Rover" locomotive,
        Great Britain (1888)
263/264 50c Locomotive *Broadlands*, Great
        Britain (1967)
265/266 60c Locomotive *Locomotion No. 1*,
        Great Britain (1825)
267/268 $1 Class "C57" locomotive, Japan
        (1937)
                        Set of 16   4·75   5·50
The first stamp in each pair shows technical drawings and the
second the locomotive at work.

1c

TUVALU

273/274 1c Class "9700" locomotive, Japan
        (1897)
275/276 15c Class "231" C/K locomotive, France
        (1909)
277/278 30c Class "640" locomotive, Italy (1907)
279/280 $1 Class "4500" locomotive, France
        (1906)
                        Set of 8   2·50   3·00
The first stamp in each pair shows technical drawings and the
second the locomotive at work.

1985

5c

TUVALU

313/314 5c Class "Churchward 28XX"
        locomotive, Great Britain (1905)
315/316 10c Class "KF" locomotive, China
        (1935)
317/318 30c Class "99.77" locomotive, East
        Germany (1952)
319/320 $1 Pearson type locomotive, Great
        Britain (1853)
                        Set of 8   2·25   2·75
The first stamp in each pair shows technical drawings and the
second the locomotive at work.

10c

TUVALU

348/349 10c Locomotive *Green Arrow*, Great
        Britain (1936)
350/351 40c Class "SD-50" diesel locomotive,
        U.S.A. (1982)
352/353 65c Locomotive *Flying Hamburger*,
        Germany (1932)
354/355 $1 Class "1070" locomotive, Japan
        (1908)
                        Set of 8   4·00   4·50
The first stamp in each pair shows technical drawings and the
second the locomotive at work.

Funafuti

Appendix

The following stamps have either been issued in excess of
postal needs, or have not been made available to the public in
reasonable quantities at face value. Miniature sheets, imperforate
stamps, etc. are excluded from this section.

1984

*Railway Locomotives (1st series). Two designs for each value, the
first showing technical drawings and the second the locomotive
at work.* 15, 20, 30, 40, 50, 60c, each × 2.
*Railway Locomotives (2nd series). Two designs for each value,
the first showing technical drawings and the second the
locomotive at work.* 5, 15, 25, 35, 40, 55, 60c, $1, each × 2.

1985

*Railway Locomotives (3rd series). Two designs for each value,
the first showing technical drawings and the second the
locomotive at work.* 5, 15, 35, 40, 50c, $1, each × 2.

1986

*Railway Locomotives (4th series). Two designs for each value, the
first showing technical drawings and the second the locomotive
at work.* 20, 40, 60c, $1.50, each × 2.

Nanumaga

Appendix

1985

*Railway Locomotives. Two designs for each value, the first
showing technical drawings and the second the locomotive at
work.* 10, 25, 50, 60c, each × 2.

Nanumea

Appendix

1984

*Railway Locomotives (1st series). Two designs for each value, the
first showing technical drawings and the second the locomotive
at work.* 15, 20, 30, 40, 50, 60c, each × 2.

1985

*Railway Locomotives (2nd series). Two designs for each value,
the first showing technical drawings and the second the
locomotive at work.* 1, 35, 50, 60c, each × 2.

Niutao

Appendix

1984

*Railway Locomotives (1st series). Two designs for each value, the
first showing technical drawings and the second the locomotive
at work.* 5, 10, 20, 40, 50c, $1, each x 2.

1985

*Railway Locomotives (2nd series). Two designs for each value,
the first showing technical drawings and the second the
locomotive at work.* 10, 30, 45, 60, 75c, $1.20, each × 2.

Nui

Appendix

1984

Railway Locomotives (1st series). Two designs for each value, the first showing technical drawings and the second the locomotive at work. 15, 25, 30, 50c, each × 2.

1985

Railway Locomotives (2nd series). Two designs for each value, the first showing technical drawings and the second the locomotive at work. 5, 15, 25c, $1, each × 2.

1987

Railway Locomotives (3rd series). Two designs for each value, the first showing technical drawings and the second the locomotive at work. 10, 25, 35, 40, 60, 75c, $1, $1.25, each × 2.

1988

Railway Locomotives (4th series). Two designs for each value, the first showing technical drawings and the second the locomotive at work. 5, 10, 20, 25, 40, 50, 60, 75c, each × 2.

Nukufetau

Appendix

1985

Railway Locomotives (1st series). Two designs for each value, the first showing technical drawings and the second the locomotive at work. 1, 10, 60, 70c, each × 2.

1986

Railway Locomotives (2nd series). Two designs for each value, the first showing technical drawings and the second the locomotive at work. 20, 40, 60c, $1.50, each × 2.

1987

Railway Locomotives (3rd series). Two designs for each value, the first showing technical drawings and the second the locomotive at work. 5, 10, 15, 25, 30, 50, 60c, $1, each × 2.

Nukulaelae

Appendix

1984

Railway Locomotives (1st series). Two designs for each value, the first showing technical drawings and the second the locomotive at work. 5, 15, 40c, $1, each × 2.
Railway Locomotives (2nd series). Two designs for each value, the first showing technical drawings and the second the locomotive at work. 5, 20, 40c, $1, each × 2.

1985

Railway Locomotives (3rd series). Two designs for each value, the first showing technical drawings and the second the locomotive at work. 10, 25, 50c, $1, each × 2.

1986

Railway Locomotives (4th series). Two designs for each value, the first showing technical drawings and the second the locomotive at work. 10, 15, 25, 40, 50, 80c, $1, $1.50, each × 2.

Vaitupu

Appendix

1985

Railway Locomotives (1st series). Two designs for each value, the first showing technical drawings and the second the locomotive at work. 10, 25, 50, 60c, each × 2.

1986

Railway Locomotives (2nd series). Two designs for each value, the first showing technical drawings and the second the locomotive at work. 5, 25, 80c, $1, each × 2.

1987

Railway Locomotives (3rd series). Two designs for each value, the first showing technical drawings and the second the locomotive at work. 10, 15, 25, 35, 45, 65, 85c, $1, each × 2.

UGANDA

East Africa
100 cents = 1 shilling

1976

173	50c Diesel train, Tanzania–Zambia Railway
174	1s Diesel train on Nile Bridge, Uganda
175	2s Diesel train at Nakuru Station, Kenya
176	3s Class "A" steam locomotive, 1896

Set of 4   2·00   1·25

1981

339†   10s Steam mail train, 1927 .... 1·40   1·40

1983

417†   50s Diesel locomotives and railway computer 45   50

1988

611 5s Class "12" light shunter steam
locomotive
612 10s Class "92" diesel-electric locomotive
613 15s Steam locomotive No. 2506
614 25s Steam tank locomotive No. 126
615 35s Class "31" steam locomotive
616 45s Class "31" steam locomotive
617 50s Class "59" Double Garratt steam
locomotive
618 100s Class "87" diesel-electric locomotive
Set of 8   1·75   2·10
MS619 Two sheets (a) 150s Class "31" steam
locomotive; (b) 150s Class "59" Double
Garratt steam locomotive
Set of 2 sheets   4·00   4·50

669† 50c Mickey Mouse on toy train   35   40

UMM AL QIWAIN

Arabian Peninsula
100 dirhams = 1 riyal

Appendix
The following stamps have either been issued in excess of
postal needs, or have not been made available to the public in
reasonable quantities at face value. Miniature sheets, imperforate
stamps, etc. are excluded from this section.

1972
Locomotives (plastic surfaced). Postage 5, 10, 20, 40, 50d; Air 6r

WHEN YOU BUY AN ALBUM LOOK FOR THE NAME "STANLEY GIBBONS"
It means Quality combined with Value for Money.

UNITED NATIONS
A. New York Headquarters
100 cents = 1 dollar

1966

161 4c Children in closed railway wagon
162 5c Children in locomotive and tender
163 11c Children in open railway wagon
Set of 3   50   35

1967

177 5c Diesel train on baggage label
178 15c Diesel train on baggage label
Set of 2   50   30

UNITED STATES OF AMERICA
North America
100 cents = 1 dollar

1869

116† 3c Steam locomotive . . . .   90·00   3·75

1898

299† $2 Eads Bridge over Mississippi, St.
Louis £1800   £600

1901

301†	2c "Empire State Express"	15·00	75
303†	5c Railway bridge below Niagara Falls	85·00	13·00

1944

919	3c "Golden Spike Ceremony, 1869" (painting by John McQuarrie)	15	8

1947

944	3c Steamlined steam locomotive	8	5

1948

958	3c Niagara Railway Suspension Bridge ..	8	5

1950

984	3c Diesel train	8	5

990	3c "Casey" Jones and railway locomotives	8	5

1952

1003	3c Horse-drawn coach, steam locomotive and diesel locomotive, Baltimore and Ohio Railway	8	5

1960

1163	4c Goods wagons at post office	8	5

1962

1195	4c Monorail, "Century 21" Expo, Seattle	8	5

1967

1303	5c Steam train on viaduct	10	5

1970

1411†	6c Toy steam locomotive	65	5

1971

1445† 8c San Francisco cable-car 25 10

1973

1512† 10c Steam train crossing Kansas
wheatfield 15 5

1517† 10c Diesel train 20 5

1975

1572† 10c Early steam and modern diesel
locomotives 20 5

1594a $5 Railway conductor's lantern .... 8·00 1·25

1976

1649† 13c Steam train on seal of Nebraska 35 20

1978

1725† 13c Steam locomotive and Jimmie
Rodgers 30 5

1979

A1748 21c Octave Chanute (civil engineer)
A1749 21c Octave Chanute (civil engineer)
and gliders
Set of 2 1·50 20

1981

1867† 2c Steam locomotive, 1870s (with "c") 5 5
1868† 3c Railway handcar, 1880s 5 5
1876† 11c Railway caboose, 1890s 20 10

1983

2030 20c Brooklyn Bridge 30 8

First American streetcar, New York City, 1832

2052　20c First American streetcar, New York
　　　　City, 1832
2053　20c Electric streetcar, Montgomery,
　　　　Alabama, 1886
2054　20c "Bobtail" horsecar, Sulphur Rock,
　　　　Arkansas, 1926
2055　20c St. Charles Streetcar, New Orleans,
　　　　1923

Set of 4 1·75 50

1985

Coal Car 1870s
13.2 Bulk Rate
USA

2158a†	2c Steam locomotive, 1870s (without "c")	5	5
2168†	13.2c Coal wagon, 1870s	15	5
2172a†	20c Cable car, 1880s	25	5
2172c†	21c Railway mail van, 1920s	25	5

1987

Stourbridge Lion 1829 USA 22

2322　22c Locomotive *Stourbridge Lion*, 1829
2323　22c Locomotive *Best Friend of
　　　　Charleston*, 1830
2324　22c Locomotive *John Bull*, 1831
2325　22c Locomotive *Brother Jonathan*, 1832
2326　22c Locomotive *Gowan and Marx*, 1839

Set of 5 1·10 20

1989

A. Philip Randolph 25
Black Heritage USA

2386　25c A. Philip Randolph (trade union
　　　　activist), railway workers and carriages　　30　5

PARCEL POST STAMPS

1912

P425†	3c Railway postal clerk	11·00	4·50
P427†	5c Steam mail train	20·00	50
P431†	25c Passenger and freight wagons at Pullman works	50·00	4·00

UPPER SENEGAL AND NIGER

West Africa
100 centimes = 1 franc

1906

As Nos. 18/22 *of Dahomey*

35†	1c General Faidherbe (builder of Dakar–St. Louis Railway)	45	60
36†	2c General Faidherbe (builder of Dakar–St. Louis Railway)	50	60
37†	4c General Faidherbe (builder of Dakar–St. Louis Railway)	60	70
38†	5c General Faidherbe (builder of Dakar–St. Louis Railway)	2·50	1·25
39†	10c General Faidherbe (builder of Dakar–St. Louis Railway)	2·50	95
40†	15c General Faidherbe (builder of Dakar–St. Louis Railway)	3·25	1·40

UPPER VOLTA

West Africa
100 centimes = 1 franc

1970

303†	50f "Expo '70" monorail coach, Osaka	1·25	25

COLLECT BIRDS ON STAMPS

New second edition available at £8.50 (p. + p. £2) from:
Stanley Gibbons Publications Ltd, 5 Parkside,
Christchurch Road, Ringwood, Hants BH24 3SH.

1979

523 65f Steam train
524 165f Diesel train
525 200f Diesel train
526 300f French high-speed train
                          Set of 4   5·00   1·10
MS527 500f Steam train .... 4·00   75

1980

548 75f Electric locomotives
549 100f Electric locomotives
                          Set of 2   2·50   1·10

573† 65f Diesel locomotive 60   25
575† 100f Mine trucks in open cast mine ...... 1·00   35

1981

599 25f Diesel railcar, Abidjan–Niger Railway
600 30f "La Gazelle" diesel train,
       Abidjan–Niger Railway
601 40f Diesel locomotive Le Belier,
       Abidjan–Niger Railway
                          Set of 3   1·10   65

1984

730 40f CC2400ch diesel train
731 100f Steam locomotive No. 1806
732 145f Steam locomotive Livingstone
733 450f Pacific Class "C51" steam
       locomotive
                          Set of 4   5·00   2·25

Appendix
The following stamps have either been issued in excess of
postal needs, or have not been made available to the public in
reasonable quantities at face value. Miniature sheets, imperforate
stamps, etc. are excluded from this section.

1973
Historic Railway Locomotives from French Railway Museum,
Mulhouse (1st series). Air 10, 40, 50, 150, 250f.

1975
Historic Railway Locomotives from French Railway Museum,
Mulhouse (2nd series). Postage 15, 25, 50f; Air 100, 200f.

URUGUAY
South America
1000 milesimos = 100 centesimos = 1 peso

1895

155† 5c Steam locomotive (red) .... 1·75   20

1897
As No. 155, but colour changed
185† 5c Steam locomotive (green) .... 1·50   15

No. 185 overprinted with palm leaf and PAZ 1897
199† 5c Steam locomotive (green) .... 1·60   1·60

1899
As No. 155, but colour changed
221a 5c Steam locomotive (blue) .... 1·50   15

1910

1360	4p Railway level crossing sign and diesel train	40	10

303†	23c Steam locomotive	3·00	50
304†	50c Steam locomotive	5·00	1·60
305†	1p Steam locomotive	7·25	2·25

1928

Surcharged **Inauguracion Ferrocarril SAN CARLOS a ROCHA 14/1/1928** *and value*

537	2c on 12c Chilian Lapwing
538	5c on 12c Chilian Lapwing
539	10c on 12c Chilian Lapwing
540	15c on 12c Chilian Lapwing

Set of 4 16·00 20·00

1930

639†	5m Rio Negro Railway Bridge	20	15

1948

991	10c River Santa Lucia Railway Bridge
992	50c River Santa Lucia Railway Bridge

Set of 2 2·75 90

1967

1349	2p S. Rodriguez (founder of first National Railway Company), steam locomotive and diesel railcar	30	10

1968

1370	10p Diesel train	40	12

1969

1401	6p Modern diesel locomotive
1402	6p Steam locomotive and diesel train

Set of 2 60 50

OFFICIAL STAMPS

1895

No. 155 overprinted **OFICIAL**

O170†	5c Steam locomotive (red)	2·50	1·00

1897

No. 185 overprinted **OFICIAL**

O203†	5c Steam locomotive (green)	2·50	1·00

1899

No. 221a overprinted **OFICIAL**

O227	5c Steam locomotive (blue)	2·50	1·00

1915

Nos. 303/5 overprinted **Oficial**

O344†	23c Steam locomotive	5·00	4·00
O345†	50c Steam locomotive	7·00	4·00
O346†	1p Steam locomotive	8·50	4·00

PARCEL POST STAMPS

1938

P971	5c Steam train	5	35
P801	10c Steam train (red)	40	25
P972	10c Steam train (purple)	55	45
P1066	10c Steam train (green)	20	40
P1067	20c Steam train (blue)	25	30
P973	20c Steam train (red)	35	35
P1068	30c Steam train (purple)	15	20
P974	30c Steam train (blue)	65	35
P1069	50c Steam train	25	30
P805	1p Steam train (red)	3·50	1·75
P975	1p Steam train (blue)	1·25	1·50
P1070	1p Steam train (green)	70	90

1945

P1046†	1p Montevideo Railway Station (blue)	3·00	3·00
P1290†	1p Montevideo Railway Station (brown)	10	5

1971

Surcharged **IMPUESTOS A ENCOMIENDAS $0.60** and diesel locomotive

P1472	60c on 6p Buoy and lighthouse	30	25

1972

Nos. 1401/2 surcharged **IMPUESTO A ENCOMIENDAS $1** and caduceus

P1507	1p on 6p Modern diesel locomotive		
P1508	1p on 6p Steam locomotive and diesel train		
	Set of 2	80	1·00

1974

P1557†	150p Steam locomotive	1·25	1·25

VENEZIA GIULIA AND ISTRIA

Southern Europe
100 centesimi = 1 lira

C. Yugoslav Military Government

1945

83†	30li Railway viaduct over the Solkan River	1·50	2·00

1946

No. 83 surcharged

97†	2li on 30li Railway viaduct over the Solkan River	2·50	2·00

POSTAGE DUE STAMPS

1945

No. 83 surcharged **PORTO 2. — Lit**

D73†	2li on 30li Railway viaduct over the Solkan River	1·50	2·00

1946

No. 83 surcharged **PORTO** and value in Lira

D87†	10li on 30li Railway viaduct over the Solkan River	1·50	1·25
D88†	20li on 30li Railway viaduct over the Solkan River	2·50	2·00
D89†	30li on 30li Railway viaduct over the Solkan River	2·50	2·00

VENEZUELA

South America
100 centimos = 1 bolivar

1959

1572† 1b Steam mail train .... 1·90 70
1575† 1b Steam mail train (air. Inscr "AEREO") 1·50 70

1964

1813† 30c Diesel train 60 35

1974

2294† 70c Tucacas Railway Station, 1911, and
projected Caracas terminal .... 1·50 50

COLLECT SHIPS ON STAMPS

The largest Stanley Gibbons thematic catalogue to date
– available at £10.95 (p. + p. £2) from:
Stanley Gibbons Publications Ltd, 5 Parkside,
Christchurch Road, Ringwood, Hants BH24 3SH.

1981

2454† 1b05 Steam locomotive, 1926 .... 90 60

1983

2491† 80c Steam locomotive No. 129, 1889 .. 1·50 90

2514 55c Central computer building, Caracas
Metro
2515 75c Metro maintenance bay
2516 95c Underground train
2517 2b Metro train at Cuno Amarillo Station,
Caracas
Set of 4 2·25 80

1987

2692† 2b Local electric train 30 15
2697† 2b25 Mainline electric train 35 20

1988

2812† 11b50 Tram and Baralt Theatre, 1888 60 30

VIETNAM

South-east Asia
100xu = 1 dong

1945

Nos. 314 and 323 of Indo-China surcharged **VIET-NAM DAN-CHU CONG-HOA BUU-CHINH** and new value

31†	50x on 1c Steam locomotive	75	75
36†	3d on 15c Steam locomotive	1·00	1·00

South Vietnam

100 cents = 1 piastre

1959

S91	1p Diesel train, Trans-Vietnam Railway		
S92	2p Diesel train, Trans-Vietnam Railway		
S93	3p Diesel train, Trans-Vietnam Railway		
S94	4p Diesel train, Trans-Vietnam Railway		
	Set of 4	3·25	1·25

1968

S326	1p50 Diesel train and route map of Trans-Vietnam Railway		
S327	3p Diesel train and route map of Trans-Vietnam Railway		
S328	9p Diesel train and permanent-way workers		
S329	20p Diesel train and permanent-way workers		
	Set of 4	4·00	1·50

North Vietnam

1956 100 cents = 1 dong
1959 100 xu = 1 dong

1956

N38	100d Crowd welcoming steam train on Hanoi–China line	
N39	200d Crowd welcoming steam train on Hanoi–China line	

N40	300d Crowd welcoming steam train on Hanoi–China line		
N41	500d Crowd welcoming steam train on Hanoi–China line		
	Set of 4	80·00	80·00

1958

N85	50d Workers reconstructing Hanoi–Saigon Railway		
N86	150d Workers reconstructing Hanoi–Saigon Railway		
	Set of 2	6·00	1·75

1959

N102	150d Mine trucks at Cam Pha coal mine	2·00	50

N112	12x Hien Luong Railway Bridge	1·10	60

1964

N315	12x Ham Rong Railway Bridge	55	30

1965

N354	12x Steam locomotive moving left		
N355	30x Steam locomotive moving right		
	Set of 2	2·10	60

1967

N492† 12x Steam locomotive .... 4·25 1·00

1968

N559† 30x "Repairing Railway Tracks"
(painting) 85 30

MILITARY FRANK STAMPS

1959

NMF112 (–) Soldier and steam train .... 6·50 2·25

OFFICIAL STAMPS

1958

NO91 50d Goods wagons at factory
NO92 150d Goods wagons at factory
NO93 200d Goods wagons at factory
Set of 3 3·75 1·50

Vietnam Republic
100 xu = 1 dong

1980

365 12x Diesel train and railway route map 15 10

1983

537 30x Class "231-300" steam locomotive
538 50x Class "230-000" steam locomotive
539 1d Class "140-601" steam locomotive
540 2d Class "241-000" steam locomotive
541 3d Class "141-500" steam locomotive
542 5d Class "150-000" steam locomotive
543 8d Class "40-300" steam locomotive
Set of 7 3·75 1·60

1985

898 1d Locomotive *Reuth*, 1840
899 1d German tank locomotive, 1900
900 2d Locomotive *Der Adler*, 1835
901 2d German passenger locomotive, 1850
902 3d German steam locomotive No. 2024,
1910
903 4d German steam tank locomotive, 1920
904 6d Bavarian State steam locomotive No.
659, 1890
Set of 7 3·00 75
MS905 10d Steam locomotive with driver ...... 1·75 45

WALLIS AND FUTUNA ISLANDS
South Pacific
100 centimes = 1 franc

1983

418 97f Gustav Eiffel, Eiffel Tower and Garabit
Railway Viaduct .... 1·60 1·25

STAMP MONTHLY
— finest and most informative magazine for all
collectors. Obtainable from your newsagent or by
postal subscription — details on request.

1986

491 74f James Watt and principle of steam
engine .... 1·40 1·10

WEST BERLIN

See under Germany

WEST GERMANY

See under Germany

WEST IRIAN

South-east Asia
100 sen = 1 rupiah

1963

No. 831 of Indonesia overprinted **IRIAN BARAT**
6† 10s Steam locomotive and sugar cane
trucks 5 5

YEMEN

Arabia
100 fils = 1 rial

1982

MS701 Two sheets 125f Diesel train (sheets
contain 7 other designs)
Set of 2 sheets 12·00 6·50

Appendix
The following stamps have either been issued in excess of
postal needs, or have not been available to the public in
reasonable quantities at face value. Miniature sheets, imperforate
stamps, etc. are excluded from this section.

1970
Inauguration of New U.P.U. Headquarters Building, Berne. 1½b
(steam locomotive)

YEMEN PEOPLE'S DEMOCRATIC REPUBLIC

Arabia
1000 fils = 1 dinar

1983

301 25f Class "P-8" steam locomotive, 1905
302 50f Class "880" steam locomotive, 1915
303 100f Class "Gt2x4/4" steam locomotive,
1923
Set of 3 3·75 1·50
MS304 Two sheets (a) 40f Class "D51" steam
locomotive, 1936, 60f Series "45" steam
locomotive, 1937, 100f Class "Pt47" steam
locomotive, 1948; (b) 200f Class "P36" steam
locomotive, 1950
Set of 2 sheets 22·00 22·00

YUGOSLAVIA

South-east Europe

Issues for Bosnia and Herzegovina
100 heller = 1 kruna

1918
No. 346 of Bosnia and Herzegovina overprinted **DRZAVA S.H.S.**
1918 1919 Bosnia i Hercegovina
2† 5h Tracks in Naretva Pass 5 15

Issues for Yugoslavia
100 paras = 1 dinar

1939

393† 1d50 + 1d50 Steam mail train .... 2·75 1·25

1940

430† 2d + 2d Loading mail van .... 5·00 3·75

1946

534 50p + 50p Railway construction
535 1d50 + 1d Railway construction
536 2d50 + 2d Railway construction
537 5d + 3d Railway construction

Set of 4 12·50 7·00

1947

563 1d + 50p Railway construction
564 1d50 + 1d Railway construction
565 2d50 + 1d50 Railway construction
566 5d + 2d Railway construction

Set of 4 2·25 1·25

1949

611 3d Steam mail train
612 5d Steam mail train
613 12d Steam mail train

Set of 3 3·25 1·50

631 2d Steam locomotive of 1849
632 3d Modern steam locomotive
633 5d Diesel train
633a 10d Electric train on bridge (orange)

Set of 4 27·50 8·25
MS633b 10d Electric train on bridge (purple) 75·00 45·00

ALBUM LISTS

Write for our latest list of albums and accessories. This
will be sent on request.

1950

662a† 50d Front of steam locomotive (violet) 45·00 16·00
714† 50d Front of steam locomotive
(turquoise) .... 2·00 10

663 3d Steam locomotive and side-dump coal
trucks .... 1·25 50

667† 5d Tracks on dock .... 1·00 10

1951

683† 100d Tracks on bank of Save River
(grey) .... 60·00 5·00
683c† 500d Tracks on bank of Save River .... 7·00 1·25

*Miniature sheet containing No. 683, but with colour changed and
imperforate*
MS684a 100d Tracks on bank of Save River
(brown) £140 £110

1958

986† 15d Tracks beneath highway overpass
(green) 35 5
900† 25d Tracks beneath highway overpass 35 5
988† 25d Goods wagon at cable factory 30 5
907† 70d Sarajevo Railway Station .... 1·00 10
908† 80d Sarajevo Railway Station .... 7·00 5
996† 300d Sarajevo Railway Station .... 1·75 30

1965

No. 988 surcharged

1173† 50d on 25d Goods wagon at cable factory 40 8

1966

Designs as Nos. 986 and 988, but with colours changed and values expressed as "0.15" etc.

1196† 15p Tracks beneath highway overpass (blue) 20 5

1201† 60p Goods wagon at cable factory 30 5

1972

1526 1d50 Locomotive No. 1 *King of Serbia*, 1882

1527 5d "Bo-Bo" electric locomotive

        Set of 2 1·00 50

1976

1725 3d20 Electric train on viaduct, Belgrade–Bar Railway

1726 8d Electric train on viaduct, Belgrade–Bar Railway

        Set of 2 90 60

1749† 8d Child's drawing of steam locomotive 50 40

1981

2002† 13d Steam locomotive towing boat on Sip Canal .... 1·25 70

1983

2072 4d Series "401" steam locomotive

2073 23d70 on 8d80 Series "442" electric locomotive

        Set of 2 80 40

1984

2136 5d Steam mail train, 1884, and Central Station, Belgrade 10 5

1986

2268† 50d Electric train 5 5

1988

2446† 1200d Electric train 40 25

YUNNAN

See under China

COLLECT MAMMALS ON STAMPS

A Stanley Gibbons thematic catalogue on this popular subject. Copies available at £7.50 (p. + p. £2) from: Stanley Gibbons Publications Ltd, 5 Parkside, Christchurch Road, Ringwood, Hants BH24 3SH.

ZAIRE

Central Africa
100 sengi = 1 kuta
100 kuta = 1 zaire

1980

977 50s Locomotive *Puffing Billy*, Great Britain
978 1k50 Buddicom locomotive No. 33,
Ⅰ France
979 5k Locomotive *Elephant*, Belgium
980 8k Locomotive No. 601, Zaire
981 50k Locomotive *Slieve Gullion*, Ireland
982 75k Locomotive *Black Elephant*, Germany
983 2z Type "1-15" locomotive, Zaire
984 5z "Golden State" express, U.S.A.

| | | *Set of* 8 | 10·50 | 10·50 |
| **MS985** | 10z Type "E.D. 75" locomotive, Zaire | 8·50 | 8·50 |

993† 250k Sir Rowland Hill with railway train
and map (on Belgian Congo No. 292)   2·50   2·50

Nos. 977/8, 981 *and* 993 *overprinted* **20 Anniversaire-
Independance — 1960–1980**

1034† 50s Locomotive *Puffing Billy*, Great
Britain 10 10
1035† 1k50 Buddicom locomotive No. 33,
France 25 25
1037† 50k Locomotive *Slieve Gullion*, Ireland 25 25
1041† 250k Sir Rowland Hill with railway train
and map (on Belgian Congo No. 292) 2·25 2·25

1985

1259† 10z Early steam locomotive 15 12
1261† 50z Modern diesel locomotive 75 70

ZAMBIA

Central Africa
100 ngwee = 1 kwacha

1968

139† 1k Kafue Railway Bridge .... 2·50 20

1974

215† 15n Kafue Railway Bridge .... 70 1·50

1975

230† 5n Knife-edge Railway Bridge 30 5

1976

253 4n Passenger train at station, Tanzania–
Zambia Railway
254 9n Diesel locomotive and copper ingot
trucks
255 15n Diesel goods train
256 25n Diesel goods train
		Set of 4	2·75	3·25
MS257	10n Clearing bush, 15n Laying tracks,		
	20n Railway workers, 25n Completed track	.. 3·50	4·00

WHEN YOU BUY AN ALBUM LOOK FOR THE NAME "STANLEY GIBBONS"

It means Quality combined with Value for Money.

1983

378† 32n Class "7" steam locomotive, 1900 .. 65 1·00

1986

472 35n Diesel train in Kasama Cutting,
Tazara Line
473 1k25 Passenger train leaving Tunnel No.
21, Tazara Line
474 1k70 Train between Tunnels Nos. 6 and
7, Tazara Line
475 5k Trains near Mpika Station, Tazara Line
Set of 4 1·40 1·75

ZANZIBAR
Indian Ocean
100 cents = 1 shilling

1949
As No. 114 of Antigua
335† 20c Silhouette of steam locomotive 25 20

ZIMBABWE
Central Africa
100 cents = 1 dollar

1983

635† 30c Electric train 50 45

1985

653 9c Class "9" locomotive No. 86
654 11c Class "12" locomotive No. 190
655 17c Class "Garratt 15A" locomotive
Isilwane
656 30c Class "Garratt 20A" locomotive *Gwaai*
Set of 4 1·75 1·40

669† 18c Electric locomotive 25 12

Subject Index

This index contains a cross reference to the stamps in the Countries Section listed, by country name and catalogue number, under the following subject headings:

Allegorical Designs
Bridges and Viaducts
Carriages
Express Trains (Named Services)
Incline Railways
Locomotives — Diesel
Locomotives — Electric
Locomotives — Gasoline and Gas Turbine
Locomotives — Steam
Mail Coaches and Mail Vans
Maps of Railway Networks
Monorails
Railway Workers and Personalities
Signs and Signals
Stations
Theme Park Trains
Toy and Model Trains
Tracks
Train Ferries
Trams and Tramways
Tunnels
Underground Railways
Universal Postal Union issues
Wagons

The sections covering locomotives are each divided into a general index and one covering individually named locomotives. Class names have not been included.

ALLEGORICAL DESIGNS
Argentine Republic 809
Austria **MS**2129
Bavaria R133/7
Belgium 1855 2274 2556 N443/60 N505/25 P63/8 P160/9
  P201/13 P259/63 P265/7 P269/70 P280/93 P341/7 P375/86
  P388/406 P409 P806/8 P856/60 P867 P876/7 P878/900
  P911/34 P1116/18 P1204/6 P1229/31 P1250/2 P1375
  P1600/2 P1678/9P1722/5 P2353 O481/6 O534/42 O620
  O677/9 O721/6 O948/53 O954 O1156/61 O1424/34a
  O1523/30 O2224/37 O2455/9
Brazil 1696
Bulgaria **MS**2731
Cameroun 376
China (British Railway Administration) BR133
China (People's Republic) 3235/6
Czechoslovakia 2618
Denmark 452 540
Ecuador 418/23 431/3 450/6 580 675 678 681 2000
France 1723
Greece 1368 1396
Guatemala 26/30 244/5
Hungary 845 1752 2717 3790
India 1237
Iran 1773
Iraq 1073/4
Italy 1450
Korea (South Korea) 697 1101
Luxembourg 1096 1127
Mexico 1614
Monaco 1035
Mozambique 934
Nicaragua 319/22 323/5 326/9 331/2 O334/39 O340/3 O344/8
  O349/55

Nigeria 166
Poland 629
Rumania 3902
Shanghai 176
Spain 547/52
Switzerland 754
Tanzania 533
Turkey 1099 1102 1106/8 1110/11 1113 1115 2439
Uruguay 537/40 P1472

BRIDGES AND VIADUCTS
Albania 1986 2220
Algeria 94 372 550
Angola 640 642
Anguilla 613
Argentine Republic 1673
Australia 142/4 705 716 864 1148 O134/5
Austria 774 799 947/8 1080 1088 1312 1882 2027/8
Belgian Congo 21 33 41 59 65 75 83 93 101
Belgium 1584
Belize **MS**798
Bermuda 536
Bohemia and Moravia 53
Bolivia 935
Brazil 1105 1159 1696 1873 2210
British Honduras 321
Bulgaria 161 176 229/30 259 420 914 1010 1453 1572 1756
  1759 2626 2634
Burma 275
Cameroun 267 290 520 539 720
Canada 282 535 892
Canal Zone 159/60
China (Republic) 289a 292/4 296 309/10 312/15 317/19 321
  349/51 361 366/70
China (Kirin and Heilungkiang)1/11
China (Sinkiang) 4/10 47/53 55/6 83/4
China (Szechwan) 1/2
China (Yunnan) 1/11
China (People's Republic) 1566 1611 1720/1 1741 1853 1868
  2647 2661 2710 2712 2750 2910/11
China (Taiwan) 180/3
Colombia 1132/3
Congo (Brazzaville) 149 169 453 783
Costa Rica 48 1206 O59
Czechoslovakia 258 273b 603/4 903/4 2130 2408 2420 2643
Dahomey 18/22 402
Ecuador 581 676 679 682 **MS**1091a/b 1175
Egypt 1396
El Salvador 754 800 O765
Eritrea 158
Ethiopia 304 319 456 617 621 806 1266
Fiji 290
Finland 1181
France 534/40 541 1056 1149 1466 1761
French Equatorial Africa 1/8 34/8 109/12 118 163
French Guinea 33/7
French Somali Coast 182/4 204 209/13 226/30 331 334
Gabon 681
Germany (French Zone) FB12 FB26 FB37
Germany (East Germany) E1878/81 E2908
Great Britain 660 1399
Greece 410 415/16 C500 C561 C591
Grenadines of St. Vincent 324
Guatemala 171 181 194 210 222 239/42 246/50 259 270/1
  909/12 1217
Honduras 186/7 190/1 229 231 235/7 242 245 305 344a 372
  O204/9 O375
Hungary 1089 1132 2024/5 2027/30 2514 2722 2943 2946
  MS3657

(BRIDGES AND VIADUCTS (Cont.))
India 1239
Iran 736 850/3 856/7 907 1149 1678 1897 1940
Iraq 336/7
Italy 871
Ivory Coast 22/6 184 464
Japan 1936/9
Jordan 904/5
Kenya 66/7 283
Kenya, Uganda and Tanganyika 115 121 141b 148b
Kiribati **MS**292
Korea (North Korea) N319 N578 N779 N1623 N2003
Latvia 162 169 241 280 **MS**277 **MS**293
Lesotho 844
Liechtenstein 80
Luxembourg 208 296a/300a 330 509 751 754 788 796 828
    986 1127 O269
Madagascar 326
Malawi 550 597
Malaysia 39
Manchukuo 97/8
Mauritania 1/5
Mexico 640 867 997 1273 1866
Middle Congo 69/77
Monaco 57 97/9 108/9 331 1901
Mongolia 118 1360
Mozambique 409 417
Mozambique Company 260 302
Netherlands 402 811 1052
Netherlands Indies 484 504
Nevis 319
New Caledonia 481
New Zealand 1368
Nigeria 44 59c 73 191
Niuafo'ou **MS**107
Norfolk Island 444
Northern Rhodesia 54/8
Norway 848
Pakistan 313
Philippines 1842
Portugal 1294/7 1672
Qatar 336
Reunion 330
Ruanda-Urundi 6 13 20 28 32
Rumania 1107/8 1423 1426 1760 1761 1898 1902 1939 1943
    2561 2835 3910 3912 4515 4932 5230
Russia 945a 1286 1312 1315 1403/4 2773 2963 3269 3506
    4509 4523 4760 4991 5079 5194
St. Lucia 666
St. Vincent 747
San Marino 961 1231
Senegal 33/8
Sierra Leone 219 265 1094
Slovakia 112
Slovenia 120
South Africa 564
Southern Cameroons 5
Southern Rhodesia 36/9 58 75 83
Spain 1107 1296 1299
Sudan 115 O59
Sweden 380
Switzerland 359 361 375b 377 493 J89 479/80 511 515 520
    563 672 1159 O387 O434 O522 O526 O531
Switzerland (International Organisations) LN46 LN51 LN53
    LN73 LB45 LB65 LB80 LB84 LB89 LE7 LE27 LE29 LE33
    LE38 LH6 LH10 LH15 LR1 LR4 LU1 LU5 LU10
Tanzania 187/8
Togo 666
Tokelau 157
Tonga **MS**989
Transkei 169 231
Travancore 72 74 O104 O107
Trieste (Zone A) 297

Trieste (Zone B) B36/a
Turkey 1070/2 1077/78 1080 1082 1100/1 1103/5 1214 1241
    1243 1338 1437 1591 1934 2387 3003 D1035/9
Uganda 173/4
United States of America 299 303 958 1303 2030
Upper Senegal and Niger 35/40
Uruguay 639 991/2
Venezia Giulia and Istria 83 97 D73 D87/9
Vietnam (North Vietnam) N112 N315
Wallis and Futuna Islands 418
Yugoslavia 633a/b 1725/6
Zaire **MS**985
Zambia 139 215 230

CARRIAGES
Antigua 765 893
Argentine Republic 2115
Austria 1937
Barbuda 772
Bhutan 726
Bulgaria 585 587 2055 2877
Chile 954
Cuba 425
Czechoslovakia 1757 2186
Finland 392
France 2284
French West Africa 73
Germany (East Germany) E536 E1509 E1578 E1580/1
    E2279/80 E2344/5 E2510 E2512 E2578/9
Ghana 869
Great Britain 1114/15
Guernsey 467
Hungary 1914
India 1070
Ivory Coast 555
Japan 547 549
Korea (North Korea) N2003 **MS**N2426
Malagasy Republic 252
Mauritius 473
Nicaragua 2160 2474 2480
Niuafo'ou **MS**107
Poland 3009
Portugal 1742 1744
Qatar 502
Russia 4291 4936 5570
St. Vincent 1163/4
Samoa **MS**704
Togo **MS**1758 **MS**1856 **MS**1860 **MS**1977
Turkey 2254
Turks and Caicos Islands 706
United States of America 1003 2386 P431

EXPRESS TRAINS FROM NAMED SERVICES
"Aerotrain-Orleans"
    Mongolia 1222
"APT" (Advanced Passenger Train)
    Antigua 606 650
    Barbuda 455 497
    Congo (Brazzaville) 848
    Grenadines of Grenada **MS**482
    Niger 767
    Tuvalu 257/8
"Asia Express"
    Manchukuo 126
"Blue Train"
    Lesotho **MS**610
"Bristolian"
    Liberia **MS**1692
"Broadway Limited"
    Sierra Leone **MS**945
"Cheltenham Flyer"
    Great Britain 1274

(EXPRESS TRAINS FROM NAMED SERVICES (Cont.))
"Cornish Riviera"
　Great Britain 1276
"Daylight Express"
　Antigua **MS**1018
　Barbuda **MS**885
　Sierra Leone 944
"Empire State Express"
　Antigua 1017
　Barbuda 884
　Gambia 753
　United States of America 301
"ET-403"
　Grenadines of Grenada 520
"Falkland Islands Express"
　Falkland Islands 500
"Flying Hamburger"
　Germany 579
　Tuvalu 352/3
"Flying Scotsman"
　Cook Islands 1028
　Great Britain 1272
　Grenada 1215
　Ivory Coast 594
　Lesotho 609
"Friendship"
　Bulgaria 2329
"Golden Arrow"
　Great Britain 1273
　Grenada 1214
"Golden State Limited"
　Zaire 984
"Grand Canyon Express"
　Antigua 1015
　Barbuda 882
"Hiawatha Express"
　Antigua 1014
　Barbuda 881
　Sierra Leone 941
"Hikari"
　Dahomey 402
　Djibouti 814
　France 1949
　Hungary 3242
　Mongolia 1221
　Qatar 336
"HST" (High Speed Train)
　Great Britain 987
　Grenadines of St. Vincent 273/4
　Liberia 1191
"ICE"
　Guinea **MS**1216 **MS**1241
　Rumania **MS**5179
"Intercity 125"
　Congo (Brazzaville) 846
"Kingston Flyer"
　Cook Islands 1022
"L'Eclair"
　Congo (Brazzaville) 957
"La Gazelle"
　Ivory Coast 812
　Upper Volta 600
"Le Belier"
　Ivory Coast 635
"MAGLEV-MLU 001"
　Dominica 1086
　Liechtenstein 931
　San Marino 1316
"Mistral"
　Grenadines of Grenada 518
　Mali 405
"Orient Express"
　Cook Islands 1029

Dominica 1093 1127
Grenada 1212
Hungary 3240
Lesotho 605
Rumania **MS**4830
"Orik"
　Czechoslovakian Army in Siberia 2 5
"Orleans"
　France 1865
"Powhattan Arrow Express"
　Antigua 1016
　Barbuda 883
"Prospector"
　Sierra Leone 943
"Rapidity"
　Mongolia 1223
"Rembrandt"
　Mali 815"Rheingold Express"
　Comoro Islands 226
　Grenadines of Grenada 519
　Sierra Leone **MS**1067
"Royal Scot"
　Great Britain 1275
"RTG"
　Mali 814
"St George Special"
　Bermuda 537
"Santa Fe"
　Grenadines of Grenada 517
"Settebello"
　Grenadines of Grenada **MS**523
"Shinkansen Tokaido Bullet"
　Bhutan **MS**736
　Congo (Brazzaville) 847
　Grenadines of Grenada 522
　Japan 1687/8
　Mali 405 813
　Nevis 225/6
　Surinam 1247 1369
"Southern Belle"
　Comoro Islands 224
"Super Chief"
　Lesotho 608
"TEE" (Trans Europe Express)
　Mongolia 821
　Switzerland 659
"TGV 001"
　Bhutan **MS**736
　Congo (Brazzaville) **MS**674 849
　Cook Islands 1027
　Djibouti 814
　France 2055 2622
　Gabon 767
　Gambia **MS**760
　Mali 816 861
　Surinam 1243
　Upper Volta 526
"The Rocket"
　Sierra Leone 942
"The White Train"
　Seychelles 754
"Trans-Siberia Express"
　Comoro Islands 223
　Grenada 1213
　Hungary 3241
"Transcamerounais"
　Cameroun 491
"Transrapid 05"
　Germany(West Germany) 1732
　Hungary 3243
"Turbotrain"
　Bhutan 701
　Canada 606/7 609

(EXPRESS TRAINS FROM NAMED SERVICES (Cont.))
"Twentieth Century Limited"
Grenada **MS**1218
"Viceroy Special"
Sri Lanka 924
"Young Socialist Express"
Germany (East Germany) E536

INCLINE RAILWAYS
Brazil 1159
Chile 939
Colombia 1109
Dominica 1092 1126
Hungary **MS**2894 3696
Isle of Man 368
Madeira 219
Portugal 2138
Russia 878
Switzerland 512 1055 O524
Switzerland (International Organisations) LB81 LE30 LH7 LR2 LU2
Togo 1749
Transvaal 215b
United States of America 1445 2172a

LOCOMOTIVES — DIESEL
A. General
Albania 1532 1986 2319
Algeria 550 975
Antigua 606 681 683 **MS**685 785 1014/15
Argentine Republic 908
Australia 278 453
Bahamas 348
Bangladesh 289
Barbuda 455 497 541 543 **MS**545 660 881/2
Belgium 1275 P689/97 P1722/5 P2064/7
Benin 1006
Bermuda 535/8
Bhutan 284 289 397 697 700 702
Bolivia 935 1048
Botswana 318
Brazil 1696 1780 2210
British Guiana 360
Bulgaria 1451 1454 2626 3497
Burkina Faso 810/15 839 850 **MS**852
Burma 274 276
Cambodia 252 254
Cameroun 267 290 377 412 453 491 539 720
Canada 436 **MS**1123 1224
Central African Empire 440
Central African Republic 47/50 360 1017 1019 1084
Ceylon 412 503/4
Chad 809
Chile 455 524
China (People's Republic) 2535 2599 2647 2697 2699 2700 2710 2797 3074
China (Taiwan) 601 908 1099 1325 1397 1623 1695
Christmas Island 15 138
Colombia 1130
Congo (Brazzaville) 149 188/9 223 248/9 326 372/4 670 672 846 848/9 952 954/7 D28
Cook Islands 1026
Cuba 1313/14 1778 2244/6 3297
Czechoslovakia 1453 1562 1974 2754 2852/3
Dahomey 342 D313
Denmark 824
Djibouti 749 752 764 804 812 855
Ecuador **MS**1091b 1110
Egypt 521 595 **MS**601 660 794 1327
Ethiopia 456 617 661/3 806 1123
Fernando Poo 252
Fiji 527/8
Finland 636 904 1116

French Territory of the Afars and the Issas 584
French West Africa 50 87
Gabon 265 284 479 550 641 681 769 **MS**771 835 903 932 964
Gambia 759
Germany 579
Germany (West Germany) 1093 1729 1740
Germany (West Berlin) B479
Germany (East Germany) E538 E655 E697 E1069 E1167 E1310 E1689 E1701 E2043 E2126
Ghana 324/7 871
Greece 1458 1790
Grenada 410 1166 1965/6 1970
Grenadines of Grenada 334 394 **MS**482 517/20
Grenadines of St Vincent 273/4 451/2 512/15 520/1 524/7 534/5
Guatemala 1218/19
Guinea 844/5 890 1252 1255/6
Guyana 401 987 1067/8 2195 2197 2199 2201 2203 2205 2207 2209 2211 2347 2349 2351 2353
Hungary 960 1441 1565 1890 1911 2030 2273 2345 2379 2717 2720 2882 3071 3073/5 3196 3210 **MS**3271 D2852
India 806
Indonesia 815 817/18 1005 1074 1193/4 1482
Iran 1116 1678 2509
Iraq 1206/7
Israel 441 688
Italy 550/2 725
Ivory Coast 596 635 812
Jamaica 327 637
Japan 898 1672
Jordan 285/8
Jordanian Occupation of Palestine P30/3
Kampuchea 490 542/3 546/8
Kenya 66/8 136 283 490
Kenya, Uganda and Tanganyika 293 358 360
Korea (South Korea) 341 354 634 743 815 876 1101
Korea (North Korea) N319 N814 N972 N1034 N1121 N1164 N1217 N1506 N1570/2 N1574 **MS**N1576 N1961 N2002 N2129 N2427
Laos 124
Lesotho 608
Liberia 731 752 1289a 1510 1590 1690/1
Luxembourg 785 1127
Macao 577
Malagasy Republic 35 221 276 725 728 **MS**730
Malawi 302/3 530/3 550 597/600 631 726
Malaysia 39 316/17 380
Maldive Islands 507 512/13
Mali 370 738 808 896 968
Malta 527
Mauritania 157 164 222 224 390/1 680
Mauritius 565
Mexico 865/6 1041/2 1614 1866 P916/17
Mongolia 229 412 545 617 671 740 821 919 1003 1062/3 1220 1353 1360 1448 1546 1584
Morocco 190 620 655
Mozambique 1016
Nauru 226 269 323
Netherlands 1558/9
Nevis 358/9 437/8
New Zealand 818/19 1422
Nicaragua 2322/4 2480 2619
Niger 497/9 1037
Nigeria 101/2 166 324 326 414
Norway 447 625
Pakistan 154 276
Philippines **MS**1028 1117/19 1140/2 1199 1331 1863 1936
Portugal 1509 1853
Rhodesia 434
Rhodesia and Nyasaland 24a
Rumania 1422 1426 2732 3032 3517 3842 3902 **MS**4541 S135/9

(LOCOMOTIVES — DIESEL (Cont.))
Russia 1555 1557 2126 2133 2299 2624/5 2773 3110 3196 3940 3960 4175 4333 4559 4781 5093 5098 5151 5163 5194 5230/1 5325 5456 5500 **MS**5509 5569
Rwanda 1186
St. Kitts 232/3
St. Vincent 746/7 794/5 1007/8
Saudi Arabia 372/6 1201
Senegal 559
Sharjah 126
Spain 1108 1295/6 1298/9 2690
Sri Lanka 1041/2
Surinam 563 764 **MS**929 1091 1245 1283
Sweden 380
Switzerland 1159
Syria 714 1509 1607 1633
Tanzania 187/9 417 445/8 533 **MS**535 541/4 **MS**566
Thailand 1057 1193 1278
Togo 375 666 961 1752 1853
Trieste (Zone A) 91
Trieste (Zone B) B35
Trinidad and Tobago 451/2
Turkey 1527 1934 2387 2389 2652 2999
Tuvalu 257/8 352/3
Uganda 173/5 417 612 618
United Nations (New York Headquarters) 177/8
United States of America 984 990 1003 1517 1572
Upper Volta 524/5 573 599/601 730
Uruguay 1349 1360 1370 1401/2 P1472 P1507/8
Venezuela 1813
Vietnam (South Vietnam) S91/4 S326/9
Vietnam 365
Yemen **MS**701
Yugoslavia 633
Zaire 984 1261
Zambia 253/6 472/5

B. Individually Named Diesel Locomotives
Dreadnought
St. Vincent 794/5
Lyntog
Denmark 355
Royal Scots Greys
St. Vincent 746/7
Zambesi
Malawi 302

LOCOMOTIVES — ELECTRIC
A. General
Algeria 372
Antigua 1101
Argentine Republic 2117
Austria 814 1364 1392 1626 1795 2027/8 2053 2099
Barbuda 951
Belgium 1584 2108 2445 2757 2779 **MS**2830 P1451/2 P1485/9 P1491/5 P1498/503 P1517/19 P1585/7 P1722/5 P2047/63a P2824/5 P2923/7 PD2703/6
Bhutan 696
Bohemia and Moravia 53
Brazil 2128
Bulgaria 1348 1452 1525 3344 3498
Burkina Faso 809 **MS**852
Canal Zone 57 61 63 156 162 251
Central African Republic 1240 **MS**1243
Chad 411
China (People's Republic) 1666 1868 2846 2909/11
China (Taiwan) 1023 1122b 1146 1168 1316 1361/2
Comoro Islands **MS**227
Congo (Brazzaville) 847
Cook Islands 1027
Costa Rica 574
Czechoslovakia 951 1561 1758 2025 2618 2851 2853
Djibouti 705

Egypt 1327
Finland 1018
France 572 1243 1249 1949 2829
French Territory of the Afars and Issas 682
Gabon 767
Germany (West Germany) 1393 1730/1 1825 1895
Germany (West Berlin) B479
Germany (East Germany) E296 E306 E1576 E2124 E2678
Grenadines of St Vincent 390/1 522/3
Guinea 1213 1215 1238 1240
Hungary 959 1035 1082 1178 2183 2335 2964 3238 3242
India 509 727 1239
Indian Forces in Indo-China N53
Ireland 580
Isle of Man 369
Italy 1275 1588 1990
Ivory Coast 598
Japan 761 988 1287 1687/8 1888
Korea (South Korea) 483 1219
Korea (North Korea) N175 N208 N358 N491 N517 N609 N720 N728 N810 N870 N970 N1005 N1013 N1015 N1017 N1020 N1083 N1110/1 N1146 N1224 N1504 **MS**N1515 N1573 N1575 N1623 N1698 N1968 **MS**N1973 N2033 **MS**N2034 N2126 N2351
Lesotho **MS**610
Luxembourg 786 1223
Malagasy Republic 146 727
Mali 405 441 464 470/1 806 813 815
Monaco 919
Mongolia 1221 1356
Nauru 131 225
Netherlands 500 977 1558
Nevis 219/22 225/6 354/5 431/2
New Caledonia 481
Nicaragua 2660
Niger 544 565 **MS**768
Pakistan 313
Panama 166 180 182 239 287 303 322 358 1144
Philippines 1466 1842 1862/3 1865
Poland 844/5 1631 1636 2417 2530 2533 3007
Portugal 1137/8 1541 1854
Qatar 502
Rumania 1762 1767 3528 3679 3854 3902 4540 5140 5206
Russia 1403/4 1416/17 2133 2738 2773 2898 3040 3172 3269 3338 3495 3506 3572 3634/5 3711 3803 4052 4509 4523 4716 5229 5232/3 5564
St. Lucia 721/2 860/1 866/7
St. Vincent 1005/6
San Marino 179/82
South Africa 564
Spain 2606 E553
Surinam 1239 1241 1243 1247
Sweden 624/5 1087 1408/9
Switzerland 474/5 479/80 512 568 577 597 659 672 1022 1122
Thailand 918/19
Togo 288
Trieste (Zone B) B36/a
Tunisia 897
Turkey 1864 2998
Upper Volta 526 548/9
Venezuela 2692 2697
Yugoslavia 633a/b 1527 1725/6 2073 2268 2446
Zimbabwe 635 669

B. Individually Named Electric Locomotives
Broadlands
Tuvalu 263/4
Electra
St. Lucia 866/7
Sea of Japan
Japan 1931
Stephenson
St. Lucia 860/1

LOCOMOTIVES — GASOLINE AND GAS TURBINE
Canada 606/7 609
Malagasy Republic 277
Mali 814 816 861
Monaco 1035
Mongolia 1222/3
Nevis 356/7
Nicaragua 2071 2478
St. Lucia 870/1

LOCOMOTIVES — STEAM
A. General
Albania 468/75 498/505 532/4
Angola 697 751
Antigua 114 392 424 682 684 1016/18
Argentine Republic 492/5 496 511 **MS**808a 828 924 2116
  OD27B/F
Ascension 52
Australia 278 715/18
Austria 813 1505 1794 1857 2099 2157 2202
Bahamas 196
Bahrain 28
Bangladesh 157 218
Barbados 267
Barbuda 160/1 542 544 883/5
Basutoland 38
Bechuanaland 138
Belgian Congo 292
Belgium 1197 1275 2826 2828/9 P69 P73 P75 P77/8 P81 P84
  P86/8 P96/121 P217/9 P294/307 P1277/95 P2505
Belize 483 796
Bermuda 130
Bhutan 264 284 289 397 536/9 695 698/9 **MS**703 735
Bohemia and Moravia 7 34 66/7
Bolivia 345 651/6 701 961 1042 1088 1164
Brazil 317/18 647/50 751/3 966 1038 1241 1267 2020/2
British Guiana 324
British Honduras 172
British Virgin Islands 126
Brunei 96
Bulgaria 418/21 438 588 744 771/2 774/a 914 953/4 1450
  1453 1874 3110 3405 3496
Burkina Faso 851
Burma 272/5
Burundi 979 987 1350 1439
Cambodia 41 43 45 47/8 253 255
Canada 283 295 330 436 535 892 1105 1134/5 1185/8 1222
  1223 1225/6 S5
Canal Zone 149 151 153 155 157 160/1 163 211 212
Cape Juby 154 163
Cayman Islands 131
Central African Empire 557
Central African Republic 671/5 832 1018/21 1084 1086 1238
  1241/2
Ceylon 410/11 442/3 503/4
Chad 756
Chamba 90
Chile 338j 431/2 956 1091 1161/2 O443
China 289a 292/4 296 309/10 312/15 317/19 321 349/51 361
  366/70 448 599/604 985 1123/7 1129/30 1134/8 1140/8
  1151 1183/93 1211 1232/7 1284/92 1312/13
China (Kirin and Heilungkiang) 1/11
China (North-east China) NE38/41 N178/81 NE197 NE230/1
  NE247/50
China (Port Arthur and Dairen) 54 59 61 62
China (Sinkiang) 4/10 22 47/50 52/3 55/6 83/4 215/16 218
  221 223 225
China (Szechwan) 1/2
China (Yunnan) 1/173
China (People's Republic — Central China) CC71/5 CC79/84
China (People's Republic — East China) EC307/17 EC320/30
  EC351/4 EC370/7
China (People's Republic — North China) NCP374/80

China (People's Republic – South-west China) SW44
China (People's Republic) 1424 1426 1430 1469/70 1474/8
  1506 1611 1669 1677 1741 1851 1853 1933 1973 2341 2479
  2504 2535 2642 2801
China (Taiwan) 86 224 225/8 233/5 304 403/4 674 1137/8
  1361/2 D151/5
Christmas Island 257
Colombia 992 1130 1367
Comoro Islands 186 221/6 372
Congo (Brazzaville) 246/7 428 450/1 453 671 846/9 D27
Cook Islands 636 690 1022/5 1028/9
Costa Rica 48 102 104/5 107/9 112 171 173 182/5 193 402/4
  461 O59
Cuba 404 412 544/6 1547 2663/8 **MS**2681 2865 3015/20
  MS3054 3082 3175 3296 3300/1 3346
Cyprus 168
Cyprus (Turkish Cypriot Posts) 202/3
Czechoslovakia 388 545 603/4 677 768 806 826 904/5 948/50
  1005 1222 1559/60 1758 2025 2051 2618 2851/2 2882
Dahomey 557/60
Denmark 354 540 851
Djibouti 750/1 779 812/13 951
Dominica 114 1088
Dominican Republic 131 477/8 1197
Ecuador 331 407 418/23 478 489 525/7 541 581 623 624 625
  660 664 676 679 682 1109 O803
Egypt 189/92 521 1327
El Salvador 39/48 49 50 51 160 222 864 881 O184 O208 O234
  O246
Eritrea 158
Ethiopia 304 319
Falkland Islands 168 497 499/500
Falkland Islands Dependencies G21
Fiji 272 290 526
Finland 392 578 635 931 **MS**1122
France 573 635 830 1737 2746
French Equatorial Africa 1/8 34/8 109/12 118 163
French Somali Coast 182/4 204 209/13 226/30 331 334 361/74
  378/85
Gabon 547 767/8 **MS**771
Gambia 166 752 755/6 759
Germany (West Germany) 1393 2112
Germany (West Berlin) B381 B473/5 B810
Germany (East Germany) E1701 E2277/8 E2342/3 E2509 E2511
  E2576/7
Ghana 175 324/7 870
Gibraltar 136
Gilbert and Ellice Islands 59
Gold Coast 140 149 158
Great Britain 1272/6
Greece 410 415/16 1412 1458 1665/8 C500 C561 C591
Grenada 168 409 628 **MS**1168 1212/17 **MS**1218 1357 1363/4
  1366/8 1629 1941/2 1944/5 1947 1949 1952/8 1960/4 1967/9
Grenadines of Grenada 28 479 **MS**482 627 **MS**635 880
Grenadines of St. Vincent 271/2 275/6 279/82 311/14 317/18
  351/6 392/3 396/7 414/19 443/6 449/50 453/8 504/7 510/11
  516/19 532/3
Guatemala 37/41 42 43a/4 46/50 51 53/5 57 59 62/75 76 77/87
  88/9 99 100 101/9 110/12 113/14 127/33 159 163 171 181
  194 210 222 239/42 246/50 259 270/1 285 291 909/12
  1217/18
Guernsey 467
Guinea 1022 1139 **MS**1142 1212 1214 1237 1239 1253/4
Guinea–Bissau 618 904/5 907/9
Guyana 2196 2200 2204 2206 2210 2212/13 2348 2352
Gwalior 110
Haiti 294/5
Honduras 108/15 686 O116/20
Hong Kong 7
Hungary 707 957/8 1030 1078 1089 1091/2 1134 1138/9 1247
  1407 1419 1437 1445 1472 1535 1740 2370 2647/53 3069/70
  3072 3240/1
India 255 343 350 362 807/9 1069 1070 1238 1240

(LOCOMOTIVES — STEAM (Cont.))
Indo-China 247/50 314 323
Indonesia J70/1 JD72/3 JD75/6 831 1193/4
Iran 736 852/3 856/7 907 1117 1149/50 1563 2002
Iraq 336/7 1208/9
Isle of Man 276
Israel 350 685/7 911
Italy 871 931 1450 1821
Ivory Coast 272 595 597 **MS**599 638 813/15
Jamaica 145 326 613/15 634/5
Japan 408 507 1305/6 1373/4 1382/3 1385/6 1395/6 1398/9
    1671 1887
Jersey 366
Jind 117
Johore 148 159
Kampuchea 544/5 **MS**669
Katanga 73 75
Kedah 72 96 108
Kelantan 57 87 100
Kenya 69
Kenya, Uganda and Tanganyika 159 292 294/5
Korea (South Korea) 129 814/15
Korea (North Korea) N113 N158 N307 N548 N621 N694/5
    N1061 N1953 **MS**N2032 N2033 N2127 N2323 N2325/6
    N2396/8 N2423/5 N2432
Kuwait 43 630/2
Labuan 116a
Leeward Islands 119
Lesotho 605/6 609
Liberia 117 1149/55 1383 1692 O130
Libya 1491/8
Luxembourg 661
Madagascar 53a/69 80 84 85/9 90/108 109 111/22 229 240
    242
Madeira 219
Malacca 18 43 54
Malagasy Republic 253 278
Malawi 301 764 766
Malaysia 315 **MS**318 1165 1168
Maldive Islands 507 512/13 1010
Mali 255/9 367/9 403/4 441 458/61 464 749/50 785 813/16
    861
Malta 251
Manchukuo 126
Marshall Islands 205
Mauritania 679 681/4 831
Mauritius 272 473 567/8
Mexico 228/30 640 869 963 1042 1273 O241/3 P732/3
Monaco 57 97/9 108/9 331 557/8 914/18 1035 1397 1675
    1702 D482/3 D700
Mongolia 118 411 544 616 755 763 918 1217/19
Montserrat 117
Mosul 1
Mozambique 759 779/84 998/1003 1028
Mozambique Company 211 228 252 254 260 302
Nabha 85
Nauru 224 325 334
Negri Sembilan 63 72
Netherlands 499 754 757a 1558
Nevis 136/7 223/4 277/8 281/4 299/302 305/8 427/8 433/4
    441/2
New Brunswick 9
New Caledonia 339 484
Newfoundland 103 183
New Zealand 619 1003/6 O147
Nicaragua 27/36 137/40 142 144/9 151/3 163 168/9 173 176
    184/6 187/8 200 203/4 205 367/78 384 727 729/30 732 748
    999 1935 2155/9 2161/3 2170 2318/21 2357 2607 2659
    2661 2663/4 Z1/15 O37/46 O197/201
Niger 527/30 563 809/12
Nigeria 64 73 412
Niuafo'ou **MS**107
North Borneo 107 136 352 387 D44

Northern Rhodesia 50
Norway 390 848 **MS**862
Nyasaland Protectorate 163
Pahang 49 79
Palau 204
Panama 571
Paraguay 589 600 636 691/5 O37 O44
Patiala 88
Penang 23 48 59
Perak 124 154
Perlis 3 33
Peru 21a 451/4 457/62 465 469 604 632 777/a 875
Philippines 777 **MS**1462 1861
Pitcairn Islands 13
Poland 629 741 876 885/6 1066 2414/15 2419/21 2531/2
    2534/7 2591 3191
Portugal 1136 1139 1541 1671/2 1852
Rhodesia 431/3
Rhodesia and Nyasaland 24a
Rumania 1422/5 1713 1760 1887 1906 1954 2006 2010/11
    2033 2036/7 2135 2159 2217 2439 2561 3031 3679 4537/9
Russia 287 597 608 643 645 670 945a/6 1002 1006 1215 1220
    1258 1312 1315 1319 1361 1374 1376 1403/4 1523/4 1556
    1759 2242 2276 2406 2963 3150 3171 3194 3479 3590 3939
    4757/61 4861/5 5697/701 5789 E590
Rwanda 756
Saar 55 70 268 277 279
St. Helena 145
St. Kitts-Nevis 82
St. Lucia 160 717/18 723/4 761/6 771/6 824/31 862/3 872/3
St. Vincent 178 752/5 758/9 792/3 798/801 806/7 834/5 840/1
    876/81 893/904 1001/2 1165 **MS**1167
San Marino 420 491 494 520 755 761 797
Sarawak 167
Saudi Arabia 195/7 214 218b/21 244/8 249/53 D232/3 D236
Selangor 111 120 133
Seychelles 154 388 754
Sharjah 125
Sierra Leone 205 219 265
Slovakia 110
Solomon Islands 77
Somaliland Protectorate 121
South Africa 183 541/4
South West Africa 96 447/50 O20
Southern Cameroons 5
Southern Rhodesia 36/9 75
Spain 534/52 1107 1297 1300 1645 2231 2528 2839
Spanish Morocco 307 316 350
Sri Lanka 821
Surinam 307 321 383 1236 1240
Swaziland 48 109/12 371 411 466/9
Sweden 173/5 195 702 1410
Switzerland 478 1021 1055
Syria 1607
Tanzania 190 430/3 449/50 545
Thailand 920/1 1094
Togo 321 961 1326 1377 1477 1702/3 1749/51 1753/8 1854/6
    1857/60 **MS**1977
Tonga 88
Transkei 229/32
Transvaal 215b
Trengganu 63 93
Trieste (Zone A) 297
Trieste (Zone B) B24/5 B33/4 B85
Trinidad and Tobago 261 557 706/8 747
Turkey 1070/2 1077/8 1080 1082 1100/1 1103/5 1214 1242
    1316 1373/5 2989 2995/7 D1035/9
Turks and Caicos Islands 217 559 628 732/5
Tuva 90
Tuvalu 241/6 253/6 259/62 267/8 273/80 313/20 354/5
Uganda 176 339 611 613/17 **MS**619
United Nations (New York Headquarters) 162

(LOCOMOTIVES — STEAM (Cont.))
United States of America 116 301 919 944 958 990 1003
1303 1512 1572 1649 1725 1867 2158a P427
Upper Volta 523 731 733
Uruguay 155 185 199 221a 303/5 1349 1402 O170 O203
O227 O344/6 P801 P805 P971/5 P1066/70 P1508 P1557
Venezuela 1572 1575 2454 2491
Vietnam (North Vietnam) N38/41 N354/5 N492 NMF112
Vietnam 537/43 899 901/5
West Irian 6
Yemen People's Democratic Republic 301/4
Yugoslavia 393 611/13 631/2 662a/3 714 1749 2002 2072
2136
Zaire 978 980 983/5 993 1035 1041 1259
Zambia 378
Zanzibar 335
Zimbabwe 653/6

B. Individually Named Steam Locomotives
Abbotsford
    Great Britain 985
Adam Brown
    Canada 1109
Aigen
    Austria 2157
Ajax
    Czechoslovakia 1557
Alexandra
    Guyana 2194 2198 2202 2208 2346 2350
Antigua
    Spain 2691
Ant
    Isle of Man 372
Archduke Charles
    Czechoslovakia 2882
Ariel
    Grenada 1943
Arima
    Trinidad and Tobago 705
Austria
    Austria 812 1392 1793
    Korea (North Korea) N2324
    Togo 1375
Baronesa
    Brazil 884 974
Bayard
    Italy 550/2
    San Marino 760
Benkei
    Japan **MS**459
Best Friend of Charleston
    Bulgaria 3159
    Gambia 758
    United States of America 2323
Bets
    Hungary 2603
Beyer Peacock
    Malta 707
Black Elephant
    Zaire 982
Black Hawk
    Bhutan 534
Black Hawthorn
    Malta 706
Blue Peter
    Grenadines of St. Vincent 285/6
Bodmin
    St. Lucia 659/60
Borsig
    Bulgaria 3162
Britannia
    Nevis 144/5

Brother Jonathan
    United States of America 2325
Caerphilly Castle
    Great Britain 986
Caesarea
    Jersey 96
Caledonia
    Isle of Man 36 371
Calugareni
    Rumania 4535
Calvados
    Jersey 94
Cardean
    Grenadines of St. Vincent 325/6
    Lesotho 607
Caroline
    Norway 390 446
Carteret
    Jersey 95
Catch-Me-Who-Can
    Grenadines of St. Vincent 315/16
Champion
    Grenada 1365
Cheshire
    St. Vincent 756/7
City of Glasgow
    St. Lucia 653/4
City of Newcastle
    St. Lucia 868/9
City of Truro
    Niger 562
Claud Hamilton
    Grenadines of St. Vincent 277/8
Cock o'the North
    Nevis 429/30
Colonel Church
    Brazil 1906
Columbia
    Chad 754
Comet
    Nevis 279/80
Coronation
    Grenadines of St. Vincent 412/13
Countess (The)
    St. Lucia 719/20
Countess of Dufferin
    Canada 1133
County of Oxford
    Nevis 132/3
Dam
    Surinam 1238
De Arend
    Netherlands 499
Der Adler
    Bulgaria 3113
    Comoro Islands 300
    Djibouti 952
    Germany 577
    Germany (West Germany) 1259
    Germany (East Germany) E538
    Grenadines of Grenada **MS**635b
    Guinea **MS**1256
    Guinea–Bissau 522
    Korea (North Korea) N2322
    Mauritania 830
    Mongolia 1216
    Nicaragua **MS**2665
    St. Lucia 725/6
    Surinam 1244 1282
    Vietnam 900
Deru
    Hungary 1564 2182

(LOCOMOTIVES — STEAM (Cont.))
De Witt Clinton
  Grenada 1959
  Togo 1378
Dom Luiz
  Portugal 1851
Dorchester
  Canada 1106
  Nevis 435/6
Drache
  Germany (West Berlin) B472
  Korea (North Korea) N2321
Duke of Normandy
  Jersey 365
Duke of Sutherland
  St. Lucia 651/2
Eagle
  Pakistan 153 755
Elephant
  Belgium 2827
  Zaire 979
Enterprise
  Jamaica 612
Erzsebet
  Bhutan **MS**539b
Eton
  St. Lucia 661/2
Evening Star
  Nevis 134/5
Experiment
  Bhutan 533
Fenchurch
  St. Vincent 874/5
Fire Fly
  Grenadines of St. Vincent 357/8
Flying Scotsman
  St. Lucia 663/4
Fryckstad
  Sweden 379 861
General (The)
  Gambia **MS**760
  Niger 564
  Surinam 1246 1318
  Togo 1376
Glen Douglas
  St. Vincent 872/3
Goliath
  Belgium P655/7
Gotland
  Sweden 862
Gowan and Marx
  United States of America 2326
Great Bear (The)
  St. Vincent 882/3
Green Arrow
  Tuvalu 348/9
Gwaai
  Zimbabwe 656
Hagley Hall
  St. Vincent 748/9
Halesworth
  Grenadines of St. Vincent 447/8
Henry B. Lock
  Isle of Man 373
Hutchinson
  Isle of Man 378
Ilmarinen
  Finland 634
  Korea (North Korea) **MS**N2327
Ince Castle
  Liberia **MS**1692
Injebreck
  Isle of Man 376

Iron Duke (The)
  Gabon 545
Isilwane
  Zimbabwe 655
J. B. Earle
  Grenadines of St. Vincent 319/20
Jenny Lind
  Bhutan 535
  Grenadines of Grenada 878
  Togo 1379
Johann Adolf
  Czechoslovakia 1758
John Bull
  Grenadines of St. Vincent 530/1
  United States of America 2324
Judge (The)
  St. Vincent 1003/4
Karlstejn
  Czechoslovakia 1558
Kestrel
  Ireland 579
Kh. Botoar
  Bulgaria 3494
King Edward II
  Liberia **MS**1692
King George V
  Nevis 146/7
King Henry VIII
  St. Vincent 744/5
King of Serbia
  Yugoslavia 1526
Kissack
  Isle of Man 37 377
Kladno
  Czechoslovakia 947 2818
L'Aigle
  Niger 813
La Callao
  Peru 578 811
La Gironde
  Mali 461
La Junta
  Cuba 2242 **MS**3179 3298
  Spain 2961
La Moye
  Jersey 367
La Portena
  Argentine Republic 907 1855
Lady
  Chad 740
Lafayette
  Bulgaria 3161
  Grenadines of Grenada 633
  Nevis 439/40
Le Belge
  Belgium P698/712 P1277
Le Continent
  Hungary 2654
Leeds United
  St. Lucia 657/8
Lemminkainen
  Finland **MS**1122
Limmat
  Switzerland 477
Lion
  Grenadines of Grenada 634
  St. Lucia 769/70
  San Marino 759
Little England
  San Marino 762
Liverpool
  Grenadines of Grenada 630

(LOCOMOTIVES — STEAM (Cont.))
Livingstone
  Upper Volta 732
Loch
  St. Vincent 893/4
Locomotion
  Gambia 808
  Great Britain 984
  Grenada 1360
  Hungary 3387
  Korea (North Korea) N2320
  San Marino 757
  Tuvalu 265/6
Lode Star
  Grenadines of St. Vincent 283/4
  Nevis 322
Lord Nelson
  St. Lucia 655/6
Lord of the Isles
  Nevis 321
  Tuvalu 247/8
Lyn
  Grenadines of St. Vincent 321/2
Macha
  Ireland 578
Maitland
  Isle of Man 380
Mallard
  Bhutan **MS**736
  Great Britain 1392
  Grenadines of Grenada 521
  Nevis 142/3
Manning Wardle
  Malta 705
M. M. Prieto
  Cuba 2243 3299
Monster
  Grenada 1948
  Grenadines of Grenada 632
Montana
  Spain 2692
Muldenthal
  Germany (East Germany) E1969
Nellie
  Nauru 268
Nord
  Chad 753
Nord Express
  Comoro Islands **MS**227
Nord L'Outrance
  Nevis 303/4
North Star
  Poland 2418
North Western
  Jersey 93
Novelty
  Grenada 1361
  St. Vincent 804/5
Odin
  Denmark 353
Orleans
  Rumania 4536
Owain Glyndwr
  St. Lucia 767/8
Papyrus
  Grenadines of St. Vincent 508/9
Pendennis Castle
  Nevis 138/9 324
Pender
  Isle of Man 38
Penydarren
  St. Vincent 802/3
Philadelphia
  Bulgaria 3163
Phoenix
  Grenada **MS**1368
Pilgrim
  New Zealand 818
Pioneer
  Hungary 3239
Planet
  Bhutan 532
Polar Bear
  Isle of Man 379

Princess
  Ireland 577
Prince August
  Sweden 863
Prince Royal
  Bulgaria 3111
Prince of Wales
  St. Vincent 838/9
Projector
  Jamaica 325 636
Puffing Billy
  Bulgaria 3112
  San Marino 756
  Zaire 977 1034
Rete Mediterranea
  Chad 755
Reuth
  Vietnam 898
Rheingold
  Central African Republic 1239
Rocket
  Bhutan 727
  Bulgaria 1449
  Cuba 3174
  Djibouti 813
  Gabon 769 **MS**771
  Gambia 754
  Great Britain 1113
  Hungary 3237
  Korea (North Korea) N2031
  Mali 403 749/50
  Mongolia 1215
  Niger 530 **MS**814 **MS**1025
  Poland 2416
  St. Lucia 665/6
  San Marino 758
  Surinam 1242
  Togo 1374
Rogers
  San Marino 764
Royal George
  Grenadines of Grenada 628
St. Aubyns
  Jersey 369
St. Heliers
  Jersey 368
Samson
  Canada 1108
Sans Pareil
  Bhutan 531
Saxonia
  Bulgaria 3160
  Germany (East Germany) E2678
Scotia
  Canada 1132
  Grenada 1860
Shamrock
  Malawi 763
Sir Lancelot
  St. Vincent 750/1
Sir William
  Mauritius 566
Slieve Gullion
  Grenadines of St. Vincent 394/5
  Zaire 981 1037
Snowdon Ranger
  Nevis 297/8
South Carolina
  Grenadines of Grenada 631
Southern Maid
  St. Vincent 836/7
Spitfire
  San Marino 763
Spuyten Duyvel
  Grenadines of St. Vincent 528/9
Stevens
  Grenadines of St. Vincent 530/1
Stourbridge Lion
  Cuba 3173
  Gambia 757
  Grenadines of Grenada 629
  Nevis 352/3
  United States of America 2323
Sutherland
  Isle of Man 35

(LOCOMOTIVES — STEAM (Cont.))
Talyllyn
  Grenadines of St. Vincent 323/4
Taw
  St. Lucia 715/16
Thistle
  Malawi 300 765
Thomas Rogers
  Gabon 546
Tip Top
  St. Lucia 858/9
Tom Thumb
  Dominica 1089
  Grenada 1950
Toronto
  Canada 1107
Tynwald
  Isle of Man 375
Washington Farmer
  Grenada 1362
Winston Churchill
  Nevis 140/1
Yantra
  Bulgaria 3493
Yatay
  Agentine Republic 2114
Yucatan
  Grenada 1951
Zbraslav
  Czechoslovakia 946

MAIL COACHES AND MAIL VANS
Algeria 307
Austria 1719 2182
Bangladesh 223 O34
Belgium 1651 P1322 P1324/5 P1450
Brazil 1738
Bulgaria P495 P502 P513
Burundi 978/9 986/7 1350 1439
Central African Empire 621
China (People's Republic) 2977
Costa Rica 669 1225
Dahomey 553
Denmark 851
Finland **MS**1122
France 821 1107
Germany (West Germany) 2199
Germany (East Germany) E397 E522 E720 E790 E2016/17
Ghana 868
Hungary 1905 1917 D3813
India 862 1342
Ivory Coast 759
Japan 1258 1885/6
Lebanon 1176
Lesotho 713
Malagasy Republic 108
Monaco 574 1883 D495
Mongolia 1213
Mozambique 1028
Niue 290/1 316/17 359/60
Poland 2640
Rumania 3511 3516 4076 5206
Russia 2380/1 3357 3568 5571 5789
St. Vincent 1159
Spain 2375
Sweden 1311
Switzerland 1112
Switzerland (International Organizations) LP11
Togo 1372
Tonga **MS**989
Tunisia 349
United States of America 2172c P425
Yugoslavia 430

MAPS OF RAILWAY NETWORKS
Albania 498/505
Angola 511/18 729 734 742
Antigua 411
Barbuda 201
Belgian Congo 292
Bolivia 332 1048
Brazil 1001 1906
Cambodia 252
Cameroun 452/3 717 736
Canada 270
Christmas Island 11 37/52 57/8 114
Colombia 1129 1131
Costa Rica 548
Czechoslovakia 2801
Egypt 528 1720
Egyptian Occupation of Palestine 87
Ethiopia 661/3
French Somali Coast 430
Gabon 681 835 964
Germany (West Germany) 1313
Germany (East Germany) E1669
Guyana 2212/13
Hong Kong 386
Hungary 1268 2335 2603 **MS**3244
Iran 908 1116 1150
Japan 1931
Jersey 22 24 49 52
Korea (South Korea) 634
Manchukuo 125
Mexico 299 433 865 996 O318 O455 O545
Monaco 330 332 334
Morocco 620
Mozambique 496/503 631 645
Netherlands 1206 1365
Newfoundland 94
Nicaragua **MS**2164
Russia 5093 5500
Saudi Arabia 1201
Slovakia 109/12
Swaziland 109/12 140 325

MONORAILS
Antigua **MS**1209
Burundi 527
Canada 1197
Central African Republic 1095
Dominica 1105
Germany (West Germany) 1754c 1774
Germany (West Berlin) B490c
Grenada 392
Guinea 860
Giunea–Bissau 906
Hungary 3243 3633
Liberia 1027
Liechtenstein 931
Maldive Islands 344
Niger 258
Pakistan 288
Rumania 3531
Russia 3198 3265
Samoa 780
Togo 531 576 745/8
United States of America 1195
Upper Volta 303

RAILWAY WORKERS AND PERSONALITIES
Albania 468/75 1294 1720 1853 2310 **MS**2312
Antigua 388
Argentine Republic 1890
Austria 799 1234
Barbuda 152/3
Belgium 1563 P996/9 P1090/113

(RAILWAY WORKERS AND PERSONALITIES (Cont.))
Brazil 966 1024 1093
Bulgaria 421 771/2 1139 2059 2254
Burkina Faso 848/50
Canada 535 673 892 1022 1105 1222
Central African Republic 1238/43
China (North-east China) NE38/41
China (People's Republic) 1972 2313 2392 2478
China (Taiwan) 403/4
Colombia 1109
Comoro Islands 496
Congo (Brazzaville) 428 951
Croatia 136
Cuba 544/6 3296
Czechoslovakia 826 984
Dahomey 18/22
Djibouti 705 813
Ecuador 1111
El Salvador 766/9
France 2392 2707 2748
French Equatorial Africa 287
French Guinea 33/7
French Territory of the Afars and the Issas 682
French West Africa 95
Germany (West Germany) 1203 1433 2285
Germany (West Berlin) B97 B122
Germany (East Germany) E130 E315 E1310 E2678 E2939
Grenada 1711
Grenadines of Grenada 907
Guatemala 1218
Guinea 890
Hungary 703/4 1030 1035 1247 1419 1426 1751 2162 2335
   2961 3013 3039 3387
India 798
Ivory Coast 22/6
Japan 1886
Korea (North Korea) N810 N970 N1066 N1392 N2126
Maldive Islands 1165 1168
Mali 1098
Mauritania 1/5
Mauritius 473
Mexico 864 963
Netherlands 1464
Nevis 318 320 323 325
Niger 496
Norway 448
Panama 470 548
Poland 2414/16 2418/19 2421 MS2547 3191
Rhodesia 488
Rumania 1713 2229 2835 2992
Russia 996 2126 2649 2963 3150 4757
Saar 429
Senegal 33/8
Spain 1106 1230 2231
Sweden 378 1086
Switzerland 352/4 J100 J112 473 1076
Togo 1682
Tonga 889
Turkey 1099 1102 1106 1108
United States of America 990 1725 A1748/9 2386
Upper Senegal and Niger 35/40
Uruguay 1349
Vietnam (South Vietnam) S328/9
Vietnam (North Vietnam) N85/6
Vietnam MS905
Wallis and Futuna Islands 418 491
Yugoslavia 534/7 563/6
Zambia MS257

SIGNS AND SIGNALS
Belgium 2520 P1203
Burma 274

Cambodia 253
Cameroun 452
Canada 572
Canal Zone 159
China 1124/6 1129/30 1134/8 1140/8 1151 1183/93 1232/7
   1284/92 1312/13
China (People's Republic – Central China) CC71/5 CC79/84
China (People's Republic – East China) EC351/4
China (Taiwan) 1023 1122b 1146 1168 D151 D153/5 D162
Czechoslovakia 826
Germany (West Germany) 1093 1145 1389
Germany (East Germany) E536 E1167 E1797 E2677
Great Britain 1272/3
Grenadines of St. Vincent 284 322 326
Hungary 1419 1472 1566 1795 1914
India 657
Iran 1115
Israel 687
Kenya 136
Korea (South Korea) 341
Netherlands 976
Poland 885
Russia 2649
Saar 59 74
Spain 544/6 1108
Switzerland 825
United States of America 990 1594a
Uruguay 1360

STATIONS
Algeria 93
Argentine Republic 1890 2023
Armenia 193/4
Austria 1092 1270 1408
Bangladesh 227 O38
Barbados 665 669
Belgium 2754 2757 P1485/1506 P1517/19 P1585/7 P1695/8
   P1787/90 P2017/20 P2180/2 P2192/2200 P2256/62 P2505
   PD2703/6 P2824/5
Bermuda 537
Brazil 2095/7 2128
Bulgaria MS2731
Burma 274
Cambodia 253/5
Cameroun 538
Canada 1071
Cape Juby 154 163
China (People's Republic) 1932/3 2684
Colombia 400 541 AR371 O503
Congo 106 950 953
Cuba 357
Cyprus (Turkish Cypriot Posts) 202
Czechoslovakia 545
Denmark 626 824
Egypt 1103
Ethiopia 618 807
Finland 329 334 382/4 538 672
France 1907 2747
Germany 755
Germany (West Berlin) B810
Germany (East Germany) E388 E638 E2680 E2940/1
Grenadines of St. Vincent 272 274 276 286 320 322
Guatemala 253 310/a 364 395
Guinea–Bissau 978
Hong Kong 384 443
Hungary 1180b 1183 1902 1904 1911 2182/3 2226 3069/75
   3092 MS3871
India 1317
Isle of Man 60
Italy 1962 1990
Ivory Coast 259 636/7
Japan 1398/9

(STATIONS (Cont.))
Kampuchea **MS**669
Kenya 68 386
Kenya, Uganda and Tanganyika 360
Korea (North Korea) N154 **MS**N1576
Lithuania 320/1
Luxembourg 612 786 1023 1096
Malawi 598
Malaysia 380
Mali 357
Monaco 1675 1702 1764 1852 1902
Mozambique 385 579
Netherlands 811
Nevis 141 143
New Caledonia 484
New Zealand 1264
Nicaragua 728 730
Niger 628
Nigeria 101
North Borneo 161 186 204 216 237 256 279 D58
Pakistan 276
Panama 1150
Poland 2530/1 2533/5 2537
Portugal 1742 1744
Rumania 1424/5 1427 2901 3913 **MS**4830
Russia 1288/9 1814/15 2081 4759 4761
St. Lucia 652 654 656 658 660 664 716 720 724
St. Vincent 747 749 753 755 877
Samoa **MS**704
San Marino 179/82 1231
Saudi Arabia 11 21 29/30 31 37/8 66 77 84/5
South West Africa 424 446
Spanish Morocco 307 316
Switzerland 474/6 661 885
Syria 814
Tanzania 189
Togo 1515
Transkei 230
Trinidad and Tobago 747
Turkey 1373/5
Uganda 175
Uruguay P1046 P1290
Venezuela 2294
Yugoslavia 907/8 996 2136

THEME PARK TRAINS
Antigua **MS**1209
Dominica 1102/8
Sierra Leone 1105 1107

TOY AND MODEL TRAINS
Antigua 615 645 1061 **MS**1209
Barbuda 467
Caicos Islands 64
Canada 962
Central African Republic 197
Comoro Islands 372
Congo (Brazzaville) 175
Cuba 2704
Dominica 929 1193
Germany (West Germany) 1506
Germany (West Berlin) B339
Germany (East Germany) E1120 E2281
Gibraltar 607
Great Britain 777 1436
Grenada 1545
Grenadines of Grenada 362 **MS**1087
Guinea–Bissau 618
Hungary 3857
Indonesia 1002
Jersey 494
Jordan 1218
Korea (North Korea) N1908 N1912 **MS**N1915 N1941

Libya 1450
Maldive Islands **MS**816
Mexico 1725
Monaco 1032/4 1373
New Zealand 610
Nicaragua 2211 **MS**2213 2246
Niger 327
Pakistan 313
Poland 841
Rumania 2385
Russia 796/7 3796
Switzerland J286
Turks and Caicos Islands 824
Uganda 669
United States of America 1411

TRACKS
Albania 569 1846 1853 2112/13 2220 2319
Algeria 1012
Angola 633
Antigua **MS**685
Australia 453
Austria 1094 1624
Barbuda **MS**545
Belgium 1611 2834 P2431/4
Belize 481
Bolivia 398 400 402
Bosnia and Herzegovina 189 346 383 385
Botswana 203 261
Brazil 286 1001 1137 1891
Bulgaria 164 179 183 491
Cameroun 376 717/19 736 943
Canada 987
Canal Zone 159 230
China (People's Republic) 2135
Costa Rica 570 1272
Croatia 32
Cuba 705 2971
Czechoslovakia 726/7 767 1486 2891
Denmark 351 400 452
Dominica 534
Ecuador 660 664 **MS**1091a
Eritrea 157 239 244
France 1057 1723 2152
French Southern and Antarctic Territories 193
Gabon 339
Germany 646 827
Germany (West Germany) 1145
Germany (West Berlin) B122 B156
Germany (East Germany) E255/6 E2679
Ghana 1231
Guatemala 252 315/16a
Iran 1115 1773
Iraq 759 762
Ireland 498
Italy 1742
Kenya 13
Korea (South Korea) 697
Korea (North Korea) N182 N864 N966 N1089
Madagascar 335
Mexico 864 995/6 1041
Mozambique 468 492/3 846 1105
Mozambique Company 210 231 248
Netherlands 1557
New Zealand 597
Nicaragua 726 731 733/5 739 741/3 745 991
Nigeria 34
Panama 357
Peru 603 614 631 656 718/21 736 776
Poland 318 492 783/4 3190
Rumania 1883 1899 1901 1940 1942 5229
Russia 1883 3635 4452 5093
South Africa 441 442/3

(TRACKS (Cont.))
Sweden 378
Switzerland J56 357 359 373b/c 375b 490 J100 473 921
  1055 O383 O430 O523
Switzerland (International Organisations) LN49aa/b LN51
  LN69 LB41 LB41b LB43 LB61 LE3 LE24 LH2
Syria 985/6
Togo 1181 1682/1685
Trieste (Zone B) B118
Trinidad and Tobago 730
Turkey 1024/6 1036/8 1056/8 1086 1090 1092 1094 1109
  1112 1114 1116 1157 1159/61 1164/6 1169 1186/7 1198
  1200 1235 1237 1286 1865 1867 1169 1935
Vietnam (South Vietnam) S91/4 S326/9
Vietnam (North Vietnam) N559
Yugoslavia 2 534/7 563/6 683 683c **MS**684a 897 900 986
  1196
Zambia **MS**257

TRAIN FERRIES
Canada 406 O9 O28
Denmark 540
Germany 645
Germany (East Germany) E537 E2139/40 E2761/2
Kenya, Uganda and Tanganyika 256
Norway 883
Panama 361
Russia 5690
Sweden 826
Turkey 2388

TRAMS AND TRAMWAYS
Allenstein 11/12 25/6
Argentine Republic 1856 2091 2099
Australia 292
Austria 559 1312 1980 2158
Barbados 667
Belgium 2745/7 2826
Brazil 1735
Bulgaria 2441/2
Canada **MS**1047 1197
Chile 802
Cuba 2726
Czechoslovakia 2286/7 2850 2883
Danzig 8/10
Dominica 1101
Ecuador 656/a
El Salvador 683/92 704 705/6 710/17 719 721 O694/703
Finland 945 1018 1151
Gambia 810
Germany 113 114/15
Germany (West Berlin) B382/3 B385
Germany (East Germany) E260 E1970 E2725/8
Great Britain 1394
Greece 784 788 1691
Grenada 396 **MS**1359
Guernsey 203/4 D33
Haiti 139/40 144 169 185/6 189 201 251/3 255 269/70 277
  279/80
Hong Kong 364 366 469 577/80
Hungary 1426 1900 2024/5 2027 2029 3576 3578 3581
Ireland 658/61
Isle of Man 17 22 80/1 83 149 365/7 370 374
Japan 1267
Korea (South Korea) 859
Lebanon 971/3
Marienwerder 25/7
Memel 30/1
Mexico 1042
Monaco 1661 1764 1802
Mongolia **MS**1233
Netherlands 812
Newfoundland 173 177

New Zealand 1360/5
Nicaragua 2662
Niger 628
Norway 946
Peru 589
Philippines 1864 1866 1937
Poland 847 2716
Portugal 1516 1518 2139
Rumania 1427 2665
Russia 1286 1405 1447 1554 1571 1678 2447 2737 5188 5192
Saar 46/7
Sierra Leone 927
South Africa 326
Spain 802 804 807 811
Sweden 937/8 1252
Switzerland 1046
Trinidad and Tobago 731
Turkey 1399 1402 1454
Turks and Caicos Islands 731
United States of America 299 303 1445 2052/5 2172a
Venezuela 2812

TUNNELS
Algeria 711/13
Austria 1626
Brazil 1629 1665 1754
Bulgaria 743 953/4 1454 1572 1756 1759
Burma 276
Cameroun 491
China (People's Republic) 2909
China (Taiwan) 1021 1122a 1145 1325
Colombia 1367
Congo (Brazzaville) 188 952
Croatia 32
Czechoslovakia 905
Ecuador **MS**1091b
Ethiopia 1266
Great Britain 1276
Grenada **MS**1218
Italy 931
Japan 898 1931
Madagascar 53a/69 80 84 85/9 90/108 109 111/22 229 240
  242
Mauritania 222 224
Mexico 995
Rumania 1883 2732 5138
Russia 287
St. Lucia 718
St. Vincent 751
Singapore 574
Slovakia 111
Swaziland 371 469
Switzerland 568 672
Syria 714
Transvaal 215b
Turkey 1244 2669
Zambia 473/4

UNDERGROUND RAILWAYS
Argentine Republic 2110/13 2139
Austria 1800
Belgium 2446
Brazil 1629 1754
Chile 1113
China (Taiwan) 1857/8
Czechoslovakia 2249 2801
Egypt 1674 1720
France 2084 2185 2748
Germany (West Berlin) B386
Grenadines of Grenada 880
Hong Kong 384/6 517
Hungary 1267/8 2517 3459
Japan 1484/5

(UNDERGROUND RAILWAYS (Cont.))
Korea (South Korea) 916 1116
Korea (North Korea) N1219/21 N1505
Mexico 1189
Netherlands 1206
Rumania 4686/7 4954 **MS**5179 5232
Russia 688/91 819/24 843/4 1280/5 1620/6 1791/4 3213/16
  4425 4901 4991 5079
San Marino 1161
Singapore 572/4
Spain 2608
Sweden 941
Tunisia 897
Venezuela 2514/17

UNIVERSAL POSTAL UNION (UPU) ISSUES SHOWING RAILWAY THEMES
Aden 32
Aden Protectorate States (Kathiri State of Seiyun) 16
Aden Protectorate States (Qu'aiti State in Hadhramaut) 16
Albania 532/4
Antigua 114 388 392 424
Ascension 52
Austria 1719
Bahamas 196
Barbados 267
Barbuda 152/3 160/1
Basutoland 38
Bechuanaland 138
Belize 483
Bermuda 130
Bhutan 264 284 289 397
Botswana 318
Brazil 1780
British Guiana 324
British Honduras 172
British Virgin Islands 126
Brunei 96
Burundi 978/9 986/7 1439
Cayman Islands 131
Chad 411
Congo (Brazzaville) 669
Cuba 3082
Cyprus 168
Czechoslovakia 2186
Dahomey 553
Dominica 114
Dominican Republic 1197
Falkland Islands 168
Falkland Islands Dependencies G21
Fiji 272
Gambia 166
Germany (East Germany) E1701
Gibraltar 136
Gilbert and Ellice Islands 59
Gold Coast 149
Grenada 168 628 635 1166
Grenadines of Grenada 28/9 479 **MS**482
Guinea 860
Hong Kong 173
Hungary 2882
Jamaica 145
Johore 148
Kedah 72
Kelantan 57
Kenya, Uganda and Tanganyika 159 360
Lebanon 1176
Leeward Islands 119
Liberia 1191
Malacca 18
Maldive Islands 507 512/13
Mali 441 464
Malta 251 527

Mauritius 272 473
Montserrat 117
Negri Sembilan 63
Nicaragua 2607
Niger 544
Nigeria 64 326
North Borneo 352
Northern Rhodesia 50
Nyasaland Protectorate 163
Pahang 49
Penang 23
Perak 120
Perlis 3
Pitcairn Islands 13
Portugal 1541
Qatar 502
Rumania 4076
Russia 1523/4
St. Helena 145
St. Kitts-Nevis 82
St. Lucia 160
St. Vincent 178
Sarawak 167
Selangor 111
Senegal 559
Seychelles 154
Sierra Leone 205
Singapore 33
Solomon Islands 77
Somaliland Protectorate 121
Spain 2528
Swaziland 48
Switzerland 885
Togo 1326
Tonga 88
Trengganu 63
Trieste (Zone B) B24/5
Trinidad and Tobago 261 451/2
Turks and Caicos Islands 217
Uganda 339
Yugoslavia 611/13
Zanzibar 335

WAGONS
Albania 1475
Australia 220 305
Austria 924 1089 1091/2 1095
Barbados 639/40
Barbuda 369
Belgium 1609 2274 2757 P2615/36
Bolivia 400
Brazil 955 1810 1942
Bulgaria 645i 645k 874 2254 2327
Cameroun 274 290
Canada 589 1203
Canal Zone 62 109 O182 D120/3
Ceylon 378 395
Chile 270 955 O283
China (People's Republic) 1614 1667 1850 2220 2232 2304
  2720 2787 2797 2845
Christmas Island 137 256
Congo (Brazzaville) 222/3 325/6
Croatia 136
Cuba 361 424 701/2 925 2088
Cyprus 176 191
Czechoslovakia 588 732 824 1269 2449
Dominica 535
Ecuador **MS**1091a/b **MS**1938
Falkland Islands 498
French Morocco 317
French Somali Coast 431
French West Africa 73
Germany 163 186 249 252 254 256 257 871 O274/5

(WAGONS (Cont.))
  Germany (West Germany) 1192
  Germany (East Germany) E60 E138 E790 E1577 E1579
    E1689 E2043 E2125 E2127
  Ghana 219 384 446 1233
  Great Britain 1115/17
  Hungary 1181 1184a 1248 1300 1304 1903 1917
  Indonesia J60 1397
  Iran 905 2461
  Iraq 760/1
  Israel 54
  Jamaica 130 528
  Kenya 286
  Korea (South Korea) 507 905
  Korea (North Korea) N191/2 N336 N364 N440 N490 N620
    N1092 N1099 N1953 N2064
  Lesotho 215
  Liechtenstein 157
  Luxembourg 207 239 **MS**359 606 807 1223 O267 O279
  Malagasy Republic 17 210
  Maldive Islands 332
  Marshall Islands 205
  Mozambique 1080
  Mozambique Company 206 220 232 250
  Nauru 130
  Netherlands 1343
  New Zealand 774 998
  Nicaragua 747 2321 2475/7 2479
  Nigeria 72/cc 81 413 517

  Pakistan 570/1
  Palau 209
  Panama 181
  Peru 601 629
  Philippines 820/1 1772
  Poland 815 873 1035 1503 2465 2467/8 3006 3008
  Portugal 1700
  Rumania 2007 **MS**2011 2125 2207 2601 2741 2744 3002
  Russia 670 949 997 1063 1216/17 1219 1321 1326 1340
    1418/19 2278 2629 3167 3340 3503 3665 3979 5565/8
  Saar 118/21 187/90 269 273 404 O127
  St. Kitts 234/6
  St. Vincent 1160/2 1166 1171
  Senegal 281
  Sierra Leone 215
  Southern Cameroons 4
  Surinam 313 319
  Sweden 1086
  Switzerland 513 518 O524 O529
  Switzerland (International Organisations) LB82 LB87 LE31 LE36
    LH8 LH13 LR5 LU3 LU8
  Togo 373
  Trinidad and Tobago 293
  Turkey 1856
  Turks and Caicos Islands 221
  United Nations (New York Headquarters) 161 163
  United States of America 1163 1868 1876 2168 P431
  Upper Volta 575
  Vietnam (North Vietnam) N102 NO91/3
  Yugoslavia 667 988 1173 1201

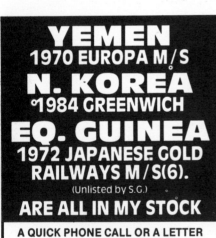